DAY HIKES AROUND
Ventura County

116 GREAT HIKES

Robert Stone
3rd EDITION

Day Hike Books, Inc.
RED LODGE, MONTANA

Published by Day Hike Books, Inc.
P.O. Box 865
Red Lodge, Montana 59068
www.dayhikebooks.com

Distributed by The Globe Pequot Press
246 Goose Lane
P.O. Box 480
Guilford, CT 06437-0480
800-243-0495 (direct order) · 800-820-2329 (fax order)
www.globe-pequot.com

Front cover photograph by Robert Stone
Back cover photograph by Linda Stone
Design by Paula Doherty

The author has made every attempt to provide accurate information in this book. However, trail routes and features may change—please use common sense and forethought, and be mindful of your own capabilities. Let this book guide you, but be aware that each hiker assumes responsibility for their own safety. The author and publisher do not assume any responsibility for loss, damage, or injury caused through the use of this book.

Cover photo: The Backbone Trail
Back cover photo: The Sandstone Trail

ALSO BY ROBERT STONE

Day Hikes On the California Central Coast

Day Hikes On the California Southern Coast

Day Hikes Around Sonoma County

Day Hikes Around Napa Valley

Day Hikes Around Big Sur

Day Hikes Around Monterey and Carmel

Day Hikes In San Luis Obispo County, California

Day Hikes Around Santa Barbara

Day Hikes Around Ventura County

Day Hikes Around Los Angeles

Day Hikes Around Orange County

Day Hikes In Sedona, Arizona

Day Hikes In Yosemite National Park

Day Hikes In Sequoia & Kings Canyon Nat'l. Parks

Day Hikes In Yellowstone National Park

Day Hikes In Grand Teton National Park

Day Hikes In the Beartooth Mountains

Day Hikes Around Bozeman, Montana

Day Hikes Around Missoula, Montana

Day Hikes On Oahu

Day Hikes On Maui

Day Hikes On Kauai

Day Hikes In Hawaii

Hiking partner, Kofax

LINDA STONE

Table of Contents

THE HIKES

Summerland • Carpinteria
South Santa Barbara County

Ojai Area

Ventura • Oxnard • Camarillo
Pacific Coast—Santa Monica Mountains

Santa Monica Mountains:
Point Mugu State Park • Rancho Sierra Vista/Satwiwa
Circle X Ranch • Leo Carrillo State Park

Thousand Oaks area
Newbury Park to Simi Hills

Westlake Village · North Ranch
Wood Ranch · Oak Park · Agoura Hills

Simi Hills
Cheeseboro/Palo Comado Canyons
Upper Las Virgenes Canyon

Los Angeles County • Simi Valley • Moorpark • Fillmore

Hiking Ventura County

Ventura County lies along the Pacific Coast between Los Angeles County and Santa Barbara County. The area has a Mediterranean-like climate, ideal for hiking year round. The county's diverse topography includes national forest land, wilderness areas, mountain ranges, and over 50 miles of coastline. Miles of hiking trails weave through the open spaces, parks, forests, and mountain ranges that together form an ecological corridor. In addition, a network of trails are accessible from the metropolitan areas, where the open spaces have been thoughtfully integrated with the development.

These hikes range in location from the Pacific Coast to the mountainous interior and national forests. The elevation dramatically changes from sea level to over 3,000 feet in the Santa Monica Mountains, which run parallel to the coast. Also running through the county are the Simi Hills, the Santa Susana Mountains, and the Topatopa Mountains. The county is bounded to the north by the Los Padres National Forest.

Now included in this greatly expanded third edition are 116 new and updated day hikes. Highlights include coastal estuaries and tidepools, long beaches backed by bluffs, waterfalls, swimming holes, forested canyons, secluded creek paths, caves, ridge walks, historic sights, filming locations, rugged outcroppings, and spectacular views.

All of these hikes can be completed within a day and are within a half hour's drive of Highway 101, the major access road. A quick glance at the hikes' summaries will allow you to choose a hike that is appropriate to your ability and intentions. An overall map on page 12 identifies the general locations of the hikes and major roads. Several other regional maps (underlined in the table of contents), as well as maps for each hike, provide the essential details. The Thomas Guide, or other comparable street guide, is essential for navigating through the urban areas. Other relevant maps are listed under the hikes' statistics if you wish to explore more of the area.

A few basic necessities will make your hike more pleasurable. Wear supportive, comfortable hiking shoes and layered clothing. Take along hats, sunscreen, sunglasses, drinking water, snacks, and appropriate outerwear. Bring swimwear and outdoor gear if heading to the beaches. Ticks may be prolific and poison oak flourishes in the canyons and shady moist areas. Exercise caution by using insect repellent and staying on the trails.

Use good judgement about your capabilities—reference the hiking statistics for an approximation of difficulty and allow extra time for exploration.

N
W E
S

(33)

SANTA BARBARA COUNTY
VENTURA COUNTY

2

(12)

(13)

11

(17-19)

(20)

(16)

8-10

(21)

(14-15)

To San Luis
Obispo and
Monterey

1 Montecito
Summerland
192 Carpinteria

(24)

(25-28) (29)

(30)

22-23 (33) Ojai

Lake
Casitas

1

2 3 4 5

150

7 (33)

(33)

Santa
Barbara

Rincon Point 6

101

Ventura R.

Ventura R.

3

38

Ventura FOOTHILL RD
(126)

34

35
36

37

HARBOR BLVD

VICTORIA AVE

VENTURA RD

CALIFORNIA

N

Lake Tahoe

San
Francisco

Monterey

Santa
Barbara — AREA MAP

Ventura

Los Angeles

San Diego

40

39

41

42

10 MILES

10 KILOMETERS

Regional Maps:

1 **Hikes 1–6:** Summerland • Carpinteria (PAGE 14)
2 **Hikes 7–33:** Ojai area (PAGE 28)
3 **Hikes 34–63:** Ventura to Point Dume (PAGE 102)
4 **Hikes 64–103:** Thousand Oaks area (PAGE 174)
5 **Hikes 104–116:** Simi Hills to Santa Susana Mtsn. (PAGE 280)

MAP of the HIKES
VENTURA COUNTY and VICINITY

Master Map

Sespe Cr.

5

116

31

32

150

Fillmore

126

Santa Paula

Santa Clara River

23

HAPPY CAMP CANYON

115

LOS ANGELES VENTURA COUNTY

Saticoy

4

Moorpark

118

110-113

ROCKY PEAK PK

To L.A.

118

23

114

Simi Valley

107-109

106

Camarillo

43

SANTA ROSA RD

89-93

105

TOPANGA CANYON

101

Oxnard

WILDWOOD

75-81

Thousand Oaks

83-88

104

To L.A.

E. 5TH

Newbury Park

64-66

67-72

82

94-97

102-103

98-101

101

LAS POSAS

LEWIS RD

POTRERO RD

44-48

73

74

Westlake Village

Agoura Hills

1

54

52-53

23

63

MALIBU CYN RD

49

50

51

YERBA BUENA

MULHOLLAND

DECKER

57

58

59

60

61

62

KANAN DUME RD

POINT MUGU STATE PARK

PACIFIC

COAST

HWY

1

LEO CARRILLO STATE PARK

55-56

To Santa Monica

Point Dume

MALIBU CREEK STATE PARK

PALO COMADO–CHEESEBORO– LAS VIRGENES CANYONS

Pacific Ocean

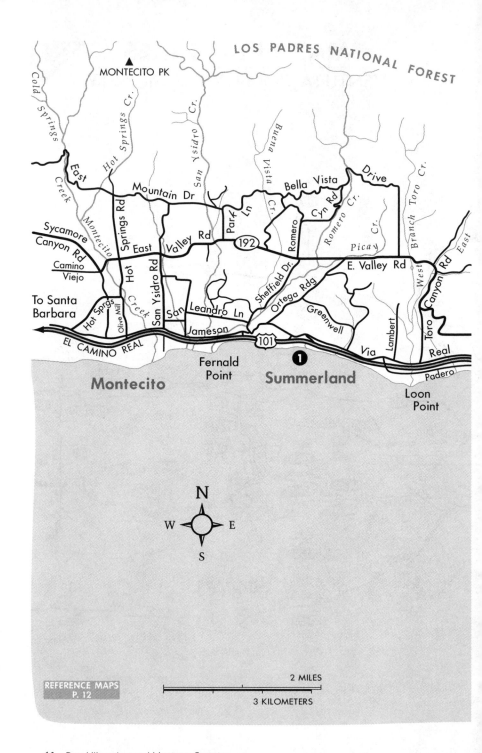

LOS PADRES NATIONAL FOREST

▲ MONTECITO PK

Cold Springs

Hot Springs Cr.

San Ysidro Cr.

Buena Vista

East Creek

Mountain Dr

Montecito

Hot Springs Rd

San Ysidro

Park Ln

Bella Vista

Drive

Cyn Rd

Romero Cr.

Branch Toro Cr.

Sycamore Canyon Rd

East

Valley Rd

192

Romero

Picay Cr.

West Canyon Rd East

Camino Viejo

Hot

San Ysidro Rd

Creek

Sheffield Dr.

Ortega Rdg

E. Valley Rd

To Santa Barbara

Hot Sprgs

Olive Mill

San

Leandro Ln

Greenwell

Lambert

Toro Real

EL CAMINO REAL

Jameson

101

Via

Padero

Fernald Point

❶

Montecito

Summerland

Loon Point

N
W · E
S

2 MILES

3 KILOMETERS

REFERENCE MAPS
P. 12

Summerland • Carpinteria
SOUTH SANTA BARBARA COUNTY

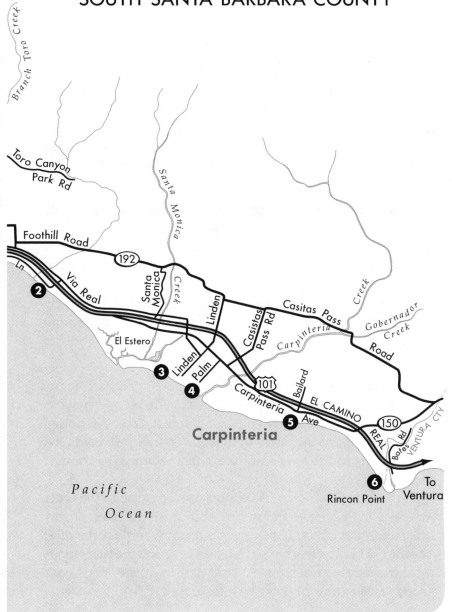

Pacific

Ocean

Carpinteria

1. Summerland Beach • Lookout Park

Hiking distance: 1-mile loop
Hiking time: 30 minutes
Elevation gain: 50 feet
Maps: U.S.G.S. Carpinteria
  Santa Barbara Front Country and Paradise Road
  Montecito Trails Foundation map

Summary of hike: Lookout Park is a beautiful grassy flat along the oceanfront cliffs in Summerland. From the four-acre park perched above the sea, paved walkways and natural forested trails lead down to a sandy beach, creating a one-mile loop. There are tidepools and coves a short distance up the coast from the beach.

Driving directions: VENTURA. From Ventura, drive northbound on Highway 101 to Summerland, and take the Evans Avenue exit. Turn left (south), cross under Highway 101 and over the railroad tracks, and go one block to Lookout Park. Park in the parking lot.

SANTA BARBARA. From Santa Barbara, drive southbound on Highway 101 and take the Summerland exit. Turn right (south), crossing the railroad tracks in one block, and park in the Lookout Park parking lot.

Hiking directions: From the parking lot, head left (east) through the grassy flat along the cliff's edge to an open gate. A path leads through a shady eucalyptus forest. Cross a wooden bridge and head to the sandy shoreline. At the shore, bear to the right, leading to the paved walkways that return up to Lookout Park.

To extend the walk, continue along the coastline to the west. At low tide, the long stretch of beach leads to coves, rocky points, and tidepools. The beach continues west past charming beachfront homes, reaching Eucalyptus Lane and the Hammonds Meadow Trailhead at 2 miles. From Lookout Park, the beach heads 1.5 miles east to Loon Point (Hike 2). ■

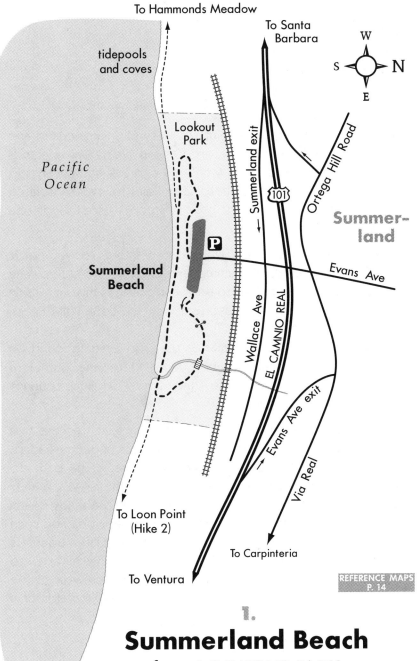

1.
Summerland Beach
from LOOKOUT PARK

2. Loon Point

Hiking distance: 3 miles round trip
Hiking time: 1.5 hours
Elevation gain: Near level
Maps: U.S.G.S. Carpinteria
Santa Barbara Front Country and Paradise Road

Summary of hike: Loon Point sits between Summerland and Carpinteria at the mouth of Toro Canyon Creek. Dense stands of sycamores, coastal oaks, Monterey cypress, and eucalyptus trees line the creek. The path to Loon Point follows an isolated stretch of coastline along the base of steep 40-foot sandstone cliffs.

Driving directions: VENTURA. From Ventura, drive north-bound on Highway 101 to Summerland, and take the Padero Lane exit. Turn left on South Padero Lane, and drive 0.4 miles, crossing Highway 101 and curving east, to the signed Loon Point Beach parking lot on the left.

SANTA BARBARA. From Santa Barbara, drive southbound on Highway 101 to Summerland, and exit on Padero Lane south. Turn right and drive 0.2 miles to the signed Loon Point Beach parking lot on the left.

Hiking directions: Take the signed Loon Beach access trail parallel to the railroad tracks. Curve to the left, under the Padaro Lane bridge, past a grove of eucalyptus trees. The path descends through a narrow drainage between the jagged, weathered cliffs to the shoreline. Bear to the right on the sandy beach along the base of the sandstone cliffs. Loon Point can be seen jutting out to sea. Follow the shoreline, reaching large boulders at Loon Point in 1.5 miles. At high tide, the water level may be too high to reach the point. At a lower tide, the beach walk can be extended from Loon Point to Lookout Park (Hike 1), an additional 1.5 miles west. ■

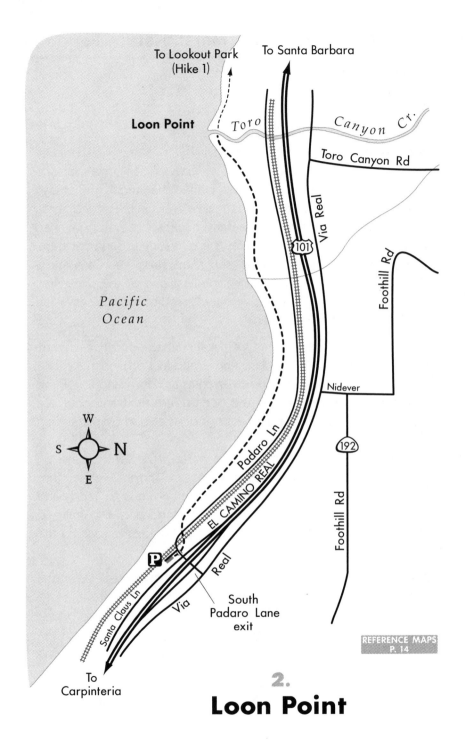

To Lookout Park
(Hike 1)

To Santa Barbara

Loon Point

Toro

Canyon Cr.

Toro Canyon Rd

Via Real

101

Foothill Rd

Pacific
Ocean

Padaro Ln

EL CAMINO REAL

Nidever

192

W

S ⊕ N

E

Foothill Rd

P

Santa Claus Ln

Via

Real

South
Padaro Lane
exit

REFERENCE MAPS
P. 14

To
Carpinteria

2.

Loon Point

3. Carpinteria Salt Marsh Nature Park

Hiking distance: 1.4 miles round trip
Hiking time: 45 minutes
Elevation gain: Level
Maps: U.S.G.S. Carpinteria

Summary of hike: The Carpinteria Salt Marsh, historically known as El Estero (*the estuary*), is one of California's last remaining wetlands. The area was once inhabited by Chumash Indians. The 230-acre estuary is fed by Franklin Creek and Santa Monica Creek. The reserve is a busy, healthy ecosystem with an abundance of sea and plant life. It is a nesting ground for thousands of migratory waterfowl and shorebirds. The Carpinteria Salt Marsh Nature Park sits along the east end of the salt marsh with a trail system, interpretive panels, and several observation decks. Dogs are not allowed.

Driving directions: VENTURA. From Ventura, drive northbound on Highway 101 to Carpinteria, and exit on Linden Avenue. Drive 0.6 miles south on Linden Avenue to Sandyland Road, the last corner before reaching the ocean. Turn right and continue 0.2 miles to Ash Avenue. Park alongside the road by the signed park.

SANTA BARBARA. From Santa Barbara, drive southbound on Highway 101 to Carpinteria, and exit on Linden Avenue. Turn right and drive 0.6 miles south on Linden Avenue to Sandyland Road, the last corner before reaching the ocean. Turn right and continue 0.2 miles to Ash Avenue. Park alongside the road by the signed park.

Hiking directions: From the nature trail sign, walk 20 yards to the west, reaching an observation deck with a group of interpretive panels. A boardwalk to the left leads to the ocean. Take the wide, meandering path to the right. Walk through the coastal scrub vegetation, parallel to Ash Avenue and the salt marsh, while passing additional interpretive panels. At the north end of the park, curve left to another overlook of the wetlands. A short distance ahead is a T-junction. The left and right forks extend a few yards; they have been fenced off to protect the fragile habitat. Cross the bridge straight ahead over 60-foot-wide Franklin Creek. After crossing, go to the right. Parallel the west side of Franklin Creek, with views into the South Marsh Preserve. Just shy of the railroad tracks, veer left and follow the north edge of the preserve to a trail split. The left fork leads a short distance to a rock platform. The right fork ends at Sandyland Cove Road. Return along the same path. ▪

3.
Carpinteria Salt Marsh Nature Park

4. Tarpits Park
CARPINTERIA STATE BEACH

Hiking distance: 1.5 miles round trip
Hiking time: 1 hour
Elevation gain: 50 feet
Maps: U.S.G.S. Carpinteria

Summary of hike: Tarpits Park is an 9-acre blufftop park at the east end of Carpinteria State Beach. The park was once the site of a Chumash Indian village. It is named for the natural tar (tarry asphaltum) that seeps up from beneath the soil. The Chumash used the tar for caulking canoes (called *tomols*) and sealing cooking vessels. Interconnecting trails cross the bluffs overlooking the steep, jagged coastline. Along Carpinteria Creek are riparian willow and sycamore woodlands. Benches are placed along the edge of the bluffs.

Driving directions: VENTURA. From Ventura, drive northbound on Highway 101 to Carpinteria, and exit on Linden Avenue. Turn right and drive 0.5 miles south on Linden Avenue to 6th Street. Turn left and go 0.2 miles to Palm Avenue. Turn right and drive one block to the Carpinteria State Beach parking lot on the right. A parking fee is required.

SANTA BARBARA. From Santa Barbara, drive southbound on Highway 101 to Carpinteria, and exit on Linden Avenue. Turn right and drive 0.5 miles south to 6th Street. Turn left and go 0.2 miles to Palm Avenue. Turn right and drive one block to the Carpinteria State Beach parking lot on the right. A parking fee is required.

Hiking directions: Two routes lead to Tarpits Park: follow the sandy beach east; or walk along the campground road east, crossing over Carpinteria Creek. At a half mile, the campground road ends on the grassy bluffs. From the beach, a footpath ascends the bluffs to the campground road. Several interconnecting paths cross the clifftop terrace. The meandering trails pass groves of eucalyptus trees and Monterey pines. A stairway leads down to the shoreline. As you near the Chevron Oil Pier, the bluffs narrow. This is a good turn-around spot.

To hike farther, cross the ravine and continue past the pier along the edge of the cliffs. The Carpinteria Bluffs and Seal Sanctuary (Hike 5) is a half mile ahead. ▦

To Ventura

To Carpinteria Bluffs and Seal Sanctuary ◢

⑤

EL CAMINO REAL

Dump Rd

Chevron Oil Pier

To Santa Barbara

101

Carpinteria Ave

Carpinteria

Carpinteria Creek

Tarpits Park

N E S W

P

San Miguel Campground

Palm Ave

entrance kiosk

P

Santa Rosa Campground

To Hwy 101

6th St

P

Santa Cruz Campground

Carpinteria State Beach

Pacific Ocean

Linden Ave

Holly Ave

Sandyland Rd

Ash

③ 3 **P**

REFERENCE MAPS
P. 14

4.
Tarpits Park
CARPINTERIA STATE PARK

5. Carpinteria Bluffs
Nature Preserve and Seal Sanctuary

Hiking distance: 2 miles round trip
Hiking time: 1 hour
Elevation gain: Level
Maps: U.S.G.S. White Ledge Peak and Carpinteria

Summary of hike: The Carpinteria Bluffs and Seal Sanctuary encompass 52 oceanfront acres with grasslands, coastal sage, and eucalyptus groves. The area has panoramic views from the Santa Ynez Mountains to the islands of Anacapa, Santa Cruz, and Santa Rosa. At the cliff's edge, 100 feet above the ocean, is an overlook of the seal sanctuary. A community of harbor seals often plays in the water below, lounging and sunbathing on the rocks and shoreline. The sanctuary is a protected birthing habitat for harbor seals during the winter and spring from December 1 through May 31. Beach access is prohibited during these months, but the seals may be observed from the blufftop.

Driving directions: VENTURA. From Ventura, drive northbound on Highway 101 to Carpinteria, and exit on Bailard Avenue. Drive one block south towards the ocean, and park at the road's end.

SANTA BARBARA. From Santa Barbara, drive southbound on Highway 101 to Carpinteria, and exit on Bailard Avenue. Drive one block south towards the ocean, and park at the road's end.

Hiking directions: From the end of the road, hike south on the well-worn path across the open meadow towards the ocean. As you near the ocean cliffs, take the pathway to the right, parallel to a row of stately eucalyptus trees. At the west end of the eucalyptus grove, bear left and cross the railroad tracks. The trail resumes across the tracks. For an optional side trip, take the beach access trail on the left down to the base of the cliffs.

Back on the main trail, continue west along the edge of the ocean bluffs to a bamboo fence—the seal sanctuary overlook. After enjoying the seals and views, return along the same path or explore the open space. ∎

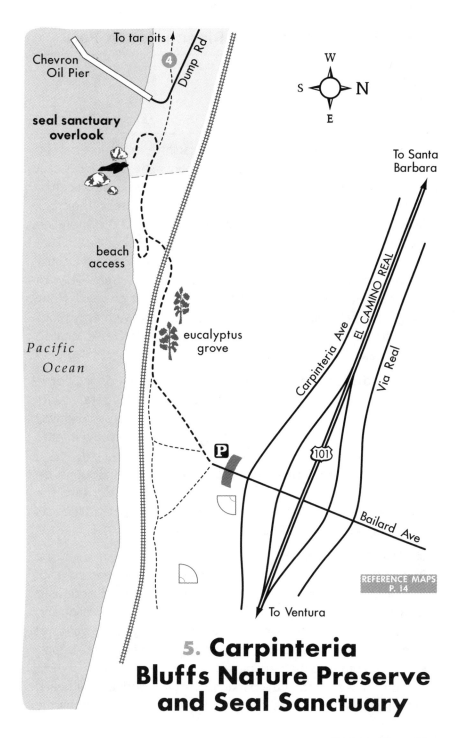

To tar pits

Chevron
Oil Pier

Dump Rd

seal sanctuary
overlook

beach
access

Pacific
Ocean

eucalyptus
grove

W
S ✦ N
E

To Santa
Barbara

Carpinteria Ave

EL CAMINO REAL

Via Real

P

101

Bailard Ave

REFERENCE MAPS
P. 14

To Ventura

5. Carpinteria Bluffs Nature Preserve and Seal Sanctuary

6. Rincon Point and Rincon Beach Park

Hiking distance: 2 miles round trip
Hiking time: 1 hour
Elevation gain: 100 feet
Maps: U.S.G.S. White Ledge Peak

Summary of hike: Rincon Point (meaning *corner* in Spanish) straddles the Santa Barbara/Ventura County line three miles east of Carpinteria. It is considered to be one of the best places to surf in California. The point is bisected by Rincon Creek. The creek flows out of the mountains and carries rocks to the shoreline, forming a cobblestone beach with tidepools. Rincon Beach Park, located on the west side of the point in Santa Barbara County, has a large grassy picnic area atop the bluffs and great views of the coastline. A stairway leads to the 1,200 feet of beach frontage. A dirt path lined with eucalyptus trees and Monterey pines leads to the tidepools and the mouth of Rincon Creek, located on the east side of the point in Ventura County.

Driving directions: VENTURA. From Ventura, drive northbound on Highway 101 to the Ventura—Santa Barbara county line, and take the Bates Road exit. Turn left and cross Highway 101 one block to the parking lots. Park in the lots on either side of Bates Road.

SANTA BARBARA. From Santa Barbara, drive southbound on Highway 101. Continue 3 miles past Carpinteria, and take the Bates Road exit to the stop sign. Turn right, and park in the lots on either side of Bates Road.

Hiking directions: WEST OF RINCON POINT: Begin from the Rincon Park parking lot on the right (west). From the edge of the cliffs, a long staircase and a paved service road both lead down the cliff face, providing access to the sandy shoreline and tidepools. Walk north along the beach, strolling past a series of tidepools along the base of the sandstone cliffs. After beachcombing, return to the parking lot.

From the west end of the parking lot, a well-defined trail heads west past the metal gate. The path is a wide shelf cut along the steep cliffs high above the ocean. At 0.3 miles, the trail reaches the railroad tracks and parallels the railroad right-of-way west to Carpinteria. Choose your own turn-around spot.

EAST OF RINCON POINT: From the Rincon Point parking lot on the east, take the wide beach access path. Descend through a shady, forested grove to the beach. Bear right on the rocky path to a small bay near the tree-lined point. This is an excellent area to explore the tidepools and watch the surfers. Return along the same route. ■

To Carpinteria

Rincon Beach
Park

EL CAMINO REAL

101

To Santa
Barbara

W

S ◆ N

E

stairs

🅿

Rincon
Point

Rincon Creek

Bates Road

🅿

Buena Fortuna St

Puesta Del Sol

SANTA
BARBARA
COUNTY

VENTURA
COUNTY

Rincon Del Mar

101

REFERENCE MAPS
P. 14

*Pacific
Ocean*

To
Ventura

6.

Rincon Point
Rincon Beach Park

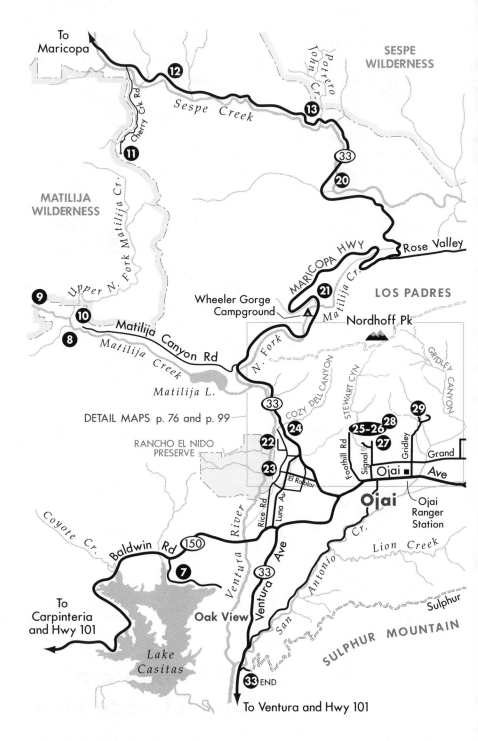

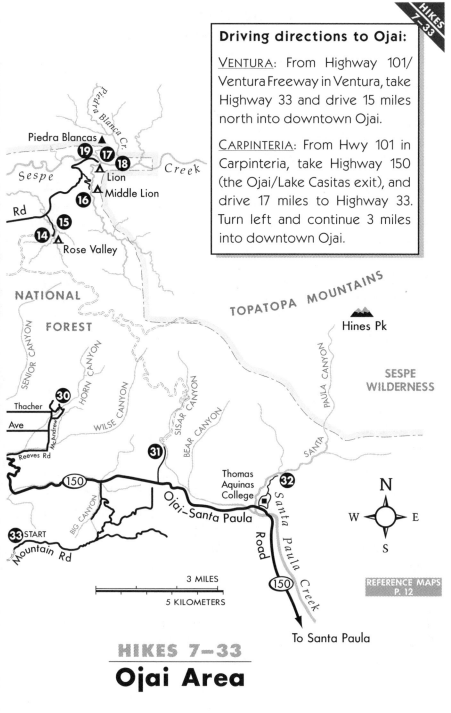

Driving directions to Ojai:

VENTURA: From Highway 101/ Ventura Freeway in Ventura, take Highway 33 and drive 15 miles north into downtown Ojai.

CARPINTERIA: From Hwy 101 in Carpinteria, take Highway 150 (the Ojai/Lake Casitas exit), and drive 17 miles to Highway 33. Turn left and continue 3 miles into downtown Ojai.

Piedra Blanca Cr.

Piedra Blancas ▲

19 **17** ▲ **18**

Sespe Creek

Lion

16 ▲ Middle Lion

Rd

15

14 ▲

Rose Valley

NATIONAL

TOPATOPA MOUNTAINS

FOREST

▲ Hines Pk

SENIOR CANYON

HORN CANYON

WILSE CANYON

SISAR CANYON

BEAR CANYON

PAULA CANYON

SESPE WILDERNESS

30

Thacher

Ave

McAndrew

Reeves Rd

SANTA

31

Thomas Aquinas College

Ojai-Santa Paula

Santa Paula Creek

32

(150)

BIG CANYON

33 START

Mountain Rd

Road

N

W ⊕ E

S

3 MILES

5 KILOMETERS

(150)

REFERENCE MAPS
P. 12

To Santa Paula

HIKES 7-33

Ojai Area

7. Shoreline Lake Trail
LAKE CASITAS RECREATION AREA
11311 Santa Ana Road · Ventura

Hiking distance: 3.6 miles round trip
Hiking time: 2 hours
Elevation gain: 100 feet
Maps: U.S.G.S. Matilija
Matilija and Dick Smith Wilderness Map Guide
Lake Casitas Recreation Area map

Summary of hike: Lake Casitas sits below the Laguna Ridge of the Santa Ynez Mountains between Ojai, Ventura, and Carpinteria. The gorgeous lake, adjacent to the Los Padres National Forest, is set among rolling hills dotted with fir, oak, and sycamore trees. The lake was created in 1959 when Coyote Creek was dammed to provide drinking and irrigation water for the surrounding communities. Santa Ana Creek and the North Fork of Coyote Creek also feed the lake. The irregularly shaped lake covers 2,500 surface acres (4.3 square miles) with 32 miles of shoreline. The reservoir is a popular fishing, boating, and camping area (with more than 400 campsites) and also has a marina. This hike follows the contours of the east side of the lake through open grasslands that include overlooks of vineyards, pockets of oaks, forested coves, and scenic vistas of the lake.

Driving directions: OJAI. From Ojai, drive 3 miles south on Highway 33 to Highway 150 (Baldwin Road). Turn right and continue 3.2 miles to Santa Ana Road and the signed Lake Casitas turnoff. Turn left and quickly veer right to the park entrance station. After paying the entrance fee, turn left and continue 1.4 miles to the parking area at the end of the road. A parking fee is required.

CARPINTERIA. From Highway 101 in Carpinteria, take Highway 150 (the Ojai/Lake Casitas exit), and drive 14 miles to Santa Ana Road and the signed Lake Casitas turnoff. Turn right and quickly veer right again to the park entrance station. After paying the

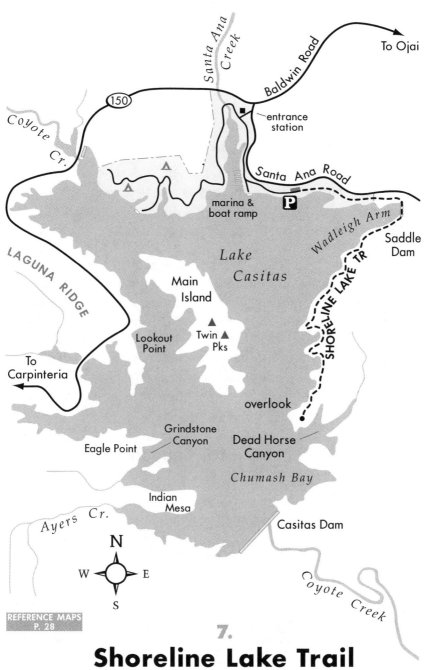

To Ojai

Santa Ana Creek

Baldwin Road

150

entrance
station

Coyote Cr.

Santa Ana Road

marina &
boat ramp

P

Wadleigh Arm

Saddle
Dam

Lake
Casitas

SHORELINE LAKE TR

Main
Island

LAGUNA RIDGE

Lookout
Point

Twin
Pks

To
Carpinteria

overlook

Grindstone
Canyon

Eagle Point

Dead Horse
Canyon

Chumash Bay

Indian
Mesa

Casitas Dam

Ayers Cr.

Coyote Creek

N

W E

S

REFERENCE MAPS
P. 28

7.

Shoreline Lake Trail
LAKE CASITAS RECREATION AREA

entrance fee, turn left and continue 1.4 miles to the parking area at the end of the road.

VENTURA. From Highway 101 in Ventura, take Highway 33 north, and drive 13 miles to Highway 150 on the left. Turn left and continue 3.2 miles to Santa Ana Road and the signed Lake Casitas turnoff. Turn left and quickly veer right to the park entrance station. After paying the entrance fee, turn left and continue 1.4 miles to the parking area at the end of the road.

Hiking directions: Take the posted trail to the east, parallel to Santa Ana Road. The path skirts the north side of the Wadleigh Arm of Lake Casitas. Follow the sloping grassland, with great views across the lake, the Topatopa Mountains, and the Santa Ynez Mountains. At the far east end of the lake, cross Saddle Dam. Continue on the southern slope of the Wadleigh Arm, overlooking vineyards and oak groves. Weave east, following the contours of the hills along minor dips and rises between pockets of oak trees and the lake. At 1.8 miles is an overlook on an oak-dotted knoll that includes a view of Twin Peaks on Main Island. A bench sits atop the knoll under a mature oak tree. The trail ends 100 yards ahead at the picnic benches on a grassy knoll above Dead Horse Canyon. After enjoying the gorgeous lake cove, return along the same trail. ∎

8. Murietta Canyon

Hiking distance: 3.4 miles round trip
Hiking time: 1.5 hours
Elevation gain: 200 feet
Maps: U.S.G.S. Old Man Mountain and White Ledge Peak
Matilija and Dick Smith Wilderness Map Guide
Sespe Wilderness Trail Map

Summary of hike: The headwaters of the 31-mile long Ventura River are formed around Ojai from San Antonio Creek, Coyote Creek, and Matilija Creek. Matilija Creek, draining from the north, delineates the boundary between the Santa Ynez Mountains to the west and the Topatopa Mountains to the north of Ojai. The

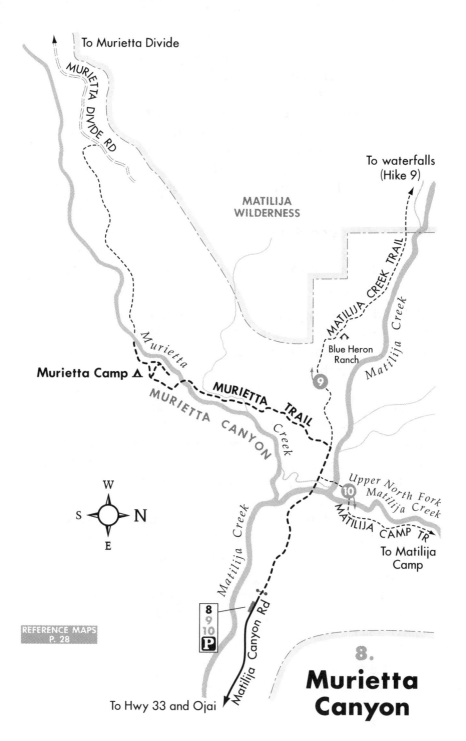

To Murietta Divide

MURIETTA DIVIDE RD

MATILIJA WILDERNESS

To waterfalls (Hike 9)

MATILIJA CREEK TRAIL

Matilija Creek

Murietta

Blue Heron Ranch

Murietta Camp ▲

MURIETTA TRAIL

MURIETTA CANYON

Creek

⑨

Matilija Creek

W
S — N
E

Upper North Fork Matilija Creek

⑩

MATILIJA CAMP TR

To Matilija Camp

Matilija Creek

8
9
10
P

Matilija Canyon Rd

To Hwy 33 and Ojai

REFERENCE MAPS
P. 28

8.

Murietta Canyon

diverse and wild landscape of the Matilija Creek watershed lies within the protected Matilija Wilderness. Hikes 8—11 explore the Matilija—Murietta Creek drainage.

The Murietta Trail begins in Matilija Canyon on the north side of Matilija Creek. The trail veers west into Murietta Canyon and follows Murietta Creek along the canyon bottom to a pristine trail camp. Murietta Camp sits on a shady wooded flat at the edge of Murietta Creek by cascades and pools. The primitive camp rests under a forest canopy dominated by cedar and oak trees.

Driving directions: OJAI. From Ojai, drive 4.9 miles north on Highway 33 (Maricopa Highway) to Matilija Canyon Road and turn left. Continue 4.8 miles to the parking area on the left by the trailhead gate.

Hiking directions: Pass the trailhead gate and follow the paved road west. Enter the Matilija Canyon Ranch, a private wildlife refuge. Stay on the road along this forest service easement. Just past the refuge the pavement ends. Cross the creek two times to views up Murrieta Canyon, Old Man Canyon, and Matilija Canyon. At 0.5 miles, just past the second creek crossing, is the signed North Fork Matilija Creek Trail to the right (Hike 10). Instead, continue another 0.2 miles to the signed Murietta Trail on the left. Leave the road and head south on the footpath towards the mouth of Murietta Canyon. Proceed to a stream crossing by pools and cascades. Rock hop across the stream channels and up a small hill, heading deeper into the canyon. Follow the creek to Murietta Camp, perched on a flat at 1.7 miles. From the camp, several trails lead down to the stream. Return along the same path.

Up the canyon from the campground, the trail enters a dense forest with a tangle of vegetation and underbrush. This unmaintained trail becomes vague and hard to follow, but leads 0.8 miles to Murietta Divide Road. Murietta Divide Road—a dirt road—leads 2.4 miles west to the 3,443-foot divide, offering great views into the Santa Ynez River Valley. ▪

9. Matilija Creek Trail

Hiking distance: 7 miles round trip
Hiking time: 3 hours
Elevation gain: 600 feet
Maps: U.S.G.S. Old Man Mountain
       Matilija and Dick Smith Wilderness Map Guide
       Sespe Wilderness Trail Map

map
page 36

Summary of hike: The Matilija Creek Trail heads up the main canyon of the Matilija Creek drainage to beautiful pools, cascades, and water slides. Large shale slabs border the creek for sunbathing beneath the steep canyon cliffs. Up the isolated and rugged canyon are several towering waterfalls.

Driving directions: OJAI. From Ojai, drive 4.9 miles north on Highway 33 (Maricopa Highway) to Matilija Canyon Road and turn left. Continue 4.8 miles to the parking area on the left by the trailhead gate.

Hiking directions: Pass the trailhead gate and follow the paved road west. Enter the Matilija Canyon Ranch, a private wildlife refuge. Stay on the road along this forest service easement. Just past the refuge the pavement ends. Cross the creek two times to views up Murrieta Canyon, Old Man Canyon, and Matilija Canyon. At 0.5 miles, just past the second creek crossing, is the signed North Fork Matilija Creek Trail to the right— Hike 10. Shortly after, a footpath on the left veers southwest along Murietta Creek—Hike 8. Stay on the main road to an intersection with another trail one mile from the trailhead. Take the right fork past a house on a Forest Service easement through the Blue Heron Ranch. For a short distance, the trail borders a beautiful, two-foot-high rock wall and fruit trees. As you approach the mountain range, cross a tributary stream at the mouth of Old Man Canyon and curve to the right. Follow the western edge of the deep, narrow canyon and cross another stream. Climb up a short hill to a perch overlooking the canyon. Take the left fork that curves around the gully, and hike down the rocky drainage. Near the canyon floor, the trail picks up again to the left. Hike

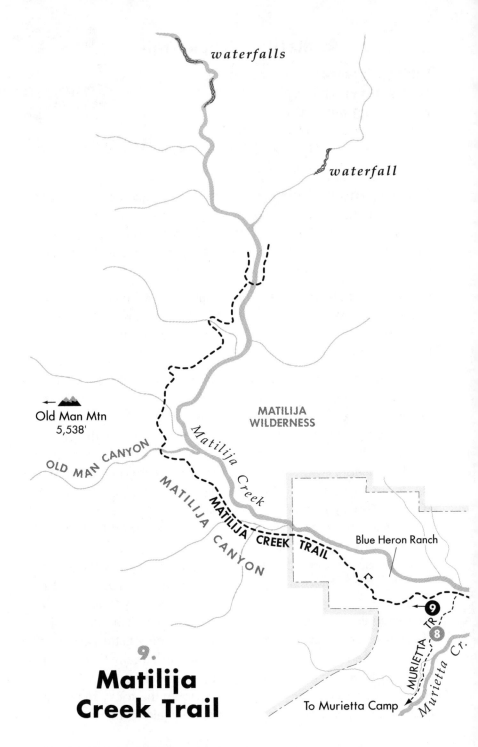

waterfalls

waterfall

MATILIJA
WILDERNESS

Old Man Mtn
5,538'

OLD MAN CANYON

Matilija Creek

MATILIJA CANYON

MATILIJA CREEK TRAIL

Blue Heron Ranch

MURIETTA TR.

Murietta Cr.

9

8

To Murietta Camp

9.
Matilija
Creek Trail

parallel to the creek along its endless cascades, pools, and rock slabs. This natural playground is the destination. Return along the same path.

To hike farther, continue up-canyon, creating your own path. There are three waterfalls ahead. Two falls are located another mile up the main canyon. Another falls is in the canyon to the northeast. Hiking may be difficult due to slippery shale and an indistinct trail. ■

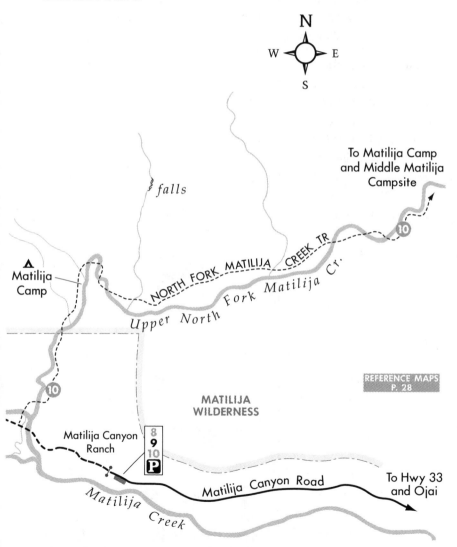

10. North Fork Matilija Creek Trail
to Matilija Camp and Middle Matilija Camp

SOUTHERN TRAILHEAD

Hiking distance: 8 miles round trip
Hiking time: 4 hours
Elevation gain: 800 feet
Maps: U.S.G.S. Old Man Mountain and Wheeler Springs
Matilija and Dick Smith Wilderness Map Guide
Sespe Wilderness Trail Map

Summary of hike: The Upper North Fork of Matilija Creek forms on the southern slopes of Ortega Hill and flows year-round. The North Fork Matilija Creek Trail runs for 9 miles through the Matilija Wilderness along the Upper North Fork of Matilija Creek, from its confluence at Matilija Creek to Ortega Hill. En route the trail passes pools, cascades, and waterfalls. This hike begins at the southern trailhead at Matilija Canyon Road and leads to Matilija Camp and Middle Matilija Camp, oak-shaded camps with large boulders, sandstone cliffs, swimming holes, and picnic areas. The easy trail winds through the lush canyon in the shade of oaks, alders, and syca-mores, crossing the

North Fork Matilija Creek Trail

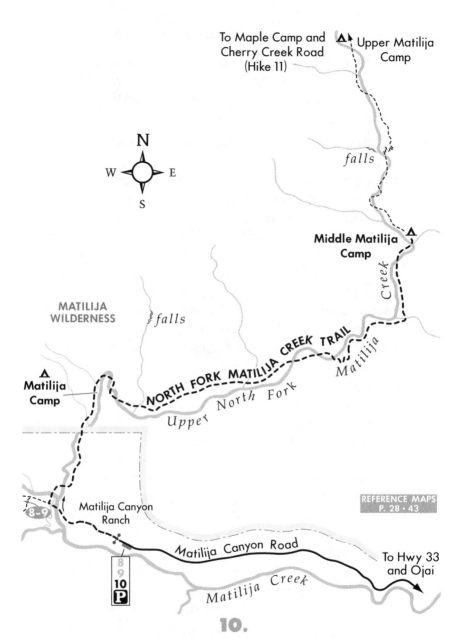

To Maple Camp and
Cherry Creek Road
(Hike 11)

Upper Matilija
Camp

N
W · E
S

falls

Middle Matilija
Camp

Creek

MATILIJA
WILDERNESS

falls

NORTH FORK MATILIJA CREEK TRAIL

Matilija

Matilija
Camp

North Fork

Upper

REFERENCE MAPS
P. 28 · 43

Matilija Canyon
Ranch

8-9

Matilija Canyon Road

To Hwy 33
and Ojai

8
9

10
P

Matilija Creek

10.

North Fork Matilija Creek Trail

to MATILIJA CAMP • MIDDLE MATILIJA CAMP
SOUTHERN TRAILHEAD

creek 14 times. (Hike 11 starts at the northern trailhead.)

Driving directions: OJAI. From Ojai, drive 4.9 miles north on Highway 33 (Maricopa Highway) to Matilija Canyon Road and turn left. Continue 4.8 miles to the parking area on the left by the trailhead gate.

Hiking directions: Pass the trailhead gate and follow the paved road west. Enter the Matilija Canyon Ranch, a private wildlife refuge. Stay on the road along this forest service easement. Just past the refuge the pavement ends. Cross the creek two times to views up Murrieta Canyon, Old Man Canyon, and Matilija Canyon. At 0.5 miles, just past the second creek crossing, leave the road and take the North Fork Matilija Creek Trail to the right. Cross a rocky wash and head north up the narrow canyon floor between steep cliffs. Hop over the Upper North Fork Matilija Creek, enter the Matilija Wilderness, and follow the east canyon wall through a canopy of riparian growth. Cross the creek again by a rock wall and boulders forming a pool. At 1.3 miles, enter Matilija Camp, a group of campsites along the creek under a grove of oaks.

Just past the campsites, cross the creek as the canyon and trail curve to the east. Cross the creek three consecutive times, and slowly gain elevation as the canyon widens. Weave through an easy and uneventful stretch away from the creek. Return to the creek by another pool at 2.6 miles. Cross to the south side of the creek and continue upstream. Cross the creek two more times by a group of pools. Traverse the south canyon wall, and climb up two switchbacks to views across the length of the canyon to Old Man Mountain. Pass more pools, small waterfalls, and cascades. Curve left and cross a tributary stream, following the bends in the canyon. Cross the creek for the thirteenth time by another pool with a 4-foot waterfall. Make the final creek crossing and enter the Middle Matilija Campsite on a grassy flat with majestic oaks at 4 miles.

To extend the hike, the trail continues 1.6 miles north to Upper Matilija Camp, 3.4 miles to Maple Camp, and 5.1 miles to the upper trailhead at the south end of Cherry Creek Road—Hike 11. ■

11. North Fork Matilija Creek Trail
from Ortega Hill to Maple Camp
and Upper Matilija Camp

NORTHERN TRAILHEAD

Hiking distance: 7 miles round trip
Hiking time: 4.5 hours
Elevation gain: 2,100 feet
Maps: U.S.G.S. Wheeler Springs
Matilija & Dick Smith Wilderness Map Guide
Sespe Wilderness Trail Map

map
page 43

Summary of hike: Perennial North Fork Matilija Creek flows 9 miles year-round from its fan-shaped drainage of multiple springs below Ortega Hill to its confluence with Matilija Creek above Matilija Lake. The North Fork Matilija Creek Trail follows the creek from the canyon's upper slopes to its confluence with Matilija Creek. This hike begins from the northern trailhead at the head of the canyon by Ortega Hill. (Hike 10 begins from the southern trailhead.) The steep path starts at an elevation of 5,000 feet and zigzags down the chaparral-covered canyon wall to the lush woodlands on the canyon floor. The trail follows the waterway past pools, small waterfalls, and vertical rock grottos while crossing the creek repeatedly. En route, the trail passes through Maple Creek, an undeveloped camp on the banks of the creek, and Upper Matilija Camp, on the edge of the creek by a small waterfall and several pools. This is a strenuous hike. The last 1.5 miles climbs 1,100 feet back to the trailhead.

Driving directions: OJAI. From Ojai, drive 27 miles north on Highway 33 (Maricopa Highway) to the unmarked Cherry Creek Road turnoff on the left. (It is located 12.4 miles past the Rose Valley Road turnoff and 6 miles past the signed Potrero John trailhead.) Turn left on the narrow and unpaved Cherry Creek Road. Wind 2.8 miles south up Cherry Canyon to the posted trailhead on the right by a large pullout on the left. This road is closed during the winter rainy season, so check with the Ojai Ranger District before heading to the trailhead.

Hiking directions: The blocked road continues south as the Ortega Trail. For this hike, pass the trailhead boulders, and descend the northwest canyon wall, overlooking the folded terrain of the surrounding mountains. Wind down the mountain to the lush canyon bottom, losing 1,100 feet in elevation over the first 1.5 miles. Once on the canyon floor, stroll through the dense riparian forest among alder, bay laurel, fir, manzanita, maple, oak, and spruce to primitive Maple Camp on the left. The camp sits along the stream under the shade of towering maple trees on a rock-strewn flat. Continue down-canyon, following the North Fork Matilija Creek past endless rock-rimmed pools. Rock-hop over the creek and recross by two pools and an eroding vertical rock formation. Cross a third time by a grotto, and weave down the rocky gorge among waterfalls, cascades, and pools. At 3.4 miles, the path drops into Upper Matilija Camp in a mixed forest on the east bank of the creek. This is our turn-around spot.

To extend the hike, the trail continues down-canyon another 1.6 miles to Middle Matilija Camp, 4.3 miles to Matilija Camp, and 5.6 miles to the southern trailhead in Matilija Canyon (Hike 10). ∎

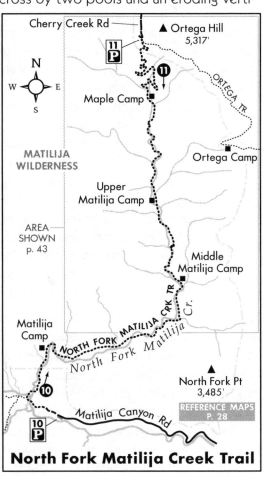

North Fork Matilija Creek Trail

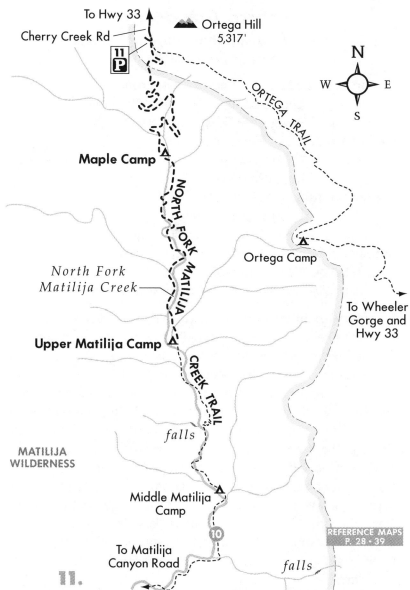

To Hwy 33

Cherry Creek Rd

Ortega Hill
5,317'

N
W · E
S

ORTEGA TRAIL

Maple Camp

NORTH FORK MATILIJA

North Fork
Matilija Creek

Ortega Camp

To Wheeler
Gorge and
Hwy 33

Upper Matilija Camp

CREEK TRAIL

falls

MATILIJA
WILDERNESS

Middle Matilija
Camp

REFERENCE MAPS
P. 28 · 39

To Matilija
Canyon Road

falls

11.

North Fork Matilija Creek Trail
from ORTEGA HILL to MAPLE CAMP
and UPPER MATILIJA CAMP
NORTHERN TRAILHEAD

12. Chorro Grande Trail
to Oak Camp, Chorro Springs Camp, and Reyes Peak Camp

Hiking distance: Oak Camp: 3.4 miles round trip
Chorro Springs Camp: 8.6 miles round trip
Reyes Peak Camp: 10.2 miles round trip

Hiking time: Oak Camp: 2 hours
Chorro Springs Camp: 5.5 hours
Reyes Peak Camp: 7 hours

map
page 46

Elevation gain: Oak Camp: 500 feet
Chorro Springs Camp: 2,350 feet
Reyes Peak Camp: 3,100 feet

Maps: U.S.G.S. Wheeler Springs and Reyes Peak
Sespe Wilderness Trail Map
Matilija and Dick Smith Wilderness Map Guide

Summary of hike: Chorro Grande Canyon is a beautiful canyon north of Ojai that stretches from Pine Mountain Ridge south to its confluence with Sespe Creek by Highway 33. Chorro Grande Creek forms on the upper southern slope of Pine Mountain and flows year-round. The Chorro Grande Trail follows the canyon for five miles along most of its length. While the first part of the trail to Oak Camp is relatively easy, the hike up to Reyes Peak Camp at the head of the canyon is a strenuous climb. The camp straddles the 7,200-foot Pine Mountain Ridge. From the summit, the staggering panoramas are phenomenal. The vistas extend across the Matilija Wilderness and Ojai Valley to the Oxnard Plain, the coastline, and the Channel Islands. Inland are views across Pine Mountain to the vast Cuyama Badlands. Reyes Peak Camp is set in a grove of ponderosa pines with huge, scattered boulders.

For a shorter hike, turn around at Oak Camp or Chorro Springs Camp (also called Chorro Grande Camp). The two primitive camps sit on the banks of the creek amongst live oaks and beautiful conifers.

Driving directions: OJAI. From Ojai, drive 25.4 miles north on Highway 33 (Maricopa Highway) to the posted trailhead on the right. (It is located 10.8 miles past the Rose Valley Road turnoff.) Park in the pullouts on either side of the highway.

Hiking directions: From the north side of the highway, head north up the chaparral-clad hillside. Climb up and over the minor draw to the west slope of Chorro Grande Canyon, overlooking the scenic canyon with beautiful sandstone outcroppings. Drop down and cross a seasonal fork of Chorro Grande Creek. Top another slope and hop over the main fork of the creek and another tributary. Head up Chorro Grande Canyon, winding through the scrub oak, manzanita, sage, pinyon pines, and yucca to the posted Oak Camp at 1.7 miles. Detour left into the camp on a creekside flat under the shade of mature oaks.

To keep hiking, return to the main trail and continue up-canyon. Follow the curves of the canyon, staying on the east side of the drainage. A half mile past Oak Camp is an unmarked junction with the abandoned Gypsum Mine Road. The road goes west and heads into Godwin Canyon. The right fork (a trail) leads to Burro Creek and Munson Creek. For this hike, cross the road, leaving the creek and canyon floor. The footpath begins its serious climb up Pine Mountain to the northeast. Zigzag up the mountain at a fairly steep grade, with views of Pine Mountain, Ortega Hill, the Matilija Wilderness, and the Sespe Creek drainage. At 4.3 miles, the trail reaches Chorro Springs Camp among Jeffrey and ponderosa pines. The camp is to the east (right) of the trail and Chorro Springs is to the west.

To continue to Reyes Peak Camp at the summit, make the final ascent, gaining 750 feet over 0.8 miles to the Pine Mountain Ridge Road by a gate. The gate is just east of the Reyes Peak Campground. The camp has picnic benches, tall ponderosa pines, and huge boulders. ▦

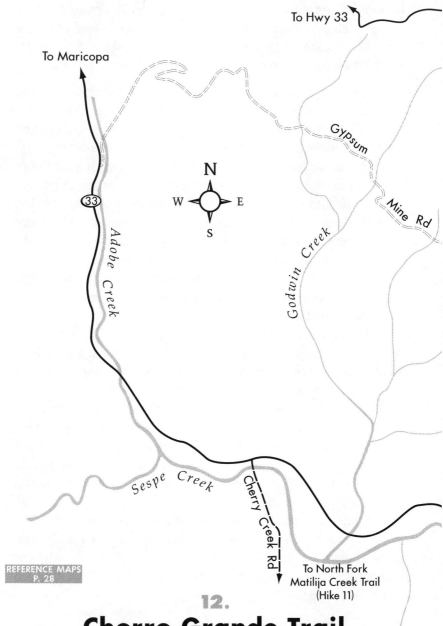

To Hwy 33

To Maricopa

Gypsum

Mine Rd

33

N
W E
S

Adobe Creek

Godwin Creek

Sespe Creek

Cherry Creek Rd

REFERENCE MAPS
P. 28

To North Fork
Matilija Creek Trail
(Hike 11)

12.

Chorro Grande Trail
to Oak Camp, Chorro Springs Camp
and Reyes Peak Camp

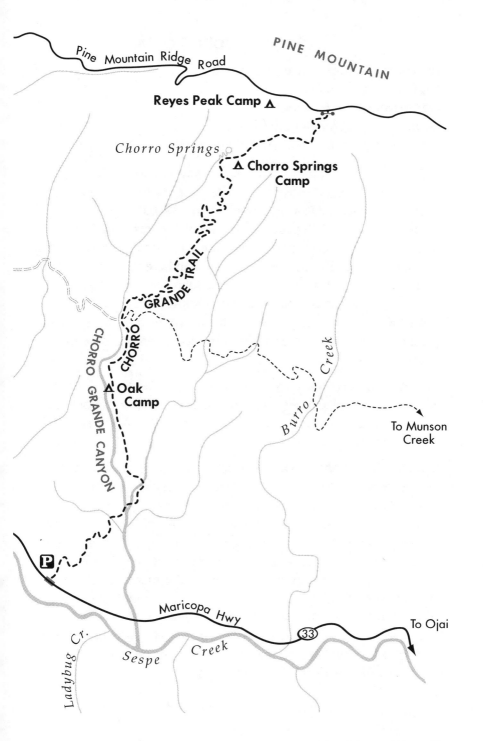

13. Potrero John Trail

Hiking distance: 4 miles round trip
Hiking time: 2 hours
Elevation gain: 600 feet
Maps: U.S.G.S. Wheeler Springs
Matilija and Dick Smith Wilderness Map Guide
Sespe Wilderness Trail Map

Summary of hike: Potrero John Canyon is tucked into the southern slopes of Pine Mountain in the 220,000-acre Sespe Wilderness, part of the Los Padres National Forest. The Potrero John Trail is an uncrowded, lightly used trail that begins at an elevation of 3,655 feet, where Potrero John Creek empties into Sespe Creek. The trail follows Potrero John Creek through a narrow gorge and up the canyon. There is also an open meadow dotted with red baked manzanita and views of the surrounding mountains. At the trail's end is Potrero John Camp, a creekside flat shaded with oaks.

Driving directions: OJAI. From Ojai, drive 21 miles north on Highway 33 (Maricopa Highway) to the trailhead parking pullout on the right side of the road. It is located on the north side of Potrero Bridge.

Hiking directions: Hike north past the trailhead sign, immediately entering the narrow, steep-walled canyon on the west side of Potrero John Creek. After three successive creek crossings, the trail enters the Sespe Wilderness. There are eight creek crossings in the first mile while passing various pools and cascades. At one mile, leave the narrow canyon and emerge into a large, open meadow. At the far side of the meadow, the trail ends at Potrero John Camp, a walk-in camp on the banks of the creek. Return to the trailhead along the same route.

To hike farther, a rough, unmaintained trail heads upstream over rocks, downfall, and underbrush. Along the way are continuous pools, cascades, and waterfalls. ▪

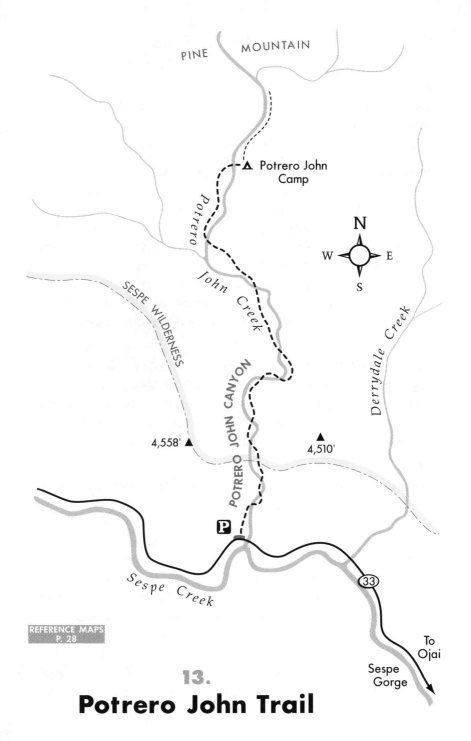

PINE MOUNTAIN

△ Potrero John
Camp

Potrero

John Creek

SESPE WILDERNESS

Derrydale Creek

N
W E
S

4,558' ▲

POTRERO JOHN CANYON

▲ 4,510'

P

Sespe Creek

33

REFERENCE MAPS
P. 28

To
Ojai

Sespe
Gorge

13.
Potrero John Trail

14. Rose Valley Falls

Hiking distance: 1 mile round trip
Hiking time: 30 minutes
Elevation gain: 300 feet
Maps: U.S.G.S. Lion Canyon
       Sespe Wilderness Trail Map

Summary of hike: Rose Valley Falls is a 300-foot, three-tiered waterfall at the northern base of Nordhoff Ridge in the Topatopa Mountains. This hike follows Rose Valley Creek up a shady canyon to the base of the lower falls, a 100-foot, multi-strand waterfall. The tall and narrow waterfall cascades through a notch over the near-vertical cliffs onto the rocks below in a cool, moss-covered grotto. This short, easy trail begins at the Rose Valley Campground at an elevation of 3,450 feet. There are also three lakes near the campground that are stocked with trout.

Driving directions: OJAI. From Ojai, drive 14.6 miles north on Highway 33 (Maricopa Highway) to the Rose Valley Road turnoff and turn right. Continue 3 miles to the Rose Valley Campground turnoff, across from the lower lake, and turn right. Drive 0.5 miles to the south end of the campground loop road to the signed trailhead by campsite number 4.

Hiking directions: Hike south past the trailhead sign, immediately entering the thick coastal live oak, bay, and sycamore forest on the well-defined trail. Cross a tributary of Rose Valley Creek, and stay on the main path as you make your way up the lush, narrow canyon. The first of several small waterfalls can be spotted on the left at 0.2 miles. Short side paths lead down to the creek by these waterfalls and pools. The trail ends at a half mile at the base of lower Rose Valley Falls, with its bridal veil beauty beneath a colorful, mossy limestone wall. Return along the same path.

To extend the hike, the Nordhoff Ridge Road (a gated road) climbs 2.1 miles west to Nordhoff Ridge, with sweeping coastal

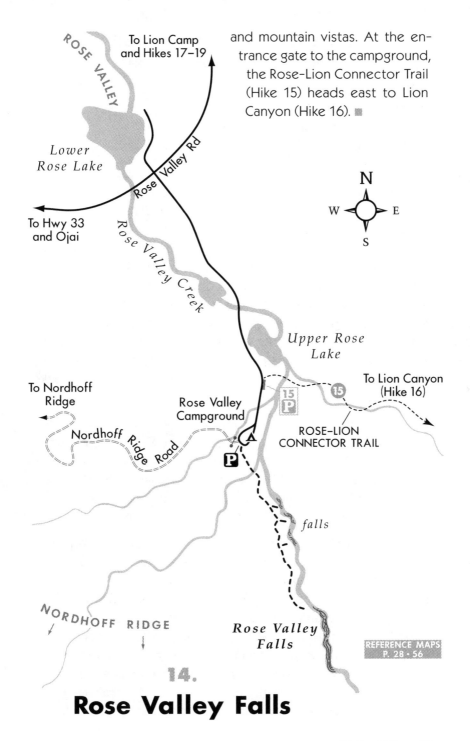

and mountain vistas. At the entrance gate to the campground, the Rose-Lion Connector Trail (Hike 15) heads east to Lion Canyon (Hike 16). ■

To Lion Camp
and Hikes 17–19

ROSE VALLEY

Lower
Rose Lake

Rose Valley Rd

To Hwy 33
and Ojai

Rose Valley Creek

N
W   E
S

Upper Rose
Lake

To Nordhoff
Ridge

Nordhoff Ridge Road

Rose Valley
Campground

15
P

15

To Lion Canyon
(Hike 16)

ROSE-LION
CONNECTOR TRAIL

P

falls

NORDHOFF RIDGE

Rose Valley
Falls

REFERENCE MAPS
P. 28 · 56

14.

Rose Valley Falls

15. Rose–Lion Connector Trail
ROSE VALLEY to LION CANYON

Hiking distance: 3.2 miles round trip
Hiking time: 1.5 hours
Elevation gain: 300 feet
Maps: U.S.G.S. Lion Canyon
       Sespe Wilderness Trail Map

Summary of hike: Rose Valley and Lion Canyon are two popular, stream-fed canyons located north of Ojai. The area has campgrounds and several hiking trails. The Rose-Lion Connector Trail is a 1.6-mile trail that links Rose Valley and Lion Canyon, offering additional hiking from either end. This hike begins from the Rose Valley Campground by Upper Rose Lake and Rose Valley Falls. The trail traverses the lower slopes of the mountain through scrubby vegetation and along a tributary stream to Lion Creek. There are overlooks with great northern views toward Pine Mountain. From Lion Creek, at the other end of the trail, the hike can be extended up the canyon to waterfalls and backcountry camps.

Driving directions: OJAI. From Ojai, drive 14.6 miles north on Highway 33 (Maricopa Highway) to the Rose Valley Road turnoff and turn right. Continue 3 miles to the Rose Valley Campground turnoff, across from the lower lake, and turn right. Drive 0.4 miles to the Rose Valley Campground sign and entrance gate. Park in the dirt pullouts or along the left (east) side of the road.

Hiking directions: From the Rose Valley Campground sign and entrance gate, head east on the posted trail. Skirt the south side of Upper Rose Lake, and cross a seasonal drainage. Weave through the draw and rolling, conical hills. Cross the streambed two more times, and ascend the south canyon slope. Traverse the hillside, climbing to the 3,700-foot saddle between Rose Valley and Lion Canyon. Begin descending into Lion Canyon, heading down a sandy slope to seasonal tributary streams. Cross the drainage and head up the hillside. Follow the drainage on a level grade, then climb and follow the north canyon slope. Drop down to Lion Creek, and cross the creek to a posted T-junction with the Lion Canyon Trail.

To extend the hike, the left fork leads 1.3 miles down-canyon to Middle Lion Campground and Rose Valley Road. The right fork—Hike 16—leads 0.6 miles to 4-Points Trail Junction, where the canyon splits. To the left is East Fork Lion Camp, a waterfall, and pool. To the right is West Fork Lion Camp and another waterfall and pool. Straight ahead, the Lion Canyon Trail climbs 1,700 feet over 3.6 miles to Nordhoff Ridge. From the 5,160-foot ridge are sweeping 360-degree panoramas of the backcountry mountains and the Ojai Valley to the Pacific Ocean. ▪

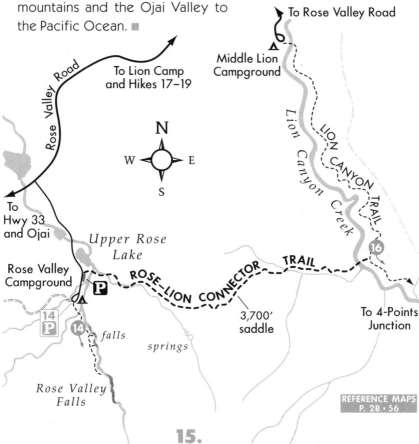

15.
Rose—Lion Connector Trail
Rose Valley to Lion Canyon

16. Lion Canyon Trail
to West Fork Lion Camp and East Fork Lion Camp

Hiking distance: 5.6 miles round trip
Hiking time: 3 hours
Elevation gain: 350 feet
Maps: U.S.G.S. Lion Canyon
       Sespe Wilderness Trail Map

Summary of hike: Lion Canyon Creek flows 6.5 miles from the upper slopes of the Topatopa Mountains through Lion Canyon, emptying into Sespe Creek. The Lion Canyon Trail follows the canyon over five miles, from Middle Lion Campground to 5,160-foot Nordhoff Ridge. The vistas expand across Ojai Valley to the ocean and Channel Islands. This hike follows the lower portion of the trail through the forested canyon along Lion Creek to a three-way trail fork, where the canyon splits at the confluence of the East Fork and West Fork. Footpaths follow each fork to shaded backcountry camps on creekside flats with lush vegetation. Both camps have a beautiful waterfall and pool that are surrounded by rounded boulders.

Driving directions: OJAI. From Ojai, drive 14.6 miles north on Highway 33 (Maricopa Highway) to the Rose Valley Road turnoff and turn right. Continue 4.8 miles to a road split. Take the right fork 0.8 miles down to the Middle Lion Campground and trailhead parking area.

Hiking directions: Walk east along the unpaved campground road, crossing Lion Canyon Creek. Take the signed trail to the right, and head south up Lion Canyon. Continue hiking gradually uphill along the east side of the canyon. At 1.3 miles is a posted junction with the Rose-Lion Connector Trail to the right, which leads to Rose Valley Campground (Hike 15). Proceed straight ahead, staying in Lion Canyon, to another creek crossing at two miles. After crossing is a three-way trail split known as Four Points Trail Junction.
    From the Four Points Trail Junction are three options. The left fork (East Fork Lion Canyon Trail) leads a half mile to East Fork

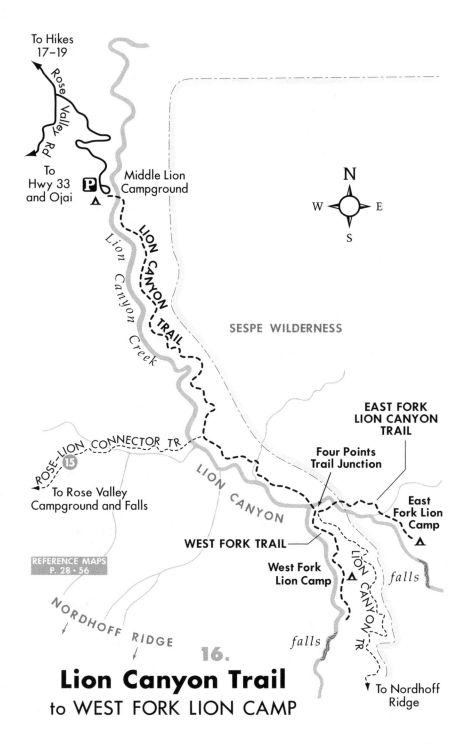

To Hikes 17–19

Rose Valley Rd

To Hwy 33 and Ojai

P

Middle Lion Campground

Lion Canyon Creek

LION CANYON TRAIL

SESPE WILDERNESS

N
W E
S

EAST FORK LION CANYON TRAIL

ROSE-LION CONNECTOR TR

15

To Rose Valley Campground and Falls

LION CANYON

Four Points Trail Junction

East Fork Lion Camp

WEST FORK TRAIL

REFERENCE MAPS P. 28 · 56

West Fork Lion Camp

LION CANYON TR

falls

NORDHOFF RIDGE

falls

To Nordhoff Ridge

16.

Lion Canyon Trail
to WEST FORK LION CAMP

Lion Camp and a waterfall and pool within the Sespe Wilderness. The Lion Canyon Trail (middle route) continues straight ahead, gaining 1,700 feet over 3.6 miles to Nordhoff Ridge. Atop the ridge are spectacular coastal and mountain views. Traversing the ridge is Nordhoff Ridge Road, a vehicle-restricted road. From the road, routes lead down the ridge into Horn Canyon and Sisar Canyon into Ojai Valley.

For now, go to the right on the West Fork Trail. Stay on the east side of the creek along the edge of the rocky hillside. Less than a half mile from the junction is West Fork Lion Camp. Rock hop up the narrow drainage a short distance past the camp to a beautiful waterfall and pool.

Return 0.4 miles to Four Points Trail Junction. Take the East Fork Lion Canyon Trail and enter the narrow canyon. Weave through the tall, reedy deer grass, used by the Chumash Indians to weave baskets. The canyon soon opens, with pockets of pines gracing the canyon slopes. Cross an ephemeral tributary to East Fork Lion Creek Camp at a half mile. Walk through the pine-dotted camp, passing a few metal grills and fire pits. Just past the camp, follow the creek, scrambling through the boulders to a box canyon and rock grotto with a waterfall and pool. Return by retracing your route. ∎

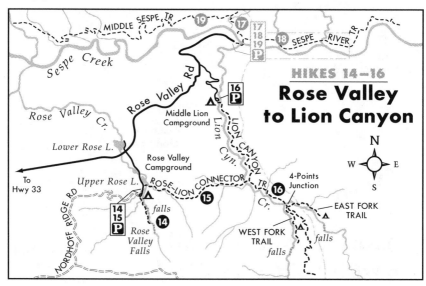

17. Piedra Blanca Formations
Piedra Blanca Camp and Twin Forks Camp

GENE MARSHALL — PIEDRA BLANCA
NATIONAL RECREATION TRAIL

Hiking distance: 6.4 miles round trip
(1.25 miles to Piedra Blanca formations)
Hiking time: 3.5 hours
Elevation gain: 600 feet
Maps: U.S.G.S. Lion Canyon
Sespe Wilderness Trail Map

map
page 60

Summary of hike: The magnificent Piedra Blanca Formations (meaning *white rock* in Spanish) are huge, weather-sculpted sandstone outcrops carved by wind and water. The impressive formations stretch for over a mile, with rounded slopes, sheer cliffs, caves, and overhangs. You can easily spend the day exploring the trails around the unique rocks, cavities, and caves. The Gene Marshall-Piedra Blanca National Recreation Trail, a 17.7-mile trail in the Sespe Wilderness, weaves through these eroded monoliths en route to a series of wilderness campsites. This hike begins at Sespe Creek and winds through the smooth, white formations, following Piedra Blanca Creek to Piedra Blanca Camp and Twin Forks Camp.

Driving directions: OJAI. From Ojai, drive 14.6 miles north on Highway 33 (Maricopa Highway) to the Rose Valley Road turnoff and turn right. Continue 4.8 miles to a road split. Take the left fork 0.9 miles down to the trailhead parking lot at the end of the road.

Hiking directions: From the signed path by the restrooms, walk towards the river gorge. Descend the slope through chaparral to an open flat. Cross the flat on the boulder-lined path to Lion Canyon Creek. Rock-hop over the creek to Sespe Creek at 0.3 miles. Wade across the river or use rocks as stepping-stones to a T-junction. The Sespe River Trail (Hike 18) goes to the right. Bear left on the Gene Marshall-Piedra Blanca National Recreation Trail, and head downstream a short distance. Curve right and climb the slope to great views of the Piedra Blanca rock outcrops straight ahead. Wind through scrub and chaparral to a posted junction. The Middle Sespe Trail (Hike 19) bears left and heads 3.5 miles west to Rock Creek, then continues another 3.5 miles west to Highway 33 by the abandoned Beaver Campground. Veer to the right, staying on the Gene Marshall-Piedra Blanca Trail. Enter the Sespe Wilderness, reaching the Piedra Blanca formations at 1.25 miles. At the formations, leave the main trail and explore the area, choosing your own route.

After the formations, the Gene Marshall-Piedra Blanca National Recreation Trail winds north through the stunning rock garden. Drop down the back side of the formations into a deep stream-fed ravine. Cross a tributary of Piedra Blanca Creek, and enter wide Piedra Blanca Canyon. Continue north, parallel to Piedra Blanca Creek, following the west edge of the canyon through a pocket of oaks and exposed scrub. Traverse the lower slope, overlooking a few pools and small waterfalls. Loop around a side canyon, and drop into a circular flat with majestic oaks and boulders on the banks of Piedra Blanca Creek at 2.9 miles. Continue up-canyon and pass a five-foot waterfall by a rock-rimmed pool. Cross the creek on large boulders, and walk 50 yards to a signed junction.

The main trail continues straight ahead 3.3 miles to Pine Mountain Lodge, nestled in the conifers. For this hike, veer right 20 yards and cross the North Fork Piedra Blanca Creek. Climb another 20 yards to the Twin Forks Camp at 3.2 miles, a small campsite on a flat bench with scattered oaks above the creek. Return by retracing your steps. ▩

18. Sespe River Trail

Hiking distance: 3.5 miles round trip
Hiking time: 2 hours
Elevation gain: 200 feet
Maps: U.S.G.S. Lion Canyon
      Sespe Wilderness Trail Map

map
page 60

Summary of hike: Sespe Creek is a wide body of water that winds 55 miles through the Sierra Madre, from Potrero Seco to the Santa Clara River in Fillmore. The creek is formed by more than thirty tributary streams and appears more like a river than a creek. It is popular for whitewater rafting and kayaking. The Sespe River Trail stretches 17 miles along the Old Sespe Road, parallel to Sespe Creek. The trail leads to Sespe Hot Springs, a natural hot springs in the Los Padres National Forest with rock-lined soaking pools. This hike follows a portion of the trail into the Sespe Wilderness on a bluff above the creek to a scenic overlook. The trail parallels the creek past deep pools and sandy flats, crossing Piedra Blanca Creek and Trout Creek.

Driving directions: OJAI. From Ojai, drive 14.6 miles north on Highway 33 (Maricopa Highway) to the Rose Valley Road turnoff and turn right. Continue 4.8 miles to a road split. Take the left fork 0.9 miles down to the trailhead parking lot at the end of the road.

Hiking directions: From the signed path by the restrooms, walk towards the river gorge. Descend the slope through chaparral to an open flat. Cross the flat on the boulder-lined path to Lion Canyon Creek. Rock-hop over the creek to Sespe Creek at 0.3 miles. Wade across the creek or use rocks as stepping stones to a T-junction. The Gene Marshall-Piedra Blanca National Recreation Trail goes to the left (Hike 17). Take the right fork on the Sespe River Trail and head downstream, parallel to the northern banks of Sespe Creek. In a half mile, the trail crosses Piedra Blanca Creek. After crossing, the trail narrows as it enters a canyon. Past the canyon, the trail widens out again and crosses Trout Creek. Along the way, side paths lead down to

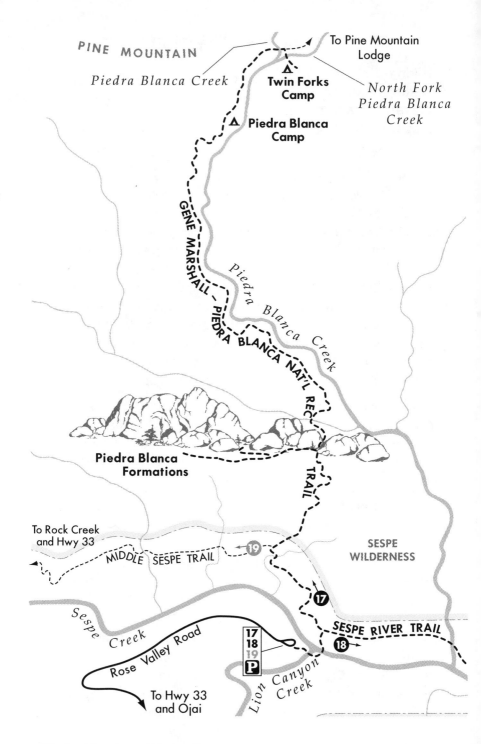

PINE MOUNTAIN

Piedra Blanca Creek

To Pine Mountain
Lodge

△ Twin Forks
Camp

*North Fork
Piedra Blanca
Creek*

△ **Piedra Blanca
Camp**

GENE MARSHALL

Piedra Blanca Creek

PIEDRA BLANCA NAT'L REC

TRAIL

**Piedra Blanca
Formations**

To Rock Creek
and Hwy 33

MIDDLE SESPE TRAIL 19

SESPE
WILDERNESS

17

Sespe Creek

Rose Valley Road

17
18
19
P

SESPE RIVER TRAIL

18

Lion Canyon Creek

To Hwy 33
and Ojai

the creek. A short distance ahead, enter the Sespe Wilderness and pass through a gate, gaining elevation to a vista overlooking the canyon. At the top of the ridge, the views open toward the mountains in the north. The ridge is the turn-around point.

To hike farther, the trail follows Sespe Creek downstream for miles, crossing the creek numerous times. The first crossing is at Bear Canyon, 4.5 miles from the trailhead. Sespe Hot Springs is another 10.5 miles past Bear Canyon. ■

HIKE 17

Piedra Blanca Formations

HIKE 18

Sespe River Trail

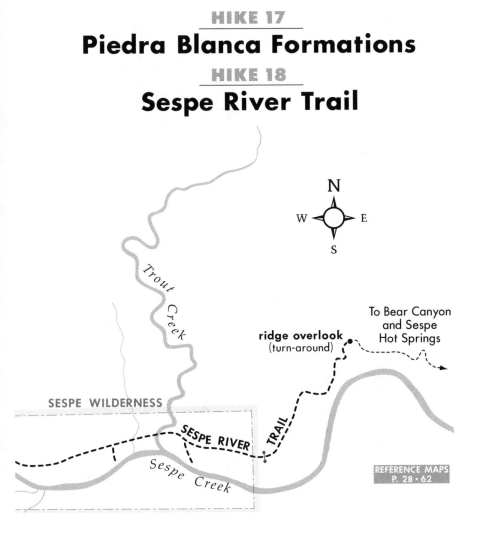

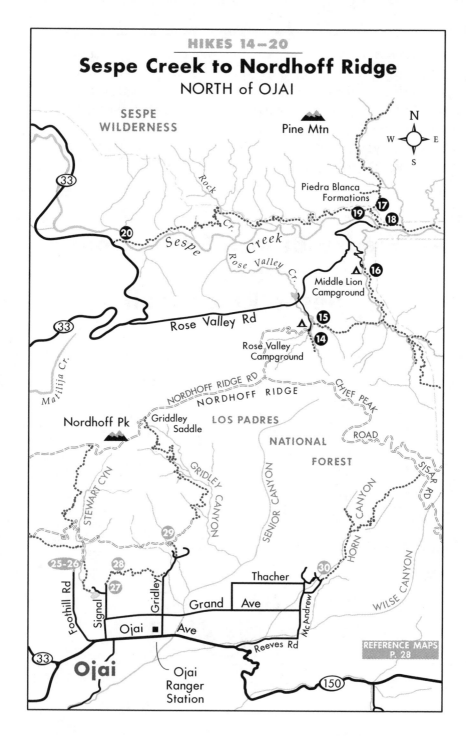

Sespe Creek to Nordhoff Ridge
NORTH of OJAI

SESPE
WILDERNESS

Pine Mtn

N
W · E
S

33

Rock

Piedra Blanca
Formations

17

19   **18**

20

S e s p e   Creek

Rose Valley Cr.

16

Middle Lion
Campground

33

Rose Valley Rd

△ **15**

14

Rose Valley
Campground

Matilija Cr.

NORDHOFF RIDGE RD

NORDHOFF RIDGE

CHIEF PEAK

Nordhoff Pk

Griddley
Saddle

LOS PADRES

ROAD

NATIONAL

SISAR RD

STEWART CYN

GRIDLEY CANYON

SENIOR CANYON

HORN CANYON

FOREST

WILSE CANYON

29

25-26

28

27

Gridley

Thacher

30

Foothill Rd

Signal

Ojai ■

Grand   Ave

McAndrew

Ave

Reeves Rd

REFERENCE MAPS
P. 28

33

Ojai

Ojai
Ranger
Station

150

19. Middle Sespe Trail

East Trailhead:
Piedra Blanca Trailhead to Rock Creek

Hiking distance: 9.6 miles round trip
Hiking time: 5 hours
Elevation gain: 250 feet
Maps: U.S.G.S. Lion Canyon
      Sespe Wilderness Trail Map
      Matilija and Dick Smith Wilderness Map Guide

*map
page 66*

Summary of hike: The Middle Sespe Trail parallels Sespe Creek from the Piedra Blanca Formations to Highway 33 by the abandoned Beaver Campground. The trail stretches 7.5 miles along the northern tier above the scenic Sespe Creek, skirting the edge of the Sespe Wilderness. Throughout the hike are sweeping vistas across the river valley to the surrounding mountains. This hike begins on the Gene Marshall–Piedra Blanca National Recreation Trail (Hike 17) at the east trailhead, then heads west on the Middle Sespe Trail. The trail traverses the vast, open terrain, crossing a series of seasonal streams to year-round Rock Creek, approximately halfway along the trail. At the beginning of the trail are great views of the stunning Piedra Blanca Formations. This hike can be combined with Hike 20 for an 8-mile shuttle hike.

Driving directions: OJAI. From Ojai, drive 14.6 miles north on Highway 33 (Maricopa Highway) to the Rose Valley Road turnoff and turn right. Continue 4.8 miles to a road split. Take the left fork 0.9 miles down to the trailhead parking lot at the end of the road.

Hiking directions: From the signed path by the restrooms, walk towards the river gorge. Descend the slope through chaparral to an open flat. Cross the flat on the boulder-lined path to Lion Canyon Creek. Rock-hop over the creek to Sespe Creek at 0.3 miles. Wade across the river or use rocks as stepping stones to a signed T-junction. The Sespe River Trail (Hike 18) goes to the right. Bear left on the Gene Marshall-Piedra Blanca National Recreation Trail, and head downstream a short distance. Curve right and climb the slope to great views of the Piedra Blanca rock outcrops straight ahead. Wind through the scrub and chaparral to a posted junction at 0.8 miles. The right fork continues on the Gene Marshall-Piedra Blanca Trail to the magnificent sandstone formations (Hike 17).

Bear left on the Middle Sespe Trail, and begin the traverse west across the open, chaparral-clad hillside. Follow the north slope above Sespe Creek, skirting the edge of the Sespe Wilderness. The far-reaching views extend across the river valley and to the eroding white rock formations in the distance. Cross a transient stream and follow the edge of a minor gully. Cross a second drainage and continue on the meandering path, crossing a few more ephemeral streams. Traverse the bench along the base of the hills. Zigzag down a few switchbacks to the water at Rock Creek at 4.8 miles. This is the turn-around point.

To extend the hike, the trail crosses the creek and climbs the slope to the west, reaching Highway 33 by the abandoned Beaver Campground, 3.5 miles beyond Rock Creek (Hike 20). ■

20. Middle Sespe Trail
West Trailhead:
Highway 33/Beaver Campground to Rock Creek

Hiking distance: 7 miles round trip
Hiking time: 3.5 hours
Elevation gain: 250 feet
Maps: U.S.G.S. Lion Canyon
Sespe Wilderness Trail Map
Matilija and Dick Smith Wilderness Map Guide

**map
page 66**

Summary of hike: The Middle Sespe Trail stretches 7.5 miles between Highway 33 and the Piedra Blanca Trail. The trail skirts the edge of the Sespe Wilderness, following the north side of Sespe Creek. Throughout the hike are far-reaching vistas of the natural terrain. This hike begins at the west end of the trail by Highway 33 and the abandoned Beaver Campground. The trail immediately crosses Sespe Creek, then follows the north side of the river valley to perennial Rock Creek, approximately halfway along the trail. En route, the trail climbs over a steep bluff with spectacular overlooks. This hike can be combined with Hike 19 for an 8-mile shuttle hike.

Driving directions: OJAI. From Ojai, drive 16.8 miles north on Highway 33 (Maricopa Highway) to the unmarked turnoff on the right. (The turnoff is located 2.2 miles past the Rose Valley turn-off.) Turn right and drive 100 yards downhill to the trailhead at the end of the road.

Hiking directions: Straight ahead, an old abandoned road leads to the defunct Beaver Campground. For this hike, do not take the road, but veer to the right of the road on the footpath. Head down the small gully to the valley floor at the banks of Sespe Creek. Rock-hop over the creek, and head east through the tall brush. Parallel the north side of the creek along the valley bottom, then traverse the elevated bench above the waterway. Cross two seasonal drainages on the undulating path to the base of Beaver Hill. Ascend the folded terrain, overlooking the valley from the hillside perches. Loop up and around a shaded side canyon to the 3,600-foot rolling hilltop. Weave across the hill-top to the east edge of the summit to a sweeping view of the river valley and surrounding mountains. Zigzag down the slope to the valley bottom and Rock Creek at 3.5 miles. This is the turn-around point.

To extend the hike, cross the waterway and continue 4 miles east, following the north side of Sespe Creek to the Piedra Blanca Formations (Hikes 17 and 19), and the Piedra Blanca Trailhead at the end of Rose Valley Road. ▪

Middle Sespe Trail

HIKE 19: East Trailhead
Piedra Blanca Trailhead to Rock Creek

HIKE 20: West Trailhead
Highway 33 to Rock Creek

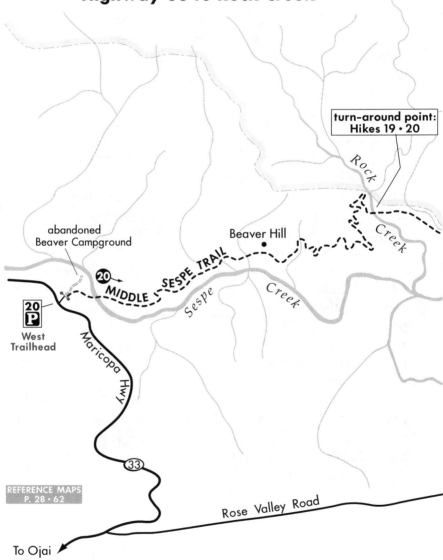

turn-around point:
Hikes 19 · 20

Rock

Creek

abandoned
Beaver Campground

Beaver Hill

MIDDLE SESPE TRAIL

Sespe

Creek

20
P
West
Trailhead

Maricopa Hwy

REFERENCE MAPS
P. 28 · 62

33

Rose Valley Road

To Ojai

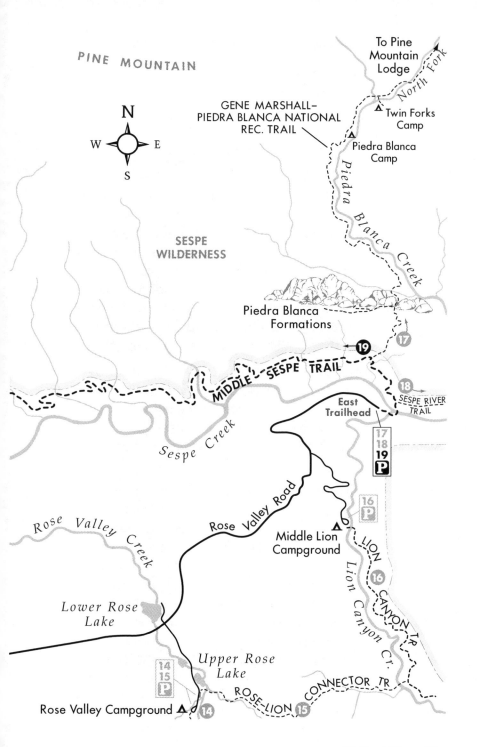

PINE MOUNTAIN

N
W E
S

GENE MARSHALL–
PIEDRA BLANCA NATIONAL
REC. TRAIL

SESPE
WILDERNESS

To Pine
Mountain
Lodge

North Fork

▲ Twin Forks
Camp

Piedra Blanca
Camp

Piedra Blanca Creek

Piedra Blanca
Formations

19

17

MIDDLE SESPE TRAIL

18

SESPE RIVER
TRAIL

East
Trailhead

Sespe Creek

17
18
19
P

16
P

Rose Valley Road

Middle Lion
Campground ▲

LION CANYON TR

Lion Canyon Cr.

16

Rose Valley Creek

Lower Rose
Lake

Upper Rose
Lake

14
15
P

Rose Valley Campground ▲

14

ROSE–LION

CONNECTOR TR

15

21. Wheeler Gorge Nature Trail

Hiking distance: 1-mile loop
Hiking time: 30 minutes
Elevation gain: 200 feet
Maps: U.S.G.S. Wheeler Springs
 Sespe Wilderness Trail Map

Summary of hike: Wheeler Gorge Nature Trail is an interpretive trail on the North Fork Matilija Creek near Wheeler Gorge Campground. The trail is an excellent introduction to the shaded creekside riparian habitats and arid chaparral plant communities that are so common throughout the area. The path winds through a small canyon gorge under sycamores, cottonwoods, willows and oaks, following the year-round creek past trickling waterfalls and bedrock pools. Free brochures from the Ojai Ranger Station correspond with numbered posts along the trail, which describe the plant life, ecology, and natural history.

Driving directions: OJAI. From Ojai, drive 8 miles north on Highway 33 (Maricopa Highway) to the Wheeler Gorge Campground on the left. Continue on the highway another 0.5 miles to the posted nature trail on the left by a locked metal gate, just before crossing the bridge over the North Fork Matilija Creek.

Hiking directions: From the trailhead map panel, take the path to the right, following the North Fork Matilija Creek upstream. Cross under the Highway 33 bridge, passing cascades, small waterfalls, and pools. Rock hop to the north side of the creek, and climb up through chaparral dotted with oaks. Follow the watercourse, passing a 12-foot waterfall between signposts 7 and 8. Cross over a rock formation, and wind through a shady tunnel of tall chaparral. Climb rock steps to a vista of Dry Lakes Ridge to the north. Curve away from the creekside vegetation, and descend on the northern slope of the arid hillside. Curve left and parallel Highway 33 from above. Drop back down to the creek, completing the loop. Recross the creek and return to the trailhead. ▪

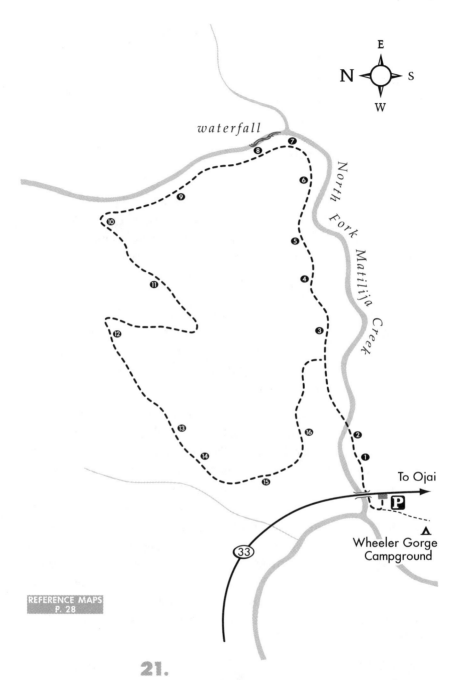

21.
Wheeler Gorge Nature Trail

22. Rice Canyon—Wills Canyon Loop
VENTURA RIVER—RANCHO EL NIDO PRESERVE

Hiking distance: 4.8-mile loop
Hiking time: 2.5 hours
Elevation gain: 400 feet
Maps: U.S.G.S. Matilija
       Matilija and Dick Smith Wilderness Map Guide
       Ventura River-Rancho El Nido Trail Map

map
page 72

Summary of hike: The Ventura River-Rancho El Nido Preserve encompasses 1,591 acres on the western side of Ojai Valley. The sprawling preserve is bordered by the Los Padres National Forest and includes three miles of the Ventura River. The preserve, purchased and managed by the Ojai Valley Land Conservancy, was opened to the public in 2003.

This hike forms a loop through two creek-fed canyons. The trail heads up Rice Canyon, parallels Rice Creek, and returns along the banks of Wills Creek. En route, the trail weaves through the Los Padres National Forest, meanders through lush riparian habitats, and leads to overlooks of the surrounding mountains.

Driving directions: OJAI. From Ojai, drive 3 miles south on Highway 33 to Highway 150 (Baldwin Road). Turn right and continue 0.2 miles to Rice Road, the third road on the right. Turn right on Rice Road, and continue 2 miles to a junction with Fairview Road. Turn left—staying on Rice Road—and drive 0.1 mile to Meyer Road. Turn left and go 0.2 miles to the signed preserve entrance at Oso Road. Veer left through the entrance gate, and drive 0.1 mile to the Rice Canyon trailhead parking lot.

VENTURA. From Highway 101/Ventura Freeway in Ventura, drive 11.2 miles north on Highway 33 towards Ojai to Highway 150 (Baldwin Road). Turn left and go 0.2 miles to Rice Road, the third road on the right. Turn right on Rice Road, and continue with the directions above.

Hiking directions: Wade or rock-hop across the Ventura River (depending on the season) by a swimming hole. Curve up the hillside to the bluff. Follow the bluff, parallel to the historic orange grove, to a bridge over Rice Creek and a junction. Begin the loop to the right on the Rice Canyon Trail. Follow the north side of Rice Creek to Canal Road, a paved access road. Cross the road and a bridge over the canal to the mouth of Rice Canyon. Drop into the shade of a sycamore, willow, and oak forest. Cross Rice Creek and head up the canyon. Cross the creek again and continue upstream through riparian vegetation. Merge with an old ranch road to a cattle gate at the Los Padres National Forest boundary. Enter the forest service land, and head uphill at a moderate grade. Follow the north canyon wall to an oak-rimmed meadow with a view of the surrounding hills. Continue west to a ridge overlooking the Ojai Valley and the Santa Ynez Mountains. Wend downhill into bucolic Wills Canyon. Pass through another cattle gate, reentering the Ojai Valley Land Conservancy tract. Continue downhill, cross El Nido Trail, and hop across Wills Creek. Veer left and follow the south edge of the creek to a junction with the Chaparral Crest Trail by the Wills Canyon footbridge.

Cross the bridge and slowly descend. Follow the course of the creek to the Fern Grotto Trail, a connector to the Chaparral Crest Trail. Stay on the Wills Canyon Trail, and steadily descend through an oak savanna. Cross Wills Creek to the mouth of the canyon and a trail junction by Canal Road. The right fork leads to the Riverview Trailhead (Hike 23). For this hike, cross Canal Road on the River Bluff Trail. Follow the east edge of the historic orange grove, parallel to the Ventura River. Cross a bridge over Rice Creek, completing the loop. Return to the trailhead, straight ahead. ▩

coast live oak

Ventura River • Rancho El Nido Preserve

HIKE 22
Rice Canyon–Wills Canyon Loop

HIKE 23
Wills Canyon–Chaparral Crest Loop

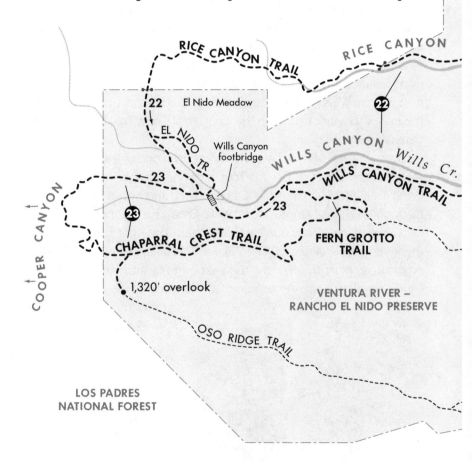

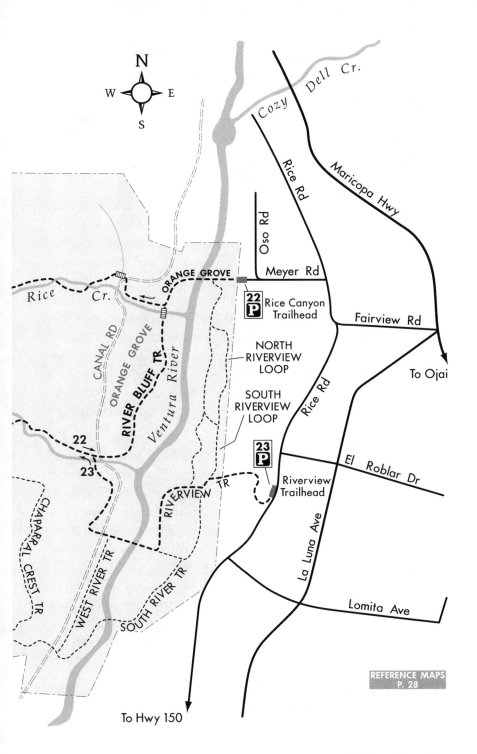

23. Wills Canyon—Chaparral Crest Loop
VENTURA RIVER—RANCHO EL NIDO PRESERVE

Hiking distance: 5.6-mile loop
Hiking time: 3 hours
Elevation gain: 700 feet

map
page 72

Maps: U.S.G.S. Matilija
Matilija and Dick Smith Wilderness Map Guide
Ventura River-Rancho El Nido Trail Map

Summary of hike: The Ventura River-Rancho El Nido Preserve is located in the Meiners Oaks area of Ojai Valley. The diverse topography includes open sandy terrain in the Ventura River basin, pockets of grasslands and meadows, chaparral hillsides exposed to the sun, riparian sycamore and willow groves, oak savanna, shaded creek-fed canyons, and year-round springs. This hike climbs through a stream-fed canyon under majestic coastal live oaks with an understory of native plants, including snowberries, Humboldt lilies, western raspberry, and hummingbird sage. The hike returns along a chaparral-covered ridge that offers exceptional vistas, including an overlook on the preserve's highest spot at 1,320 feet.

Driving directions: OJAI. From Ojai, drive 3 miles south on Highway 33 to Highway 150 (Baldwin Road). Turn right and continue 0.2 miles to Rice Road, the third road on the right. Turn right on Rice Road, and continue 1.4 miles to the posted Riverview Trailhead parking lot on the left, directly across the street from the horse boarding facility. The parking lot is located between Lomita Avenue and just south of El Roblar Drive.

VENTURA. From Highway 101/Ventura Freeway in Ventura, drive 11.2 miles north on Highway 33 towards Ojai to Highway 150 (Baldwin Road). Turn left and go 0.2 miles to Rice Road, the third right turn. Turn right on Rice Road, and continue with the directions above.

Hiking directions: Walk past the trailhead gate, and head down the slope on the Riverview Trail to the valley floor. Wind through the oak-dotted flatland with 360-degree vistas of the surrounding mountains. Cross the open terrain and several dry creekbeds to a posted trail split. The right fork leads to the Rice Canyon trailhead (Hike 22). Bear left for 20 yards, and curve right to another junction. Again, the right fork leads to the Rice Canyon trailhead. Bear left and head south to a fork. Go to the right, crossing rocky streambeds and passing pockets of bamboo to the Ventura River. Wade or rock-hop across the river (depending on the season) to Canal Road, a paved access road. Cross the road, staying on the trail, and curve right, parallel to the sycamore-lined stream. Follow the base of the oak-covered hillside to a junction by a bench and the historic orange grove at the mouth of Wills Canyon. The River Bluff Trail crosses Canal Road and heads north between the orange grove and the Ventura River to the Rice Canyon trailhead (Hike 22).

For this hike, bear left and head up Wills Canyon. Drop down and cross Wills Creek. Stroll through the pastoral oak savanna to the Fern Grotto Trail, a connector to the Chaparral Crest Trail. Begin the loop straight ahead, staying on the shaded canyon floor to the Wills Canyon footbridge. Cross the bridge to a posted junction with the Chaparral Crest Trail. Bear left and climb the north wall of the side canyon to a ridge with sweeping mountain vistas at the Los Padres National Forest boundary. Enter the Forest Service land, and traverse the ridge across the head of the canyon above Cooper Canyon on the right. Curve left and follow the south rim of Wills Canyon to a trail split. Detour right on the Oso Ridge Trail 220 yards to the preserve's highest point at the 1,320-foot overlook. From the summit are views of Lake Casitas, the coastal ridge, the Pacific Ocean, Ojai Valley, the Santa Ynez Mountains, the Topatopa Mountains, and Sulphur Mountain.

Return to the Chaparral Crest Trail and follow the ridge, steadily descending to a posted junction. Bear left on the Fern Grotto Trail, leaving the exposed ridge to the shade of the oaks. Complete the loop at Wills Creek. Bear right and retrace your steps along the creek, back to the trailhead. ▨

North of Ojai

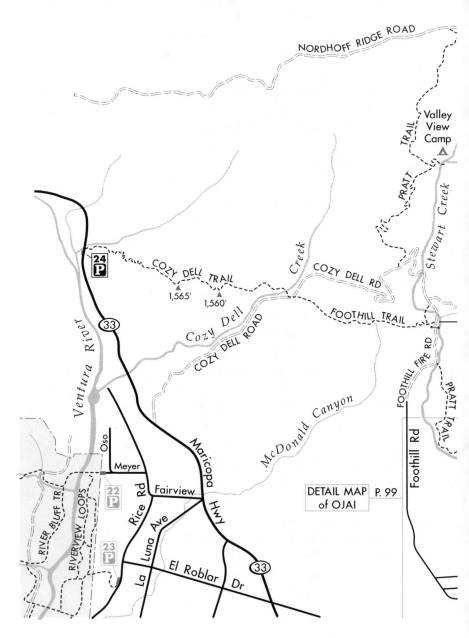

NORDHOFF RIDGE ROAD

Valley
View
Camp

PRATT TRAIL

Stewart Creek

24 P

COZY DELL TRAIL

1,565'   1,560'

Creek

COZY DELL RD

Cozy Dell

COZY DELL ROAD

FOOTHILL TRAIL

Ventura River

33

McDonald Canyon

FOOTHILL FIRE RD

PRATT TRAIL

Foothill Rd

Oso

Meyer

River Bluff Tr

Riverview Loops

22 P

Rice Rd

Fairview

Maricopa Hwy

DETAIL MAP P. 99
of OJAI

23 P

La Luna Ave

El Roblar Dr

33

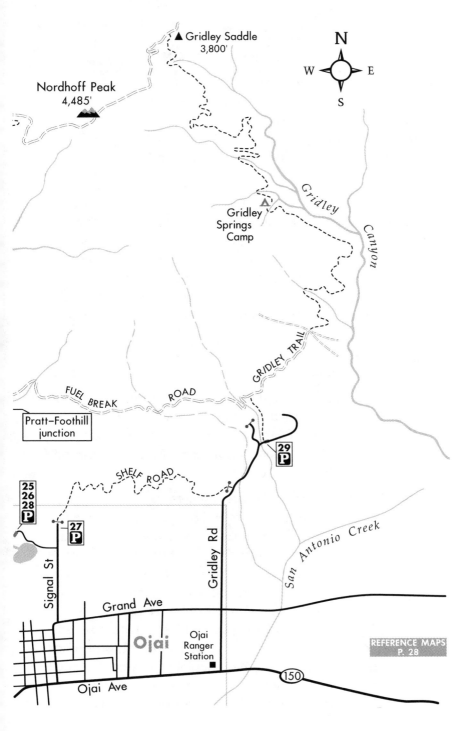

N
W E
S

▲ Gridley Saddle
3,800'

Nordhoff Peak
4,485'

Gridley Canyon

⌂ Gridley
Springs
Camp

GRIDLEY TRAIL

FUEL BREAK ROAD

Pratt-Foothill
junction

29 P

SHELF ROAD

25 26 28 P

27 P

Signal St

Gridley Rd

San Antonio Creek

Grand Ave

Ojai

Ojai
Ranger
Station

Ojai Ave

150

REFERENCE MAPS
P. 28

24. Cozy Dell Trail
to COZY DELL CANYON

Hiking distance: 4 miles round trip
Hiking time: 2 hours
Elevation gain: 700 feet
Maps: U.S.G.S. Matilija
       Matilija and Dick Smith Wilderness Map Guide
       Sespe Wilderness Trail Map

Summary of hike: The Cozy Dell Trail is on the west end of Ojai on the lower slopes of the Topatopa Mountains. The trail climbs up several switchbacks through a small, shaded canyon to vista points with panoramic views in every direction. There are great views into the Ojai Valley to the south and the surrounding peaks of the Santa Ynez and Topatopa Mountains. From the overlooks, the trail drops into the beautiful and forested Cozy Dell Canyon by Cozy Dell Creek. The trail ties in with the Foothill Trail and Cozy Dell Road. The hike can be extended with Hike 26 for a 7.2-mile loop hike.

Driving directions: OJAI. From Ojai, drive 3.4 miles north on Highway 33 (Maricopa Highway) to the Cozy Dell trailhead parking pullout on the left (west) side of the road. The pullout is located by a bridge, a packing house, and a Forest Service trailhead sign.

Hiking directions: From the parking area, cross the highway to the trailhead, which is south of the packing house along the right side of the metal railing. Take the well-defined trail east, and head up the canyon. A short distance ahead is a series of 18 switchbacks, gaining 600 feet up the south edge of the canyon. At one mile, the trail reaches its peak at a 1,565-foot saddle, giving way to an open area with breathtaking views. Proceed downhill towards Cozy Dell Canyon and back up to a second saddle with more outstanding views at 1,560 feet. Drop back into the oak trees, descending 200 feet into forested Cozy Dell Canyon, Cozy Dell Creek, and a T-junction with Cozy Dell Road. One hundred yards to the left (east) is a posted junction with

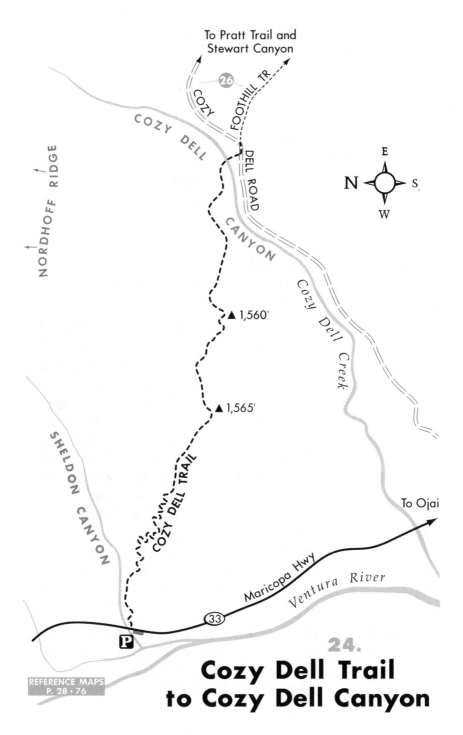

To Pratt Trail and
Stewart Canyon

26

COZY
DELL ROAD
FOOTHILL TR.

COZY DELL

CANYON

Cozy Dell Creek

NORDHOFF RIDGE

N E S W

▲ 1,560'

▲ 1,565'

SHELDON CANYON

COZY DELL TRAIL

To Ojai

Maricopa Hwy

33

Ventura River

P

24.

Cozy Dell Trail
to Cozy Dell Canyon

REFERENCE MAPS
P. 28 · 76

the Foothill Trail (Hike 27). This is the turn-around spot. Return by retracing your steps.

To hike farther, the fire road continues to the Pratt Trail and Foothill Fire Road at Stewart Canyon—Hikes 25 and 26. ▨

25. Pratt Trail
Stewart Canyon to Valley View Camp
STEWART CANYON

Hiking distance: 6.6 miles round trip
Hiking time: 3.5 hours
Elevation gain: 2,000 feet
Maps: U.S.G.S. Ojai and Matilija
       Matilija and Dick Smith Wilderness Map Guide
       Sespe Wilderness Trail Map

Summary of hike: Stewart Canyon, at the north edge of downtown Ojai, is the gateway to a network of magnificent hiking trails in the Los Padres National Forest. The Pratt Trail heads up Stewart Canyon, leading 4.6 miles and gaining 3,000 feet in elevation to Nordhoff Ridge, one mile west of the old fire lookout tower. The lower canyon connects to several trails, including the Foothill Trail to Cozy Dell Canyon (Hike 26), the Cozy Dell Trail to Highway 33 (Hike 24), and the Ojai Fuel Break Road to Gridley Road (Hike 28). This hike winds up the lower canyon, following Stewart Creek for 1.3 miles through a eucalyptus grove, meadows, and landscaped rock gardens. The trail continues up the mountain slope to Valley View Camp, a beautiful forested camp in a serene grotto on the banks of Stewart Creek. The primitive camp sits beneath a vertical, moss-covered rock wall. Throughout the hike are vistas of picturesque Ojai Valley, but none are available at the aptly named Valley View Camp.

Driving directions: OJAI. From downtown Ojai, drive 0.8 miles north up Signal Street (on the west side of the arcade) to the Pratt/Foothill Trailhead sign by the water tower. Turn left and drive 0.2 miles to the parking area on the left.

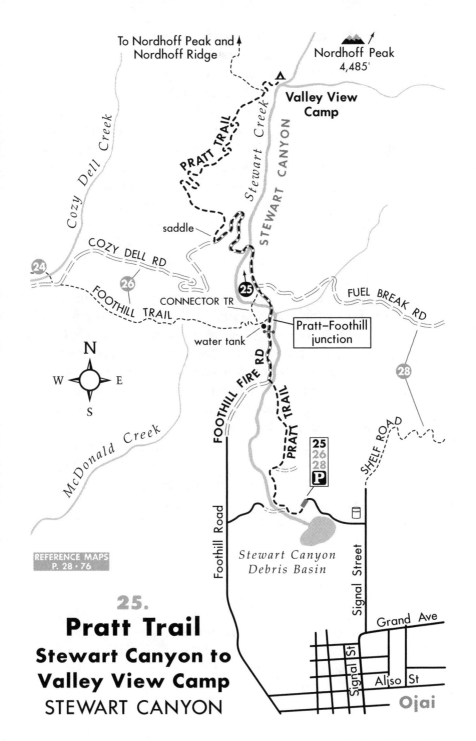

To Nordhoff Peak and
Nordhoff Ridge

Nordhoff Peak
4,485'

Valley View
Camp

Stewart Creek

STEWART CANYON

PRATT TRAIL

Cozy Dell Creek

saddle

COZY DELL RD

24

26

FOOTHILL TRAIL

CONNECTOR TR

FUEL BREAK RD

25

Pratt–Foothill
junction

water tank

28

FOOTHILL FIRE RD

N
W — E
S

McDonald Creek

PRATT TRAIL

25
26
28
P

SHELF ROAD

REFERENCE MAPS
P. 28 · 76

Foothill Road

Stewart Canyon
Debris Basin

Signal Street

25.
Pratt Trail
Stewart Canyon to
Valley View Camp
STEWART CANYON

Grand Ave

Signal St

Signal St

Aliso St

Ojai

Hiking directions: Take the posted Pratt Trail and curve north up Stewart Canyon. Parallel Stewart Creek, following the trail signs. Weave through the tall brush on the distinct rock-embedded path. Veer left and walk through a eucalyptus grove, following the east wall of Stewart Canyon to a plateau above the canyon with a picnic table. From this overlook are great views of the Ojai Valley and Sulphur Mountain. Descend into the canyon, staying on the rock-lined path past a few hillside homes, a creekside rock garden, and a paved road crossing. Cross Stewart Creek and take the Foothill Fire Road to the right, following the trail signs. Continue on the paved, narrow road along a beautiful rock wall. Pass a gate and water tank, where the pavement ends, to the posted Pratt and Foothill Trail junction on the left (Hike 26).

Stay on the Pratt Trail—straight ahead—climbing a quarter mile to a Y-fork on a wide, rounded flat at 1.3 miles. (Just shy of the Y-fork, the Foothill Connector Trail takes off to the left.) The Fuel Break Road, a connector trail to Gridley Road (Hike 28) curves to the right. Stay to the left and continue north, steadily climbing to a 2,050-foot saddle and a signed junction at 2 miles. Straight ahead, the trail descends into Cozy Dell Trail and leads 2.5 miles to Highway 33 (Hike 24). Bear sharply to the right on the footpath signed for Nordhoff Peak. Climb to views that span across Cozy Dell Canyon to Lake Casitas and the Pacific Ocean. Zigzag up four switchbacks, and follow the narrow path perched on the near-vertical cliffs. There is a spectacular bird's-eye view down Stewart canyon to Ojai and across Sulphur Mountain to Point Mugu in the Santa Monica Mountains. At 3.2 miles, on a left bend, is a unmarked but distinct Y-fork. The Pratt Trail continues to the left, leading another 1.4 miles and an additional thousand feet in elevation to Nordhoff Ridge. For this hike, veer right and descend 0.2 miles into the shady forest. Weave down five switchbacks to the end of the trail at Valley View Camp, a small primitive camp on the banks of Stewart Creek. Return by retracing your steps. ■

26. Pratt Trail to
Foothill Trail—Cozy Dell Road Loop
STEWART CANYON · COZY DELL CANYON

Hiking distance: 5.8-mile loop
Hiking time: 3 hours
Elevation gain: 1,200 feet
Maps: U.S.G.S. Ojai and Matilija
Matilija and Dick Smith Wilderness Map Guide
Sespe Wilderness Trail Map

map
page 85

Summary of hike: This loop hike follows Stewart Creek up the canyon, passing meadows and rock gardens to the Foothill Trail. The route heads west through McDonald Canyon and drops into pastoral Cozy Dell Canyon by the creek. Cozy Dell Road winds up the forested canyon, climbing to sweeping overlooks beneath Nordhoff Peak.

Driving directions: OJAI. From downtown Ojai, drive 0.8 miles north up Signal Street (on the west side of the arcade) to the Pratt/Foothill Trailhead sign by the water tower. Turn left and drive 0.2 miles to the parking area on the left.

Hiking directions: Take the posted Pratt Trail and curve north up Stewart Canyon. Parallel Stewart Creek, following the trail signs. Weave through the tall brush on the distinct rock-embedded path. Veer left and walk through a eucalyptus grove, following the east wall of Stewart Canyon to a plateau above the canyon with a picnic table. From this overlook are great views of the Ojai Valley and Sulphur Mountain. Descend into the canyon, staying on the rock-lined path past a few hillside homes, a creekside rock garden, and a paved road crossing. Cross Stewart Creek and take the Foothill Fire Road to the right, following the trail signs. Continue on the paved, narrow road along a beautiful rock wall. Pass a gate and water tank, where the pavement ends, to the posted Pratt and Foothill Trail junction on the left.

Begin the loop to the left and climb rock steps, ascending the east-facing hillside to a trail split with the Foothill Connector Trail. Curve left and continue uphill along the short switchbacks, with great views down Stewart Canyon and across Ojai Canyon to Sulphur Mountain. Cross a saddle to views of Lake Casitas and the Santa Ynez Mountains. Drop into McDonald Canyon and cross another saddle. Descend a sloping meadow bordered by oaks. Head into Cozy Dell Canyon to the Cozy Dell Road. (A hundred yards to the left is the Cozy Dell Trail—Hike 24.) Bear right on the fire road towards the posted Pratt Trail, meandering through the rolling, forested glen. Steadily climb out of the canyon to a junction on a saddle. Bear left and continue uphill, curving right around the mountain to a posted junction with the Pratt Trail to Nordhoff Peak. Stay on the fire road to the right, and head downhill into Stewart Canyon to an open flat and road split. The left fork is the Fuel Break Road to Gridley Road (Hike 28). Descend to the right a quarter mile and complete the loop. Return down Stewart Canyon to the trailhead. ▪

27. Shelf Road

STEWART CANYON • GRIDLEY CANYON

Hiking distance: 3.5 miles round trip
Hiking time: 1.5 hours
Elevation gain: 200 feet

map page 88

Maps: U.S.G.S. Ojai
Matilija and Dick Smith Wilderness Map Guide
Sespe Wilderness Trail Map

Summary of hike: Shelf Road is an old, unpaved road that traverses the cliffs several hundred feet above the northern edge of Ojai. The road, connecting Signal Street with Gridley Road, is gated at both ends. The Los Padres National Forest is on the north side of the trail, and orange groves line the south side. It is a hiking, biking, and jogging path that is popular with the locals. The path has several scenic overlooks with great views of the city of Ojai, ten-mile long Ojai Valley, and Sulphur Mountain

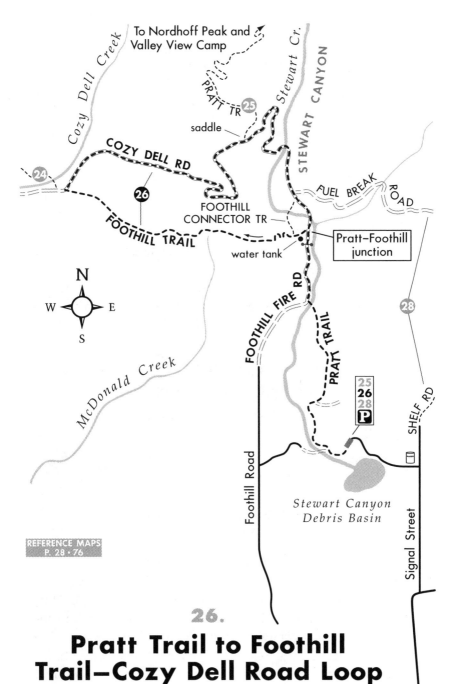

To Nordhoff Peak and
Valley View Camp

Cozy Dell Creek

Stewart Cr.

STEWART CANYON

PRATT TR 25

saddle

COZY DELL RD

24

26

FUEL BREAK ROAD

FOOTHILL
CONNECTOR TR

FOOTHILL TRAIL

water tank

Pratt–Foothill
junction

N
W   E
S

FOOTHILL FIRE RD

PRATT TRAIL

28

McDonald Creek

25
26
28
P

SHELF RD

Foothill Road

*Stewart Canyon
Debris Basin*

Signal Street

REFERENCE MAPS
P. 28 • 76

26.
Pratt Trail to Foothill
Trail–Cozy Dell Road Loop
STEWART CANYON • COZY DELL CANYON

across the valley. This is an out-and-back hike on Shelf Road. For a longer loop hike, Shelf Road can be combined with the Fuel Break Road and the Pratt Trail—Hike 28—for a 6.4-mile loop.

Driving directions: OJAI. From downtown Ojai, drive one mile north up Signal Street (on the west side of the arcade) to the trailhead gate at the end of the road. Park along the side of the road.

Hiking directions: Hike north past the gate and up the abandoned road. The road curves east, passing orange trees and avocado groves. Shelf Road follows the contours of the cliffs, snaking its way to the east above the city. At 1.7 miles, the trail ends at another entrance gate by Gridley Road. Return to the trailhead along the same route.

For the longer loop hike, continue north up Gridley Road and return on the Fuel Break Road, following the reverse directions for Hike 28. ■

28. Pratt Trail—Fuel Break Road— Shelf Road Loop
STEWART CANYON • GRIDLEY CANYON

Hiking distance: 6.4-mile loop
Hiking time: 3.5 hours
Elevation gain: 900 feet

*map
page 88*

Maps: U.S.G.S. Ojai and Matilija
Matilija and Dick Smith Wilderness Map Guide
Sespe Wilderness Trail Map

Summary of hike: The Fuel Break Road runs parallel to Ojai Valley a thousand feet above the city of Ojai. The views from above the valley are fascinating. The 1.5-mile fire road, built by the forest service in 1962, connects Stewart Canyon and the Pratt Trail on the west with Gridley Canyon on the east. This hike begins on the Pratt Trail and climbs up Stewart Canyon. The route then traverses the folded mountain layers on the Fuel Break Road to Gridley Road. The hike returns along Shelf Road, forming an easy, scenic loop. The Fuel Break Road is a backcountry hike while Shelf Road is more of an easy social stroll. Both fire roads are vehicle restricted.

Driving directions: OJAI. From downtown Ojai, drive 0.8 miles north up Signal Street (on the west side of the arcade) to the Pratt/Foothill Trailhead sign by the water tower. Turn left and drive 0.2 miles to the parking area on the left.

Hiking directions: Take the posted Pratt Trail and curve north up Stewart Canyon. Parallel Stewart Creek, following the trail signs. Weave through the tall brush on the distinct rock-embedded path. Veer left and walk through a eucalyptus grove, following the east wall of Stewart Canyon to a plateau above the canyon with a picnic table. From this overlook are great views of the Ojai Valley and Sulphur Mountain. Descend into the canyon, staying on the rock-lined path past a few hillside homes, a creekside rock garden, and a paved road crossing. Cross Stewart Creek and take the Foothill Fire Road to the right, following the trail signs. Continue on the paved, narrow road along a beautiful rock wall. Pass a gate and water tank, where the pavement ends, to the posted Pratt and Foothill Trail junction on the left (Hike 26). Stay on the Pratt Trail—straight ahead—climbing a quarter mile to a Y-fork on a wide, rounded flat at 1.3 miles. (Just shy of the Y-fork, the Foothill Connector Trail takes off to the left.) The Pratt Trail veers to the left and climbs to Valley View Camp and Nordhoff Ridge (Hike 25). For this hike, stay to the right on the Fuel Break Road.

Traverse the hillside on a winding course through the folded hills. Continue zigzagging eastward to a trail gate and posted junction on the right. The Gridley Trail (Hike 29) continues on the road to the left. Take the footpath to the right, and descend the narrow drainage 0.4 miles to the top of Gridley Road. Follow Gridley Road downhill one-third mile to the Shelf Road trailhead on the right. Take Shelf Road and head west 1.7 miles to the Signal Street gate. The trailhead turnoff is 0.2 miles ahead to the water tower. Bear right and complete the loop back at the trailhead parking area. ▪

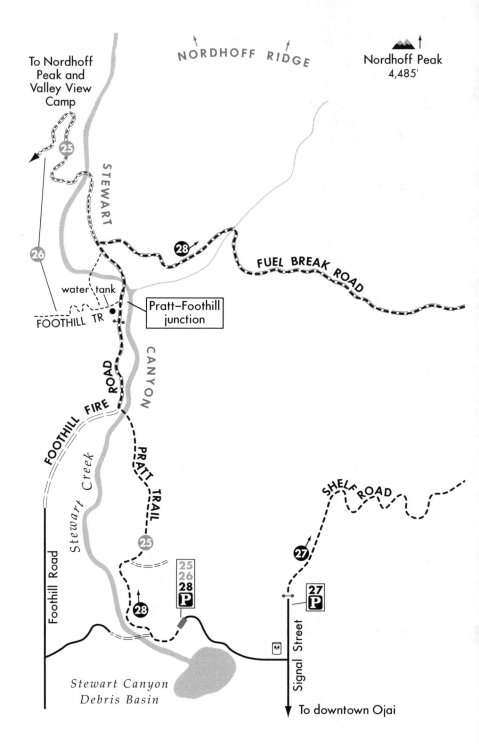

To Nordhoff Peak and Valley View Camp

NORDHOFF RIDGE

Nordhoff Peak
4,485'

STEWART

FUEL BREAK ROAD

water tank

Pratt–Foothill junction

FOOTHILL TR

CANYON

FOOTHILL FIRE ROAD

Stewart Creek

PRATT TRAIL

Foothill Road

SHELF ROAD

25
26
28
P

27
P

Signal Street

Stewart Canyon Debris Basin

To downtown Ojai

HIKE 27
Shelf Road
HIKE 28
Pratt Trail–Fuel Break Road–
Shelf Road Loop
STEWART CANYON • GRIDLEY CANYON

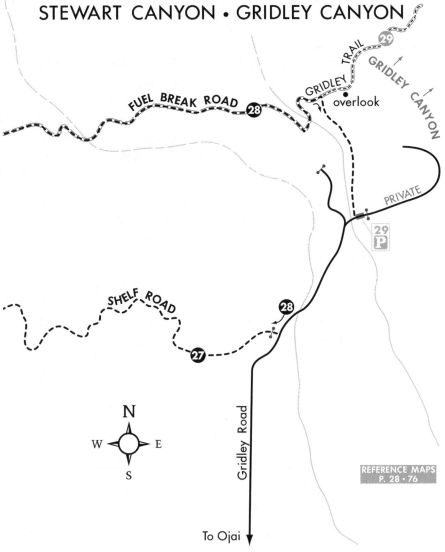

29. Gridley Trail
to Gridley Springs Camp

Hiking distance: 6 miles round trip
Hiking time: 3 hours
Elevation gain: 1,200 feet
Maps: U.S.G.S. Ojai
      Matilija and Dick Smith Wilderness Map Guide
      Sespe Wilderness Trail Map

Summary of hike: The Gridley Trail begins at the northern edge of Ojai in the foothills of the Topatopa Mountains. The trail follows a fire road into Gridley Canyon and climbs six miles to Gridley Saddle atop Nordhoff Ridge, 1.1 miles northeast of Nordhoff Peak and the lookout tower. This hike goes to Gridley Springs Camp, a primitive campsite by Gridley Springs and a stream halfway to the ridge. En route, the trail follows the shady northwest slope of the canyon.

Driving directions: OJAI. From downtown Ojai, drive one mile east on Highway 150 (Ojai Avenue) to Gridley Road and turn left. Continue 1.5 miles to the end of Gridley Road, and park by the signed trailhead on the left.

Hiking directions: Take the signed trail on the west up a draw through the tall, native brush. Continue up the footpath 0.4 miles to the Fuel Break Road (Hike 28). There is a beautiful overlook of the Ojai Valley and Sulphur Mountain on the right. The left fork leads 1.5 miles to the Pratt Trail in Stewart Canyon (Hike 25). Head to the right up the unpaved, vehicle-restricted fire road past avocado orchards on the steep slopes. The road curves around the contours of the mountain as the canyon narrows. Continue to a five-way junction of dirt ranch roads in Gridley Canyon. Take the center left fork, following the trail sign. At two miles, the trail is perched high above the deep canyon and enters a small side canyon at the confluence of two streams. Gridley Springs Camp is at the first sharp switchback by a horse watering trough. This is the turn-around spot.

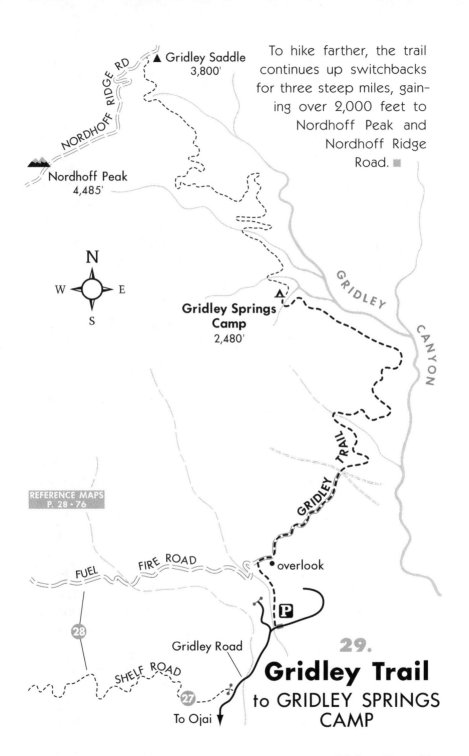

Gridley Saddle
3,800'

To hike farther, the trail continues up switchbacks for three steep miles, gaining over 2,000 feet to Nordhoff Peak and Nordhoff Ridge Road.

NORDHOFF RIDGE RD

Nordhoff Peak
4,485'

N
W E
S

GRIDLEY CANYON

Gridley Springs Camp
2,480'

GRIDLEY TRAIL

REFERENCE MAPS
P. 28 · 76

FUEL   FIRE ROAD

overlook

P

28

Gridley Road

SHELF ROAD

27

To Ojai

29.
Gridley Trail
to GRIDLEY SPRINGS CAMP

30. Horn Canyon Trail

Hiking distance: 3 miles round trip
Hiking time: 1.5 hours
Elevation gain: 600 feet
Maps: U.S.G.S. Ojai
Sespe Wilderness Trail Map

Summary of hike: Horn Canyon is a stream-fed canyon northeast of Ojai in the Topatopa Mountains. The Horn Canyon Trail parallels Thacher Creek through a forested canyon that is lush with sycamores, alders, and oaks. The trail, which is partially a service road, crosses the creek four times to a rocky gorge. At the gorge, the trail is rugged and far less used, leading past a continuous series of cascades, pools, and small waterfalls.

Driving directions: OJAI. From downtown Ojai, drive 2.3 miles east on Highway 150 (Ojai Avenue) to Reeves Road and turn left. Continue 1.1 mile to McAndrew Road and turn left again. Drive one mile and enter the Thacher School grounds. The trailhead parking area is 0.4 miles ahead, bearing right at all three road splits.

Hiking directions: From the parking area, take the unpaved service road northeast past the gate and kiosk into Horn Canyon. There are two creek crossings in the first half mile. After the second crossing, the service road enters the forest and the trail narrows. At one mile, cross the creek again and climb up the west wall of the canyon while enjoying the great views of Horn Canyon and the creek below. Just before the fourth creek crossing, leave the main trail and take the left path, heading up Horn Canyon along the west side of the creek. The trail is replaced by faint paths that crisscross the creek in a scramble past pools, cascades, and small waterfalls. Choose your own turn-around spot, and return along the same path.

To hike farther, at the fourth creek crossing, continue on the Horn Canyon Trail across the creek. The trail steeply climbs out of the canyon to the Pines Campsite under the shade of Coulter pines, one mile ahead, and on to Sisar Road, 2.4 miles farther. ▓

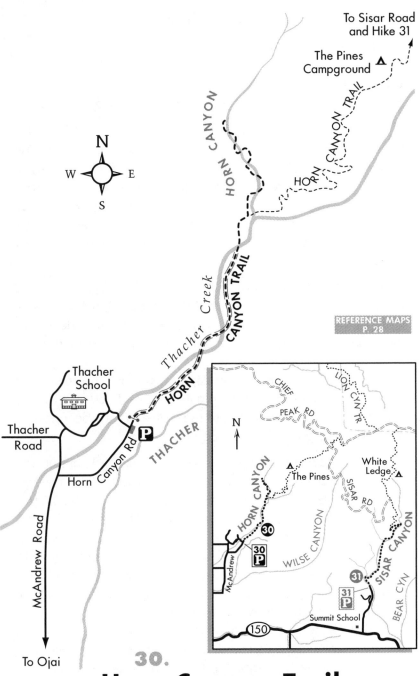

To Sisar Road
and Hike 31

The Pines
Campground

HORN CANYON TRAIL

HORN CANYON

HORN CANYON TRAIL

N
W · E
S

Thacher Creek

HORN CANYON TRAIL

REFERENCE MAPS
P. 28

Thacher
School

Thacher
Road

P

THACHER

Horn

Canyon Rd

McAndrew Road

CHIEF PEAK RD

LION CYN TR

N

HORN CANYON

The Pines

White
Ledge

SISAR RD

WILSE CANYON

30
P

SISAR CANYON

McAndrew

31
P

BEAR CYN

Summit School

150

To Ojai

30.
Horn Canyon Trail

31. Sisar Canyon

Hiking distance: 4 miles round trip
Hiking time: >2 hours
Elevation gain: 1,000 feet
Maps: U.S.G.S. Ojai & Santa Paula Peak
Sespe Wilderness Trail Map

Summary of hike: Sisar Canyon begins in the Upper Ojai Valley, halfway between Ojai and Santa Paula. The Sisar Canyon Trail follows Sisar Creek among large boulders and sheer rock walls, through a canopy of oaks, sycamore and bay laurel trees. The hike up this beautiful canyon involves two stream crossings and a scenic overlook with views across the Upper Ojai Valley to Sulphur Mountain.

Driving directions: OJAI. From downtown Ojai, drive 7.8 miles east on Highway 150 towards Santa Paula. Turn left on Sisar Road along the eastern side of Summit School. Drive one mile to the trailhead gate, bearing right at the road split. Park on the side of the road.

SANTA PAULA. From Santa Paula, drive 8.7 miles northwest on Highway 150 towards Ojai. Turn right on Sisar Road, just before Summit School. Drive one mile to the trailhead gate, bearing right at the road split. Park on the side of the road.

Hiking directions: Hike north past the trailhead gate up the fire road. Sisar Creek is to the right of the road. Within minutes, the trail crosses the creek by small waterfalls and pools. The trail steadily gains elevation up Sisar Canyon. At one mile, recross Sisar Creek. Continue up canyon, parallel to the creek, to a sharp left bend in the trail. The trail leaves the creek and begins to climb out of the canyon to an overlook and another switchback curving to the right. The overlook is the turn-around point for this hike. To return, follow the same trail back.

To hike farther, the trail continues up the ridge for 3.5 miles to White Ledge Camp, a forested streamside camp. The trail eventually crosses the Topatopa Ridge into the Sespe Wilderness. En route to the camp, Sisar Road makes a sharp bend south and heads east to Horn Canyon (Hike 30). ▨

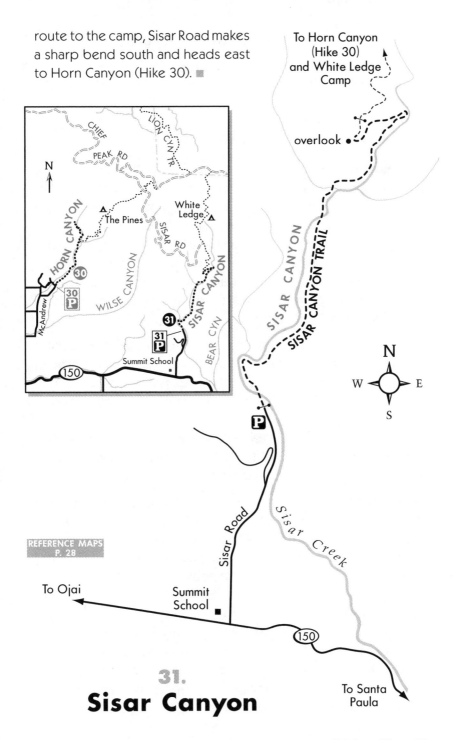

31.
Sisar Canyon

32. Santa Paula Canyon

Hiking distance: 6—8 miles round trip
Hiking time: 3—4 hours
Elevation gain: 750—900 feet
Maps: U.S.G.S. Santa Paula Peak
Sespe Wilderness Trail Map

Summary of hike: The Santa Paula Canyon Trail in the Topa-topa Mountains is among the most beautiful and popular hikes in the Ojai area. The trail begins by walking through picturesque Saint Thomas Aquinas College into Santa Paula Canyon. The hike follows Santa Paula Creek up a shady, forested canyon past a number of deep bedrock pools and cascades surrounded by rugged mountain views. The trail leads to The Punchbowl, a scenic, narrow gorge with waterfalls and pools between Big Cone Camp and Cross Camp.

Driving directions: OJAI. From downtown Ojai, drive 11 miles east on Highway 150 towards Santa Paula. Park in the trailhead parking area on the right side of the road, just east of the bridge over Santa Paula Creek. The parking area is across from Thomas Aquinas College.

SANTA PAULA. From Santa Paula, drive 5.7 miles northwest on Highway 150 towards Ojai to the trailhead parking area on the left. The parking area is across from Thomas Aquinas College.

Hiking directions: From the trailhead parking lot, hike 500 feet up and across the road, entering Thomas Aquinas College. Stay on the paved road, heading north towards the far end of the campus. Near the top, take the road veering off to the right. Walk through the gate and past Ferndale Ranch. The road ends in front of two rusty oil rigs. Curve around to the left, then enter forested Santa Paula Canyon along the creek. Cross to the north side of the creek, and head up-canyon under sycamore and al-der trees to a fire road at 1.2 miles. Continue up the fire road. Recross the creek at two miles, and begin switchbacking up the mountain. The trail levels off before dropping down into Big Cone Camp, located on a shaded terrace above Santa Paula Creek. At the far end of the grassy flat, the narrow path descends to Santa Paula Creek in a sandstone gorge. Detour to the left, leaving the main trail, and head 30 yards downstream to a side canyon on the right. A 25-foot waterfall and pool are twenty yards up this canyon. Large boulders lining the pool are perfect for sitting and viewing the falls. This is a good turn-around point for a 6-mile round-trip hike.

To continue, return to the main trail. Cross to the north side of the East Fork Santa Paula Creek, and climb up to a junction. The right fork parallels the East Fork on an unmaintained trail to Cienega Camp and Santa Paula Peak. Take the left fork and head north up Santa Paula Canyon on the Last Chance Trail. Pass the top of the waterfall and a series of pools, falls, and water chutes for a half mile to spruce-shaded Cross Camp. This is the turn-around spot for an 8-mile round-trip hike.

To hike farther, the trail continues up canyon for another 6 miles to the Topatopa Ridge and Hines Peak. ■

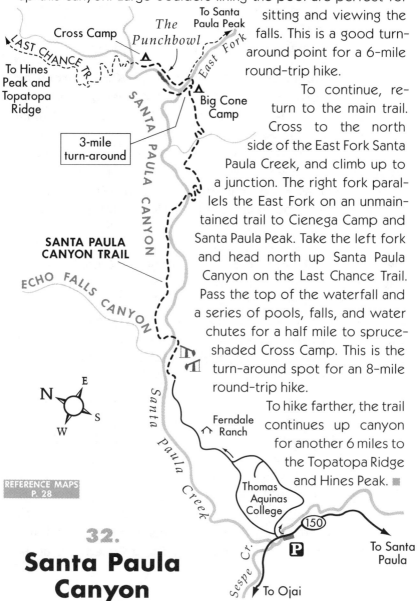

To Santa Paula Peak

The *Punchbowl*

Cross Camp

LAST CHANCE TR.

To Hines Peak and Topatopa Ridge

SANTA PAULA CANYON

East Fork

Big Cone Camp

3-mile turn-around

SANTA PAULA CANYON TRAIL

ECHO FALLS CANYON

N E S W

Santa Paula Creek

Ferndale Ranch

Thomas Aquinas College

150

REFERENCE MAPS P. 28

P

To Santa Paula

Sespe Cr.

To Ojai

32.

Santa Paula Canyon

33. Sulphur Mountain Road Recreation Trail

Hiking distance: 10 miles one way (shuttle)
Hiking time: 4 hours
Elevation loss: 2,200 feet
Maps: U.S.G.S. Ojai and Matilija
       Sespe Wilderness Trail Map

map
page 100

Summary of hike: Sulphur Mountain rises 2,700 feet along the south side of Ojai, forming the southern border of Ojai Valley. The prominent 11-mile-long mountain stretches from the Ventura River on the west to Santa Paula Creek on the east. San Antonio Creek flows along the north base of the mountain. Sulphur Mountain Road—a gated hiking, biking, and equestrian road—follows the ridge across the length of Sulphur Mountain, connecting Highway 150 in upper Ojai Valley with Highway 33 in Casitas Springs.

This popular hike is a 10-mile downhill shuttle route from the eastern trailhead to the shuttle car near the confluence of San Antonio Creek and the Ventura River. The journey across the oak-dotted ridgeline has gorgeous alternating views. To the south and west are views of the Conejo Valley, Point Mugu, the Pacific Ocean, Lake Casitas, and the Channel Islands. To the north are views of the Ojai valley, the Topatopa Mountains, and the Los Padres National Forest.

Driving directions: SHUTTLE CAR: Leave a shuttle car at the end of the hike: From Highway 101/Ventura Freeway in Ventura, drive 7.5 miles north on Highway 33 towards Ojai to Sulphur Mountain Road and turn right. Continue 0.4 miles to the locked gate. Park the shuttle car alongside the road.

TRAILHEAD: Return to Highway 33 and continue north to Ojai. From downtown Ojai, drive 6.4 miles east on Highway 150 towards Santa Paula. Turn right on Sulphur Mountain Road, and continue 4.6 miles up the winding road to a locked gate at the trailhead.

Hiking directions: From the trailhead gate, head west on the paved, vehicle-restricted road. Follow the ridgetop road, which begins at an elevation of 2,600 feet. Enjoy the southwest views of Santa Paula and the Santa Clara River Valley. Continue along the shadeless ridge, overlooking Ojai Valley through open hills and meadows while slowly losing elevation. At 1.5 miles, the pavement ends and the well-graded dirt road meanders through pastureland with grazing cattle. Panoramic vistas span southward to the coastal foothills, the Oxnard Plain, the Pacific Ocean, and the Channel Islands. Gradually but steadily descend, staying atop the oak-dotted ridgecrest, to great views of Lake Casitas to the west. The final two miles are steeper, dropping 1,500 feet into an oak forest. As you near the trail's end, the serpentine road descends over a cattle guard and past a gate to the shuttle car parking area by the Casitas Springs trailhead. ▨

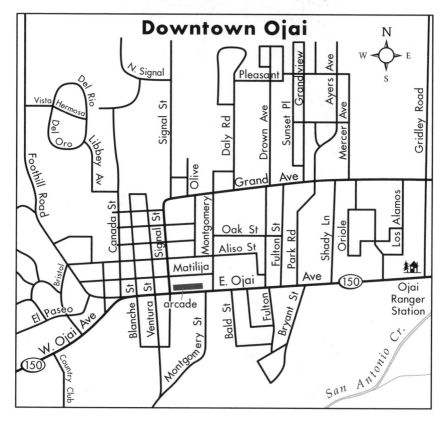

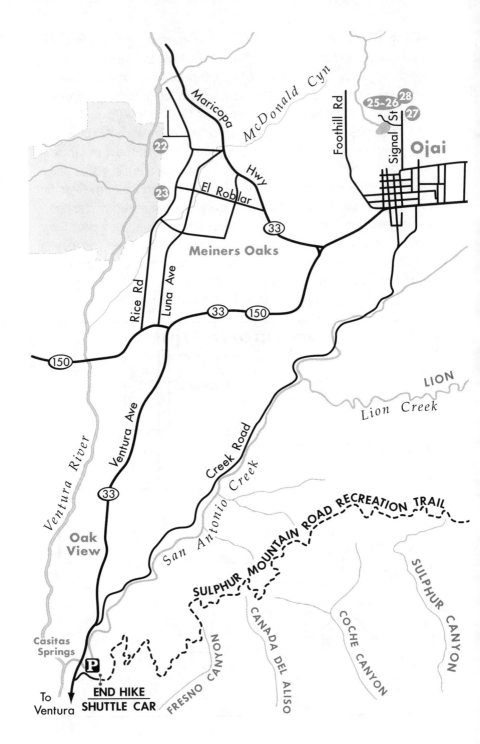

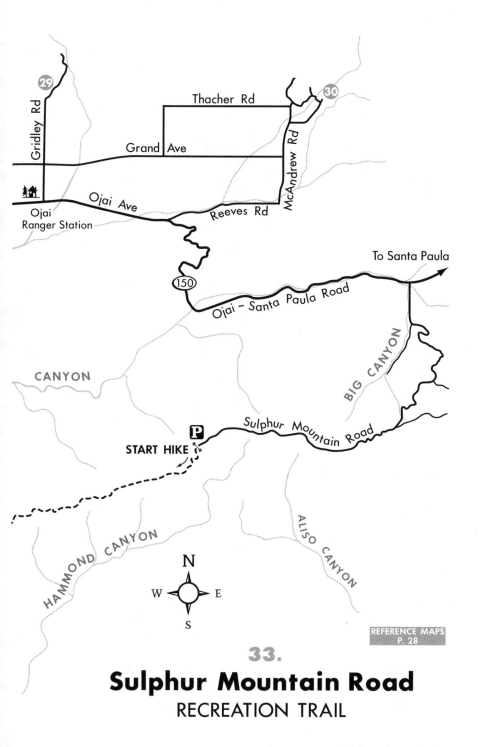

33.

Sulphur Mountain Road
RECREATION TRAIL

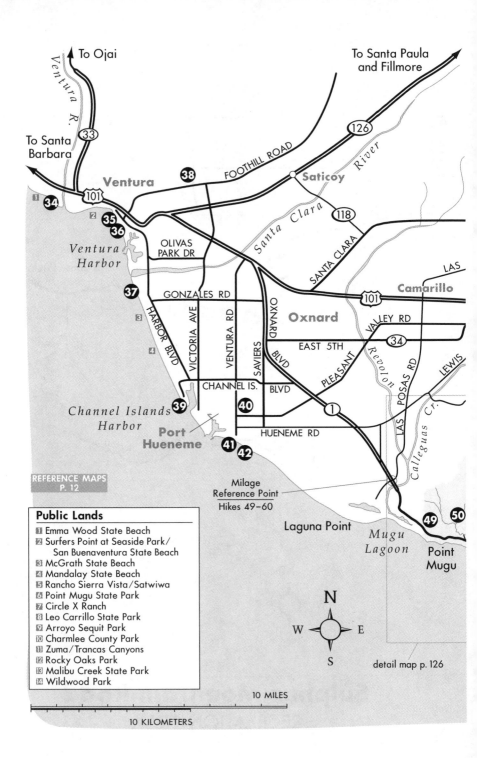

To Ojai

Ventura R.

To Santa Barbara

To Santa Paula and Fillmore

(33)

(126)

Ventura River

Santa Clara River

Ventura (38) FOOTHILL ROAD **Saticoy**

(101) (118)

(34) (35) (36)

Ventura Harbor

OLIVAS PARK DR

SANTA CLARA

LAS

Camarillo

(37) GONZALES RD

(101)

VICTORIA AVE

VENTURA RD

OXNARD BLVD

Oxnard

VALLEY RD (34)

EAST 5TH

SAVIERS

PLEASANT

Revolon

LAS POSAS RD

LEWIS

CHANNEL IS. BLVD

Channel Islands Harbor (39)

(40)

Calleguas Cr.

Port Hueneme

HUENEME RD

(41) (42)

(1)

REFERENCE MAPS P. 12

Milage Reference Point Hikes 49–60

Laguna Point

Mugu Lagoon

(49) (50)

Point Mugu

Public Lands

1. Emma Wood State Beach
2. Surfers Point at Seaside Park/ San Buenaventura State Beach
3. McGrath State Beach
4. Mandalay State Beach
5. Rancho Sierra Vista/Satwiwa
6. Point Mugu State Park
7. Circle X Ranch
8. Leo Carrillo State Park
9. Arroyo Sequit Park
10. Charmlee County Park
11. Zuma/Trancas Canyons
12. Rocky Oaks Park
13. Malibu Creek State Park
14. Wildwood Park

N

W E

S

detail map p. 126

10 MILES

10 KILOMETERS

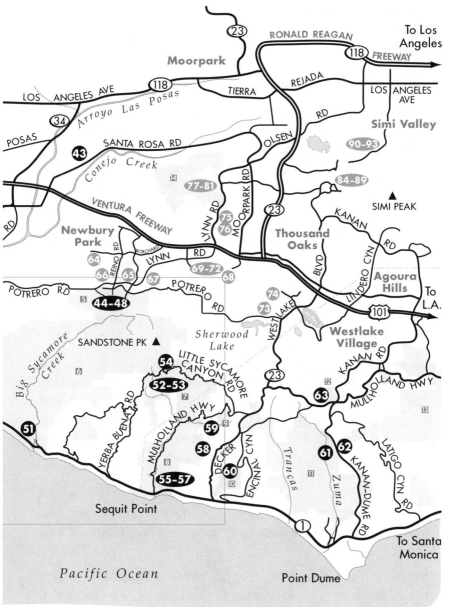

Ventura to Point Dume
Pacific Coast–Santa Monica Mountains

34. Emma Wood State Beach and Seaside Wilderness Park
Ocean's Edge—River's Edge Loop

Hiking distance: 2-mile loop
Hiking time: 1 hour
Elevation gain: Level
Maps: U.S.G.S. Ventura
　　　　Emma Wood State Beach map

Summary of hike: Emma Wood State Beach, located minutes from the city of Ventura, encompasses 152 acres near the mouth of the Ventura River. The state beach includes a campground, sand and cobblestone beaches, tidepools, sand dunes, a fresh-water marsh, and thick riparian foliage. At the mouth of the river is an estuary where the freshwater from the river mixes with the salt water of the sea. Seaside Wilderness Park is adjacent to Emma Wood State Beach and the estuary. It is an undeveloped 22-acre park with a quarter mile of ocean frontage. The Ocean's Edge Trail begins in Emma Wood State Beach and follows the coastline past tidepools, into the estuary, and along the sur-rounding wetlands of Seaside Wilderness Park. The level loop hike returns along the Ventura River on the River's Edge Trail.

Driving directions: VENTURA. Driving northbound on the Ventura Freeway/Highway 101 in Ventura, take the California Street exit. Drive a few blocks north to Main Street. Turn left and drive 1.2 miles through downtown Ventura to the Emma Wood State Beach entrance, just before reaching the northbound Highway 101 on-ramp. Turn left and drive 0.4 miles to the far end of the parking lot. A parking fee is required.

Driving southbound on the Ventura Freeway/Highway 101, take the Main Street/Ventura exit. At the end of the off-ramp, turn right and quickly turn right again into the posted Emma Wood State Beach.

Hiking directions: Take the paved walking path towards the railroad tracks and ocean. Cross through a tunnel under

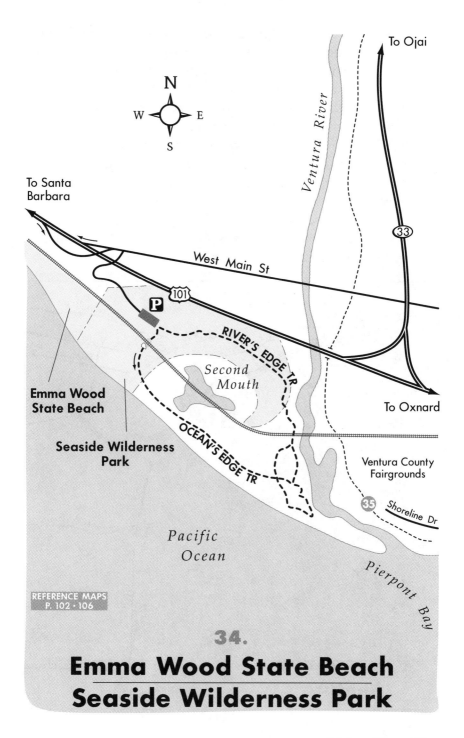

34.
Emma Wood State Beach
Seaside Wilderness Park

the tracks. Follow the natural path through the chaparral to the rocky oceanfront. Bear left on the Ocean's Edge Trail and stroll the coastline south. Cross a sandy stretch by the Second Mouth estuary, a former outlet of the Ventura River. Walk past the estuary and climb the low dunes to a network of connecting trails in Seaside Wilderness Park at the Ventura River.

Bear left on the River's Edge Trail through riparian vegetation and groves of Monterey pines and palms. Parallel the north banks of the river in the Lower Ventura River Estuary. Cross over the railroad tracks, heading upstream to a bench overlooking a bend in the river. Curve away from the river on the wide path, weaving through a tunnel of trees. Cross the grassy picnic area, completing the loop at the parking lot. ▪

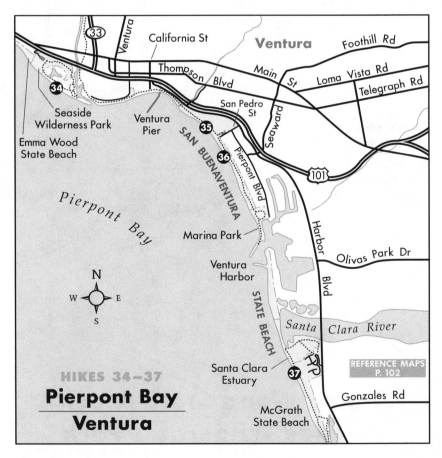

35. San Buenaventura State Beach to the Ventura River Estuary

Hiking distance: 4 miles round trip
Hiking time: 2 hours
Elevation gain: Level
Maps: U.S.G.S. Ventura

map
page 108

Summary of hike: San Buenaventura State Beach is an ocean-front park extending two miles along Pierpont Bay. This hike begins at the park headquarters and follows the coastline west on a paved walking and biking path. The trail passes through Promenade Park (a grassy park at the edge of the beach), Surfers Point at Seaside Park (a popular surfing spot at the south end of Figueroa Street), and Ventura County Fairgrounds Beach (a rock and cobble beach). The hike ends at a wetland estuary where the Ventura River joins the ocean. For a longer walk along the beach, Hike 36 continues along San Buenaventura State Beach on a footpath to the south, ending at Ventura Harbor and Marina Park.

Driving directions: VENTURA. From the Ventura Freeway/Highway 101 in Ventura, exit on Seaward Avenue and head west to Harbor Boulevard. Turn right and drive 0.4 miles to San Pedro Street. Turn left and go 0.2 miles to the San Buenaventura State Beach parking lot on the right. A parking fee is required.

Hiking directions: Walk 50 yards towards the ocean and sand dunes. Take the paved walking and biking path to the right, heading northbound parallel to the dunes. At a half mile, the path closely parallels Harbor Boulevard. Cross a bridge over a lagoon formed by the San Jon Barranca drainage, reaching the Ventura Pier at just over a mile. For a short detour, walk up the steps and stroll 1,700 feet out to sea on the wooden pier.

Back at the shoreline, continue west of the pier through land-scaped Promenade Park, fronted by a wide, sandy beach. The sand soon gives way to the rocky shoreline at Surfers Point along Seaside Park and the Ventura County Fairgrounds Beach,

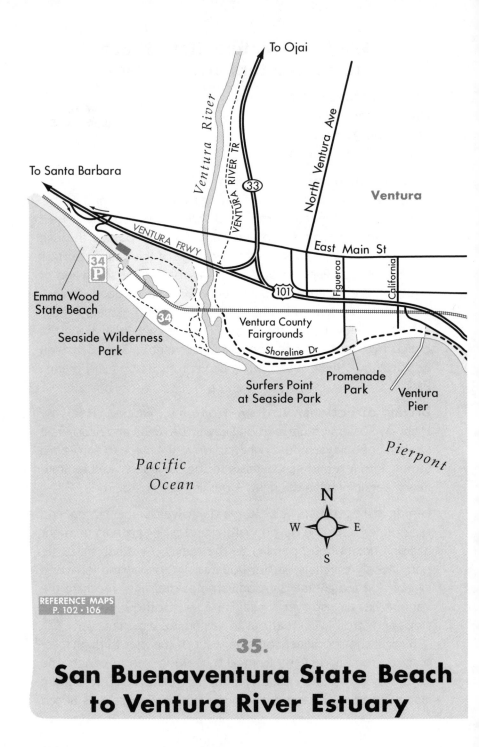

35.

San Buenaventura State Beach to Ventura River Estuary

lined with palms. At the west end of the pathway, the trail turns inland along the Ventura River and estuary. Across the river is Seaside Wilderness Park and Emma Wood State Beach (Hike 34). This is the turn-around point.

To extend the hike north, the Ventura River Trail crosses under Highway 101 and jogs through Ventura to a paved path. The trail continues to Foster Park off of Highway 33, where it becomes the Ojai Valley Trail. It continues 9.5 miles uphill on the old Southern Pacific Railroad bed to Libbey Park in downtown Ojai. ▨

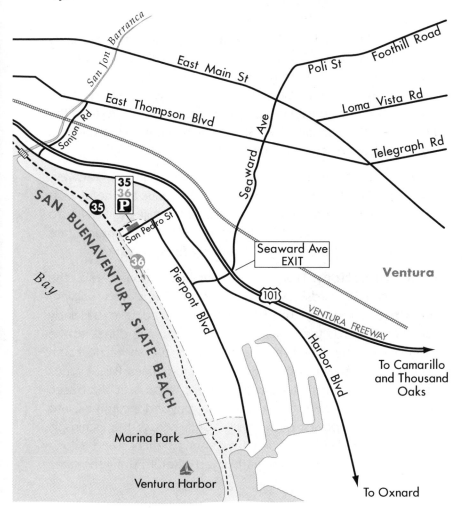

36. San Buenaventura State Beach to Marina Park and Ventura Harbor

Hiking distance: 2.4 miles round trip
Hiking time: 1.5 hours
Elevation gain: Level
Maps: U.S.G.S. Ventura and Oxnard

Summary of hike: San Buenaventura State Beach extends for two miles along the Ventura coastline along a low dune ridge. Nestled near the southern end of the state beach is Marina Park, a 15-acre, palm-studded oceanfront park on the north peninsula of Ventura Harbor. The grassland park has sandy beaches, seagulls, playground equipment, and benches fronting the harbor. The well-developed harbor was carved out of the dunes and has two separate marinas. Marina Park is a great spot for observing boats coming in and out of the harbor. To extend the walk along San Buenaventura State Beach, a paved walking and biking path heads north from the parking lot—Hike 35.

Driving directions: VENTURA. From the Ventura Freeway/Highway 101 in Ventura, exit on Seaward Avenue and head west to Harbor Boulevard. Turn right and drive 0.4 miles to San Pedro Street. Turn left and go 0.2 miles to the San Buenaventura State Beach parking lot on the right. A parking fee is required.

Hiking directions: From the parking lot entrance, take the paved path 50 yards towards the beach. The paved walking/biking path curves right (north)—Hike 35. Instead, take the sandy footpath towards the low dunes. Climb over the dunes to the shoreline by the rock breakwater. Follow the shoreline south, parallel to the beachfront homes behind the dunes. Pass a series of four rock groins that extend offshore to protect the beach from erosion. Continue along the shore, beyond the homes, into Marina Park. A paved path heads south across the peninsula to the Ventura Harbor Channel by sitting benches and a lone cypress. The trail ends at the harbor jetty. Return along the same route. ▓

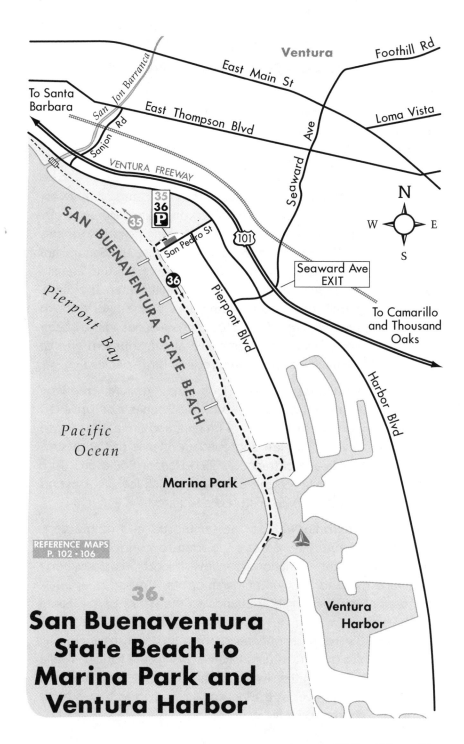

36.

San Buenaventura State Beach to Marina Park and Ventura Harbor

37. McGrath State Beach
Santa Clara Estuary Natural Preserve

Hiking distance: 0.7-miles to 4 miles round trip
Hiking time: 45 minutes—2 hours
Elevation gain: Level
Maps: U.S.G.S. Oxnard
McGrath State Beach map

Summary of hike: McGrath State Beach is located on the west end of Oxnard just south of Ventura. Rolling sand dunes, stabilized with vegetation, line the two-mile long coastline of this 295-acre park. The northern 160 acres comprise the Santa Clara Estuary Natural Preserve, where fresh water from the 94-mile Santa Clara River mixes with the ocean's salt water. The Santa Clara Nature Trail follows the south banks of the river through the estuary and wildlife refuge, crossing low dunes to the ocean. McGrath Lake, a small freshwater lake at the southern end of McGrath State Beach, attracts hundreds of bird species.

Driving directions: VENTURA. From the Ventura Freeway/Highway 101 in Ventura, take the Victoria Avenue exit. Drive 0.6 miles south to Olivas Park Drive. Turn right and drive 2.4 miles to Harbor Boulevard. Turn left and continue 1.1 mile to the posted McGrath State Beach entrance at 2211 Harbor Boulevard. Turn right and go 0.2 miles to the trailhead parking lot, just beyond the entrance station. A parking fee is required.

Hiking directions: Walk to the far (north) end of the parking lot and curve right. Cross a wooden footbridge and enter a riparian habitat of sandbar willow thickets, cottonwoods, coastal scrub, and freshwater marsh plants. A raised boardwalk winds through the fragile wetlands to the banks of the Santa Clara River.

Return 30 yards and continue on the path downstream to a levee. A path to the left returns to the parking area for a half-mile loop. Continue along the river and climb over the sand dunes to the mouth of the river at the ocean. This is a good turn-around spot for a shorter, 0.7-mile walk.

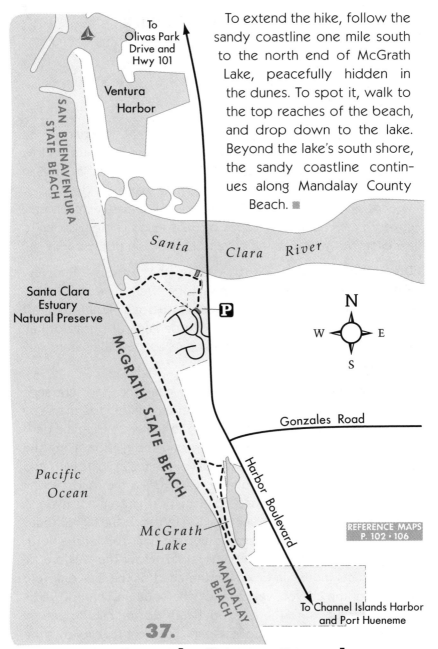

To extend the hike, follow the sandy coastline one mile south to the north end of McGrath Lake, peacefully hidden in the dunes. To spot it, walk to the top reaches of the beach, and drop down to the lake. Beyond the lake's south shore, the sandy coastline continues along Mandalay County Beach. ▩

To
Olivas Park
Drive and
Hwy 101

Ventura
Harbor

SAN BUENAVENTURA STATE BEACH

Santa Clara Estuary Natural Preserve

Santa   Clara   River

P

N
W ← → E
S

Gonzales Road

Pacific
Ocean

McGRATH STATE BEACH

Harbor Boulevard

REFERENCE MAPS
P. 102 · 106

McGrath
Lake

MANDALAY BEACH

To Channel Islands Harbor
and Port Hueneme

37.

McGrath State Beach
SANTA CLARA ESTUARY NATURAL PRESERVE

38. Arroyo Verde Park

Hiking distance: 3-mile loop
Hiking time: 1.5 hours
Elevation gain: 200 feet
Maps: U.S.G.S. Saticoy

Summary of hike: Arroyo Verde Park is a 129-acre park in the city of Ventura. The park sits in a small canyon between Barlow Canyon to the west and Sexton Canyon to the east in the San Miguelito Hills. On the south end of the park is a developed 14-acre open grassy area. To the north is a natural, chaparral-covered canyon area. A series of trails lead up the hillsides to excellent views above the developed portion of the park.

Driving directions: VENTURA. From the Ventura Freeway/Highway 101 in Ventura, exit on Victoria Avenue. Head 2.2 miles north to the end of Victoria Avenue at Foothill Road. Turn left and continue 0.7 miles to Arroyo Verde Park, opposite of Day Road. Turn right into the park entrance. Park past the nature center in the first lot.

Hiking directions: The trail begins near the park entrance across the lawn from the Arroyo Verde Center. You may also pick up the trail by crossing the lawn to the west from the parking lot. The trail heads north, traversing the hillside along the forested route. At 0.8 miles, the trail descends at Vista Bluff and meets the park road by Redwood Glen. Cross the road, picking up the backcountry trail, and continue north into the canyon. A short distance ahead is a junction. The left fork, the higher route, loops around the hillside and rejoins the right fork at the north end of the canyon. The two paths rejoin below The Wall, a 600-foot vertical mountain boxing in the head of the canyon. From the end of the canyon, veer to the right (southeast) for 50 yards to another junction. The left fork heads up the hillside, returning along the eastern side of the park. The right fork follows the canyon floor, returning along the most direct route. ▪

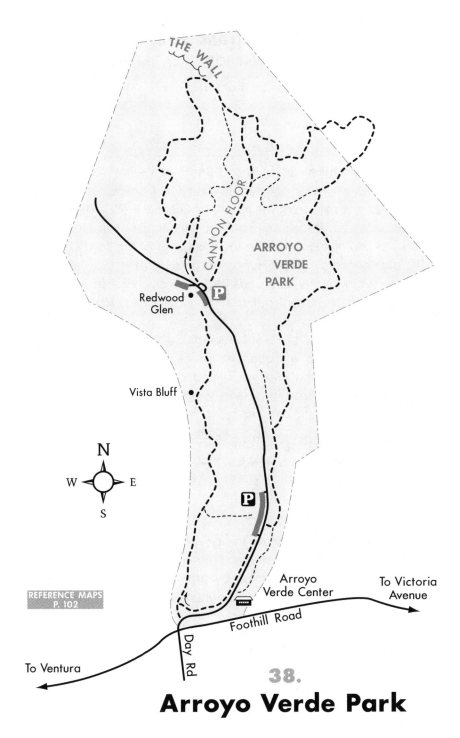

THE WALL

CANYON FLOOR

ARROYO
VERDE
PARK

Redwood
Glen

P

Vista Bluff

N
W   E
S

P

Arroyo
Verde Center

To Victoria
Avenue

Foothill Road

Day Rd

To Ventura

38.
Arroyo Verde Park

39. Silver Strand Beach

CHANNEL ISLANDS HARBOR to LA JANELLE PARK

Hiking distance: 2.5 miles round trip
Hiking time: 1.5 hours
Elevation gain: Level
Maps: U.S.G.S. Oxnard

Summary of hike: Silver Strand Beach is a white sand beach that fronts a small pocket community in Oxnard. The beach stretches one mile from the mouth of Channel Islands Harbor to Point Hueneme, at the mouth of Port Hueneme Harbor. La Janelle Park sits on Point Hueneme at the south end of the sandy beach. The park borders the Port Hueneme Naval Construction Battalion Center, which nearly surrounds Port Hueneme Harbor. This hike strolls along the oceanfront from Channel Islands Harbor to La Janelle Park.

In April of 1970, the S.S. La Jenelle, a 12,000-ton pleasure ship, ran aground in a storm. The wreck, just offshore of Point Hueneme, was filled with rocks and converted into a fishing jetty. The park and offshore area is now a popular fishing and surfing spot.

Driving directions: VENTURA. From the Ventura Freeway/ Highway 101 in Ventura, take the Victoria Avenue exit. Drive 6.6 miles south to the end of Victoria Avenue at the junction with San Nicholas Avenue. Park in the lot on the right, just before reaching San Nicholas Avenue.

Hiking directions: Follow the paved Channel Islands Harbor walking path southwest on the elevated rock jetty. Pass Ocean Drive to the sandy beachfront by the lifeguard station. At the end of the path are benches for watching the surf and the boat traffic through the harbor. Head south, strolling along the wide sandy beach fronted by homes. At the south end of the beach is Point Hueneme, jutting out to sea with two rock jetties. (The west jetty is built upon the S.S. La Jenelle ruins.) A fence separates La Janelle Park from the military center.

Return along the same route or follow the fenceline on the unpaved road to Ocean Drive. Bear left on Ocean Drive, returning to the Channel Islands Harbor. ■

Oxnard

To Hwy 101

Victoria Ave

HOLLYWOOD BEACH

Channel Islands Harbor

N
W ✦ E
S

Port Hueneme
Naval Construction
Battalion Center

BREAKWATER

P

San Nicholas Ave

lifeguard
station

SILVER STRAND BEACH

Island View Ave

Ocean Drive

**Port
Hueneme**

Pacific Ocean

Port Hueneme Harbor

Sawtelle

REFERENCE MAPS
P. 102

Point Hueneme

S.S. La Janelle Jetty

**La Janelle
Park**

41

To Port
Hueneme
Beach Park

39.
Silver Strand Beach
CHANNEL ISLANDS HARBOR
to LA JANELLE PARK

40. Bubbling Springs Recreational Greenbelt

Hiking distance: 3.6 miles round trip
Hiking time: 2 hours
Elevation gain: Level
Maps: U.S.G.S. Oxnard
The Thomas Guide—Ventura County

Summary of hike: Bubbling Springs Park is a long, narrow greenbelt extending from Port Hueneme's inner residential area to the ocean at Port Hueneme Beach Park. A 1.5-mile walking and biking path winds through the landscaped recreational corridor alongside tranquil Bubbling Springs, a tree-shaded drainage channel.

Driving directions: OXNARD. From the Ventura Freeway/ Highway 101 in Oxnard, take the Ventura Road exit, and drive 6 miles south to Bard Road. Turn left and drive 0.3 miles to Bubbling Springs Park. Turn right on Park Avenue and park in the spaces on the left.

Heading southbound on the Ventura Freeway/Highway 101 in Oxnard, take the Wagon Wheel Road exit, and turn right a half block to Ventura Road. Turn left and drive 6 miles south to Bard Road. Turn left and drive 0.3 miles to Bubbling Springs Park. Turn right on Park Avenue and park in the spaces on the left.

Hiking directions: Cross the grassy park by the ball fields to the paved hiking and biking path on the east edge of the greenbelt. Take the path to the right. Head south alongside Bubbling Springs, lined with eucalyptus trees. At 0.3 miles is a bridge crossing over the stream to an open parkland. The path stays on the east side of the waterway, passing the community center to Pleasant Valley Road at 0.6 miles. Cross the intersection at Ventura Road, and continue on the signed walking path. Curve left, crossing a bridge over the creek, and follow the tree-lined watercourse downstream to Port Hueneme Road at 1.1 mile. Cross the boulevard and continue south, parallel to the creek and Surfside Drive. Another bridge crosses the creek to an expansive grassy section of Bubbling Springs Linear Park and its baseball fields. The streamside trail meanders through palm tree groves to Surfside Drive. Cross the road to Port Hueneme Beach Park, where the trail ends. To extend the hike along the coastline, continue with Hike 41 or 42. ■

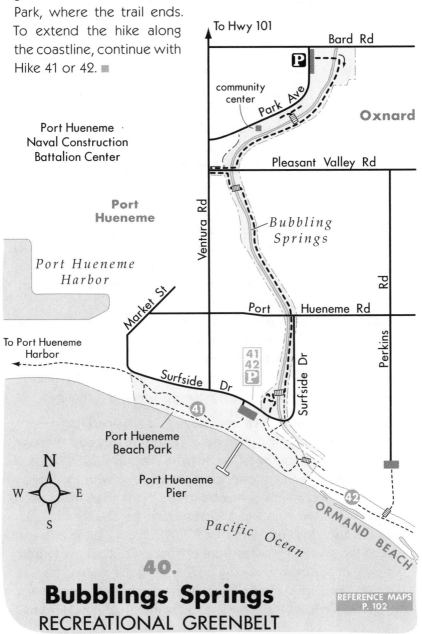

40.
Bubblings Springs
RECREATIONAL GREENBELT

REFERENCE MAPS
P. 102

41. Port Hueneme Beach Park

Hiking distance: 2.5 miles round trip
Hiking time: 1.5 hours
Elevation gain: Level
Maps: U.S.G.S. Oxnard

Summary of hike: Port Hueneme Beach Park is a well-maintained, landscaped park to the southeast of the 1,600-acre Port Hueneme Naval Construction Battalion Center. The 50-acre park has a wide sandy beach and a T-shaped recreational pier that extends 1,240 feet out to sea. From the pier are great views of the Ventura County coastline, the Channel Islands, and the Santa Monica Mountains at Point Mugu. A path runs along the edge of the beach, ending at the harbor entrance of the naval complex.

Driving directions: OXNARD. Heading northbound on the Ventura Freeway/Highway 101 in Oxnard, take the Ventura Road exit, and drive 7 miles south to Surfside Drive at the beachfront. Turn left and drive 0.2 miles to the beach parking lot on the right. A parking fee is required.

Heading southbound on the Ventura Freeway/Highway 101 in Oxnard, take the Wagon Wheel Road exit, and turn right a half block to Ventura Road. Turn left and drive 7 miles south to Surfside Drive at the beachfront. Turn left and drive 0.2 miles to the beach parking lot on the right. A parking fee is required.

Hiking directions: Take the paved, palm-lined path curving south and looping by Bubbling Springs, the shady drainage channel. Heading southeast, away from the walkway, is Ormand Beach—Hike 42, an undeveloped natural area with low rolling sand dunes and a wide sandy beach that extends 3 miles along the coast. For this walk, head west through Port Hueneme Beach Park and towards Port Hueneme Pier. Stroll out on the pier and take in the sweeping vistas from offshore. Continue west from the pier, either beachcombing or following the walking path to the west end of Surfside Drive. Beyond the walkway, a wide gravel path follows the shoreline to the mouth of Port Hueneme

Harbor. The harbor lies between the oceanfront jetty boulders and the shipping docks. At the harbor channel is the Port Hueneme Lighthouse, originally built in 1874 and rebuilt in 1941. Return by retracing your steps. ■

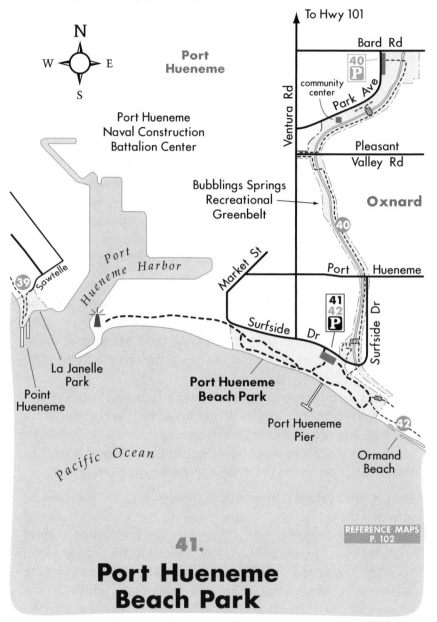

41.
Port Hueneme Beach Park

42. Ormand Beach

Hiking distance: 4 miles round trip
Hiking time: 2 hours
Elevation gain: Level
Maps: U.S.G.S. Oxnard and Point Mugu

Summary of hike: Ormand Beach is a 865-acre undeveloped beach in Oxnard that is off the beaten track. The beach stretches nearly 5 miles, from Port Hueneme Beach Park to Point Mugu Naval Air Station. It is backed by acres of farmland and has an extensive dune structure. The beach also includes a salt marsh wetland preserve, mudflats, and a freshwater lagoon fed by ground water and agricultural runoff. The preserve is on the Pacific Flyway, a 2,000-mile migratory route providing habitat for birds between Alaska and Latin America. The wetlands are also a nesting ground for the endangered western snowy plover, California least tern, and the California brown pelican. This coastal walk explores the dunes and coastal wetlands, following water channels parallel to the ocean.

Driving directions: OXNARD. Heading northbound on the Ventura Freeway/Highway 101 in Oxnard, take the Ventura Road exit, and drive 7 miles south to Surfside Drive at the beachfront. Turn left and drive 0.2 miles to the beach parking lot on the right. A parking fee is required.

Heading southbound on the Ventura Freeway/Highway 101 in Oxnard, take the Wagon Wheel Road exit, and turn right a half block to Ventura Road. Turn left and drive 7 miles south to Surfside Drive at the beachfront. Turn left and drive 0.2 miles to the beach parking lot on the right. A parking fee is required.

Hiking directions: From the far south end of the parking lot, take the paved path to a wooden bridge crossing Bubbling Springs. Just before the bridge, curve right on the wide gravel path. Follow the bank of the water channel to the lagoon. Head south on the sandy dune/channel between the lagoon and the ocean. Stroll through the wetland bird sanctuary, parallel to the water channel, to another bridge. The bridge crosses over the water channel and heads inland to Perkins Road and a parking lot at the wastewater treatment plant. (This is another access to Ormand Beach, located 0.6 miles south from Hueneme Road.) Continue south on the isolated coastal stretch through the wetlands to the fenced boundary of Point Mugu Naval Air Station. An asphalt path parallels the naval station and crosses a bridge to Arnold Road, the southern beach access parking lot at the end of the road (1.7 miles south of Hueneme Road). Return along the same route. ▓

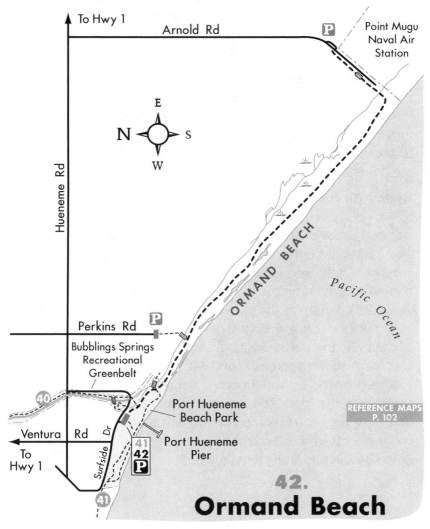

42.
Ormand Beach

REFERENCE MAPS
P. 102

43. Mission Oaks Park Trail

Hiking distance: 2 miles round trip
Hiking time: 1 hour
Elevation gain: 100 feet
Maps: U.S.G.S. Camarillo

Summary of hike: The Mission Oaks Park Trail leads through a natural area with hills and canyons connecting Mission Oaks Community Park and Mission Verde Park. Mission Oaks Park is a developed park with baseball fields, tennis courts, and a picnic area. Mission Verde Park is a grassy hilltop flat overlooking the open space. The forested trail parallels a seasonal waterway.

Driving directions: CAMARILLO. From the Ventura Freeway/Highway 101 in Camarillo, take the Pleasant Valley Road/Santa Rosa Road exit. Drive 1.6 miles north to Oak Canyon Road and turn left. Continue 0.4 miles—crossing Mission Oaks Boulevard—to Mission Oaks Community Park. Park in the lot to the left near the tennis courts.

Hiking directions: From the parking lot, walk between the tennis courts and Mission Oaks Boulevard to the trailhead. The path leads downhill and crosses a wooden footbridge to a five-way junction. Continue straight ahead on the main path. After crossing a drainage creek, the trail curves to the right. Take the narrow side path on the left that leads up the hill into Mission Verde Park. Return to the main trail, and continue north to a trail split. Take the left fork up the draw. Near the northwest corner of the park, the trail heads up a short hill to a junction. The left fork leads to Woodcreek Road. Take the right fork east across the head of the canyon. Descend back down into the canyon, completing the loop. Retrace your steps to the five-way junction. Take the right fork through the tunnel under the road. The trail curves 0.4 miles through a wooded area and ends at Santa Rosa Road. Return along the same path. ∎

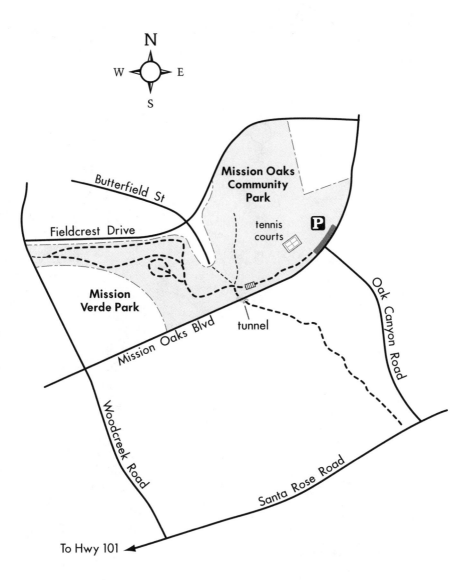

43.
Mission Oaks
Park Trail

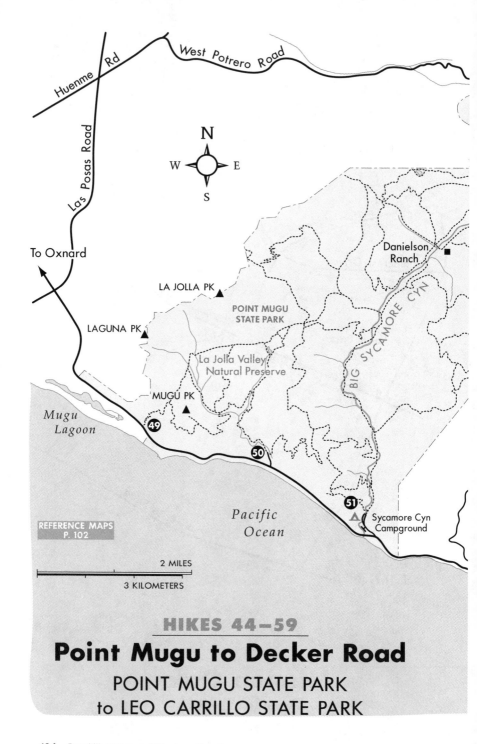

Huenme Rd

West Potrero Road

Las Posas Road

N
W   E
S

To Oxnard

Danielson Ranch

LA JOLLA PK ▲

POINT MUGU
STATE PARK

LAGUNA PK ▲

La Jolla Valley
Natural Preserve

BIG SYCAMORE CYN

MUGU PK ▲

*Mugu
Lagoon*

49

50

*Pacific
Ocean*

51

Sycamore Cyn
Campground

REFERENCE MAPS
P. 102

2 MILES

3 KILOMETERS

HIKES 44–59
Point Mugu to Decker Road
POINT MUGU STATE PARK
to LEO CARRILLO STATE PARK

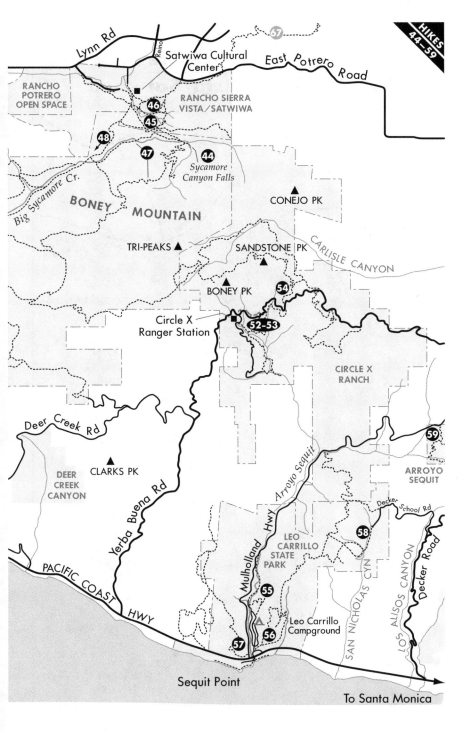

RANCHO POTRERO OPEN SPACE

Lynn Rd

Reino

Satwiwa Cultural Center

East Potrero Road

57

46

45

RANCHO SIERRA VISTA/SATWIWA

48

47

44

Sycamore Canyon Falls

Big Sycamore Cr.

BONEY MOUNTAIN

CONEJO PK ▲

CARLISLE CANYON

TRI-PEAKS ▲

SANDSTONE PK ▲

BONEY PK ▲

54

Circle X Ranger Station ■

52-53

CIRCLE X RANCH

Deer Creek Rd

59

DEER CREEK CANYON

CLARKS PK ▲

ARROYO SEQUIT

Yerba Buena Rd

Mulholland Hwy

Arroyo Sequit

Decker School Rd

58

LEO CARRILLO STATE PARK

SAN NICHOLAS CYN

LOS ALISOS CANYON

Decker Road

PACIFIC COAST HWY

55

57

56

Leo Carrillo Campground

Sequit Point

To Santa Monica

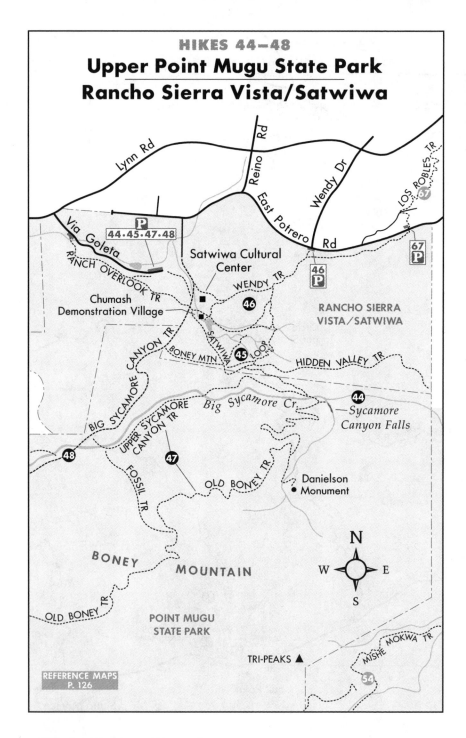

HIKES 44–48
Upper Point Mugu State Park
Rancho Sierra Vista/Satwiwa

Lynn Rd

Reino Rd

Wendy Dr

East Potrero Rd

LOS ROBLES TR

67

P
44·45·47·48

Via Goleta

RANCH OVERLOOK TR

Satwiwa Cultural Center

WENDY TR

46

46
P

67
P

Chumash
Demonstration Village

RANCHO SIERRA
VISTA/SATWIWA

BIG SYCAMORE CANYON TR

BONEY MTN TR

SATWIWA LOOP

45

HIDDEN VALLEY TR

44

UPPER SYCAMORE CANYON TR

Big Sycamore Cr.

Sycamore
Canyon Falls

48

47

FOSSIL TR

OLD BONEY TR

Danielson
Monument

BONEY

MOUNTAIN

N
W   E
S

OLD BONEY TR

POINT MUGU
STATE PARK

TRI-PEAKS ▲

MISHE MOKWA TR

54

REFERENCE MAPS
P. 126

44. Boney Mountain Trail to Sycamore Canyon Falls

RANCHO SIERRA VISTA/SATWIWA
POINT MUGU STATE PARK

Hiking distance: 3 miles round trip
Hiking time: 1.5 hours
Elevation gain: 350 feet
Maps: U.S.G.S. Newbury Park
      Santa Monica Mountains West Trail Map
      N.P.S. Rancho Sierra Vista/Satwiwa map

map page 131

Summary of hike: The Boney Mountain Trail climbs up the west slope of Boney Mountain at the upper reaches of Point Mugu State Park. This hike follows the lower portion of the trail to Sycamore Canyon Falls (also known as Rancho Sierra Vista Falls), a layered waterfall with a series of cascades set in a shaded, fern-filled grotto. The waterfall is surrounded by deep sandstone walls, lush vegetation, and small pools in the shade of a dense sycamore, bay, maple, and oak forest. The hike begins north of Point Mugu State Park in the Rancho Sierra Vista/Satwiwa area. The area is located at an early ranching site and on former Native American Indian land.

Driving directions: NEWBURY PARK. From the Ventura Freeway/Highway 101 in Newbury Park, exit on Wendy Drive. Drive 2 miles south to Lynn Road. Turn right and continue 1.7 miles to Via Goleta, the park entrance road. Turn left and drive 0.7 miles to the main parking lot at the end of the road.

Hiking directions: Take the posted trail past the restrooms a quarter mile to the service road at the Satwiwa Native American Indian Cultural Center. Bear right on the road, entering Point Mugu State Park. As you approach the ridge overlooking Big Sycamore Canyon, take the Boney Mountain Trail to the left along the brink of the canyon. Climb a short hill, passing the Satwiwa Loop Trail on the left, and continue around a ridge to a trail split. Take the right fork, descending down to the forested canyon floor. Stay on the main trail and cross the streambed, where the trail switchbacks sharply to the right. Instead of taking this horseshoe turn to the right (Hike 47), bear to the left, taking the footpath 100 yards to a stream crossing and the waterfall. Return along the same trail, or take one of the many trail options around the cultural center. ■

45. Ranch Overlook Trail—Satwiwa Loop
RANCHO SIERRA VISTA/SATWIWA

Hiking distance: 2.5-mile loop
Hiking time: 1.5 hours
Elevation gain: 300 feet

map
page 133

Maps: U.S.G.S. Newbury Park
      Santa Monica Mountains West Trail Map
      N.P.S. Rancho Sierra Vista/Satwiwa map

Summary of hike: Rancho Sierra Vista/Satwiwa is located at the northern boundary of Point Mugu State Park and the south edge of Newbury Park. The historical site is named for its two cultural legacies. For thousands of years it was the ancestral land of the Chumash and Gabrielino Indians. It was also a horse and cattle ranch named Rancho Sierra Vista. In 1980, an area of the parkland, part of the Santa Monica Mountains National Recreation Area, was designated as the Native American Indian Cultural Center and Natural Area. The site hosts a network of hiking trails. This hike loops through the rolling grasslands and chaparral to the hills that surround the meadow.

Driving directions: NEWBURY PARK. From the Ventura Freeway/Highway 101 in Newbury Park, exit on Wendy Drive. Drive 2 miles south to Lynn Road. Turn right and continue 1.7 miles to Via Goleta, the park entrance road. Turn left and drive 0.7 miles to the main parking lot at the end of the road.

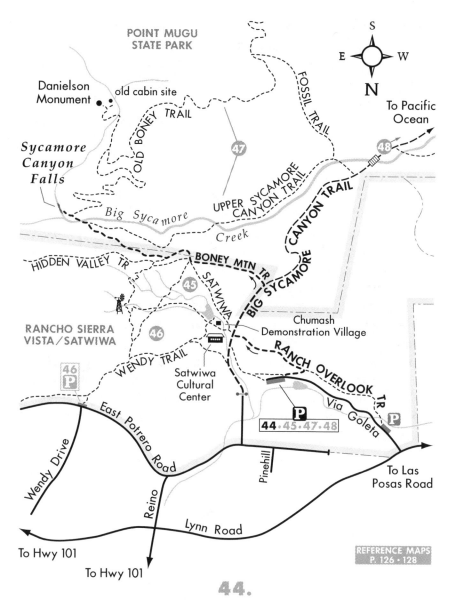

44.

Boney Mountain Trail to Sycamore Canyon Falls

RANCHO SIERRA VISTA/SATWIWA
POINT MUGU STATE PARK

Hiking directions: Walk back up the entrance road 0.1 mile to the posted Ranch Overlook Trail on the left. Bear left and climb the hill overlooking Rancho Sierra Vista, the Satwiwa Natural Area, the jagged Boney Mountain ridge, and Big Sycamore Canyon. Follow the ridge east to a junction with the main park road. To the right is the head of Big Sycamore Canyon (Hike 48), and left leads to Potrero Road.

Cross the road over two bridges to the cultural center on the left and a Chumash demonstration village on the right. Take the signed Satwiwa Loop Trail, passing an old cattle pond on the right. Cross the grasslands toward the windmill, which can be seen on the hillside ahead. As you near the windmill, drop into an oak-shaded ravine and cross a seasonal stream. Climb a short distance to the windmill and a junction. Bear to the right and traverse the upper slope of the meadow to a Y-fork. Stay to the left on the Hidden Valley Connector Trail. Head 50 yards to a magnificent overlook of Hidden Valley and Big Sycamore Canyon. Go to the right and follow the ridge downhill to a trail split. The left fork leads to Sycamore Canyon Falls (Hike 44). Continue straight to a 3-way trail split at the top of the meadow. Take the middle fork, completing the loop at the cultural center. Cross the road and return to the parking area on the wide gravel path. ■

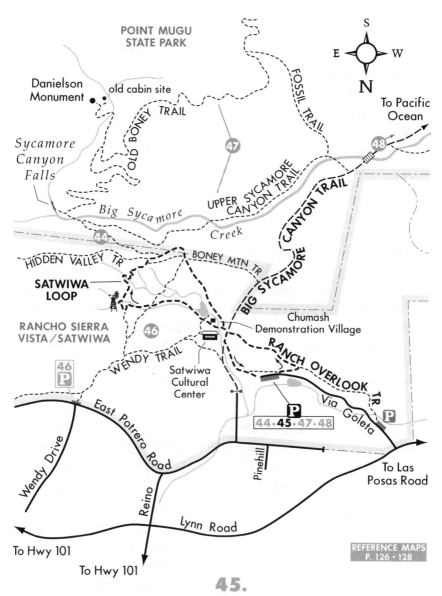

POINT MUGU
STATE PARK

Danielson
Monument

old cabin site

OLD BONEY TRAIL

Sycamore
Canyon
Falls

Big Sycamore Creek

47

UPPER SYCAMORE
CANYON TRAIL

FOSSIL TRAIL

To Pacific
Ocean

48

CANYON TRAIL

BIG SYCAMORE

44

HIDDEN VALLEY TR

BONEY MTN TR

SATWIWA
LOOP

RANCHO SIERRA
VISTA/SATWIWA

46

WENDY TRAIL

Chumash
Demonstration Village

RANCH OVERLOOK TR

46
P

Satwiwa
Cultural
Center

P

44·45·47·48

Via Goleta

P

East Potrero Road

Wendy Drive

Reino

Pinehill

To Las
Posas Road

Lynn Road

To Hwy 101

To Hwy 101

REFERENCE MAPS
P. 126 · 128

45.

Ranch Overlook Trail—
Satwiwa Loop

RANCHO SIERRA VISTA/SATWIWA
POINT MUGU STATE PARK

46. Wendy–Satwiwa Loop Trail
RANCHO SIERRA VISTA/SATWIWA

Hiking distance: 2.2-mile loop
Hiking time: 1 hour
Elevation gain: 200 feet
Maps: U.S.G.S. Newbury Park
      Santa Monica Mountains West Trail Map
      N.P.S. Rancho Sierra Vista/Satwiwa map

Summary of hike: Rancho Sierra Vista/Satwiwa sits on the bluffs at the head of Big Sycamore Canyon on the northern boundary of Point Mugu State Park. The Satwiwa Native American Indian Natural Area was occupied for thousands of years by the Chumash and Gabrielino Indians. Big Sycamore Canyon was part of a Chumash trade route to the ocean. Satwiwa, the name of the Chumash village, means *the bluffs*. This hike explores the open rolling terrain covered with chaparral and grasslands and the forested ravines with oaks and sycamores. The prominent volcanic cliffs of Boney Mountain are in view throughout the hike. Boney Mountain is the highest promontory of the Santa Monica Mountain range.

Driving directions: NEWBURY PARK. From the Ventura Freeway/Highway 101 in Newbury Park, exit on Wendy Drive. Drive 2.7 miles south to Potrero Road. Park in the parking area straight ahead, across the road.

Hiking directions: Head southwest past a signed junction with the Los Robles Connector Trail, and cross the grassy slopes dotted with oaks and sycamores. At 0.3 miles is a signed junction, the start of the loop. Leave the Wendy Trail for now, and bear left towards the windmill. Climb a short, steep hill to another junction. Again bear left, reaching the windmill and a junction at a half mile. Both trail forks follow the Satwiwa Loop Trail. The left fork leads to the Boney Mountain Trail. Take the right fork, and descend through a narrow ravine under an oak-shaded canopy. Cross the drainage and follow the open slopes, passing an unsigned path. Curve around the hillside to a 4-way junction by a pond. Straight ahead is the cultural center. The left fork leads to the pond. Bear right and climb to a junction at the crest of the hill. Take the right fork, staying on the Wendy Trail. Traverse the hillside northeast and complete the loop. ▪

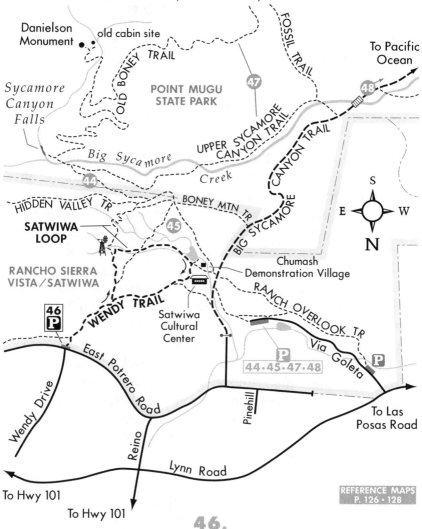

REFERENCE MAPS
P. 126 · 128

46.

Wendy—Satwiwa Loop Trail
RANCHO SIERRA VISTA/SATWIWA
POINT MUGU STATE PARK

47. Old Boney Trail to Danielson Monument

BONEY MOUNTAIN STATE WILDERNESS and POINT MUGU STATE PARK

Hiking distance: 7.8-mile loop
Hiking time: 4 hours
Elevation gain: 1,000 feet
Maps: U.S.G.S. Newbury Park
Tom Harrison Maps: Point Mugu State Park Trail Map
N.P.S. Rancho Sierra Vista/Satwiwa map

Summary of hike: The Boney Mountain State Wilderness area occupies the eastern portion of Point Mugu State Park. The centerpiece of the preserved area is Boney Mountain, a rocky, jagged formation that rises 1,500 feet above Sycamore Canyon. The scenic mountain contains four of the highest peaks in the coastal Santa Monica Range, including well-known Sandstone Peak (Hike 54). This hike follows the Old Boney Trail in Upper Sycamore Canyon to the Danielson Monument, a stone monument with a metal arch honoring Richard Danielson. Danielson donated the ranch to the National Park Service for preservation as an open space. Near the monument is the old cabin site of Richard Danielson Jr., where the rock fireplace still remains. En route to the monument, the trail passes Sycamore Canyon Falls, a 70-foot cascade in a lush box canyon along the riparian corridor of Big Sycamore Creek. The hike weaves through open grassland, wooded forests, a stream-fed canyon, and mountain overlooks with close-up views of the sheer rock face of Boney Mountain.

Driving directions: NEWBURY PARK. From the Ventura Freeway/Highway 101 in Newbury Park, exit on Wendy Drive. Drive 2 miles south to Lynn Road. Turn right and continue 1.7 miles to Via Goleta, the park entrance road. Turn left and drive 0.7 miles to the main parking lot at the end of the road.

Hiking directions: Take the posted trail past the restrooms a quarter mile to the service road at the Satwiwa Native American

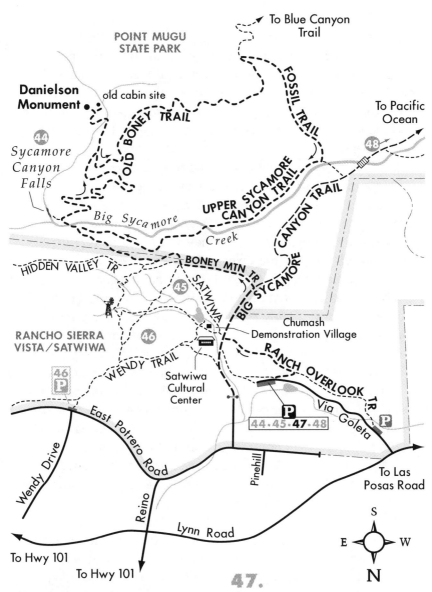

To Blue Canyon Trail

POINT MUGU STATE PARK

Danielson Monument

old cabin site

OLD BONEY TRAIL

FOSSIL TRAIL

To Pacific Ocean

44

Sycamore Canyon Falls

UPPER SYCAMORE CANYON TRAIL

48

CANYON TRAIL

Big Sycamore

Creek

BIG SYCAMORE

HIDDEN VALLEY TR

BONEY MTN TR

SATWIWA

45

RANCHO SIERRA VISTA/SATWIWA

46

Chumash Demonstration Village

WENDY TRAIL

RANCH OVERLOOK TR

46 P

Satwiwa Cultural Center

P 44·45·47·48

Via Goleta

P

Wendy Drive

East Potrero Road

Reino

Pinehill

To Las Posas Road

Lynn Road

To Hwy 101

To Hwy 101

S

E W

N

REFERENCE MAPS
P. 126 · 128

47.
Old Boney Trail to Danielson Monument

BONEY MOUNTAIN STATE WILDERNESS
POINT MUGU STATE PARK

116 Great Hikes – **137**

Indian Cultural Center. Bear right on the road, entering Point Mugu State Park. As you approach the ridge overlooking Big Sycamore Canyon, take the Boney Mountain Trail to the left along the brink of the canyon. Climb a short hill, passing the Satwiwa Loop Trail on the left, and continue around to a ridge to a trail split. Take the right fork, descending down to the forested canyon floor and a junction with the Upper Sycamore Canyon Trail at 1.3 miles, our return route.

Begin the loop straight ahead under a canopy of oaks, syca-mores, and bay laurel to a U-shaped right bend. Detour 100 yards to the left to seasonal Sycamore Canyon Falls in a rock-walled box canyon. Return to the Old Boney Trail, and continue up the hillside on the north flank of Boney Mountain to an overlook of Sycamore Canyon, the Oxnard Plain, and the Channel Islands. Inland views extend to the Los Padres National Forest. Steadily climb to a posted junction and views of the rounded rock for-mations of upper Boney Mountain. Detour 0.3 miles on the left fork, dropping down and crossing a seasonal drainage to the Danielson Monument at the end of the trail. To the right is the old cabin site with the remaining rock chimney and fireplace.

Return to the Old Boney Trail, and walk through the tall brush, gaining elevation while passing occasional overlooks that span from Point Mugu State Park to the Pacific Ocean. Gradually de-scend to a signed junction with the Fossil Trail at 4.4 miles. Straight ahead, the Old Boney Trail leads 2.1 miles to the Blue Canyon Trail, part of the Backbone Trail. (To the west, the Backbone Trail con-nects to the Danielson Ranch in Big Sycamore Canyon—Hike 48. To the east, the trail leads to Sandstone Peak—Hike 54.)

For this hike go to the right on the Fossil Trail, and descend into the stream-fed canyon. Follow the east canyon wall downstream, passing dozens of shell fossils embedded in the rock along the path. Near the bottom, enter an oak grove to a T-junction with the Upper Sycamore Canyon Trail. The left fork leads 0.1 mile to the Big Sycamore Canyon Fire Road/Trail. Bear right and head east, following the canyon floor. Complete the loop at 6.5 miles, 0.2 miles shy of Sycamore Canyon Falls. Bear left and retrace your steps 1.3 miles back to the trailhead. ▪

48. Big Sycamore Canyon Trail
POINT MUGU STATE PARK

Hiking distance: 8.4 miles one way (car shuttle)
Hiking time: 3 hours
Elevation loss: 900 feet

map page 140

Maps: U.S.G.S. Newbury Park, Camarillo and Point Mugu
      Tom Harrison Maps: Point Mugu State Park Trail Map
      Santa Monica Mountains West Trail Map
      N.P.S. Rancho Sierra Vista/Satwiwa map

Summary of hike: The Big Sycamore Canyon Trail is a one-way, mountains-to-the-sea journey. The canyon was originally part of the Chumash Indian trade route. The trail, now a partially paved service road, connects Newbury Park with the Sycamore Canyon Campground at the Pacific Ocean. The hike parallels Big Sycamore Creek through the heart of 15,000-acre Point Mugu State Park in a deep, wooded canyon under towering sycamores and oaks.

Driving directions: OXNARD. Shuttle Car: From the Pacific Coast Highway/Highway 1 and Las Posas Road in southeast Oxnard, drive 5.8 miles southbound on the PCH to the posted Big Sycamore Canyon entrance on the left. Turn left and park in the day-use pay parking lot 0.1 mile ahead on the left. (Parking is free in pullouts along the PCH.)

    To the Trailhead: From the shuttle car parking lot, drive 5.8 miles northbound on the Pacific Coast Highway/Highway 1 to Las Posas Road. Take Las Posas Road 2.9 miles north to Hueneme Road—turn right. Continue one mile to West Potrero Road and turn right. Drive 5.4 miles to Via Goleta and turn right (En route, West Potrero Road becomes Lynn Road). Drive 0.7 miles on Via Goleta to the parking lot at the end of the road.

Hiking directions: Take the posted trail past the restrooms a quarter mile to the service road at the Satwiwa Native American Indian Cultural Center. Bear right on the road, entering Point Mugu State Park, to a junction with the Boney Mountain Trail on the left.

Continue straight and begin the winding descent on the paved road to the canyon floor. The trail crosses a wooden bridge over the creek to the Hidden Pond Trail junction on the right. This is an excellent single track alternative trail that rejoins the Big Sycamore Canyon Trail 1.7 miles down canyon. On the alternative trail, there is a split at 2.2 miles. Take the left fork to the Sycamore Camping and Picnic Area. At 3 miles is a signed "beach" path on the right. This is where the alternative trail rejoins the service road. Just past the junction is the Danielson Ranch. Past the ranch, the trail is unpaved. Continue south down the forested canyon, past the Backbone Trail and the Overlook Trail (Hike 51) to the gate. From the gate, a paved road leads back to the shuttle car. ■

BACKBONE TRAIL

To Sandstone Peak
(Hike 54)

POINT MUGU
STATE PARK

OLD BONEY TR

FOSSIL

BIG

Danielson
Monument ●

44

47

*Sycamore
Canyon Falls*

BONEY
MTN TR

45

46

P

44·45·47·**48**

START

Satwiwa Cultural Center

East Potrero Road

Wendy

Reino

Via
Goleta

Lynn Road

REFERENCE MAPS
P. 126 · 128

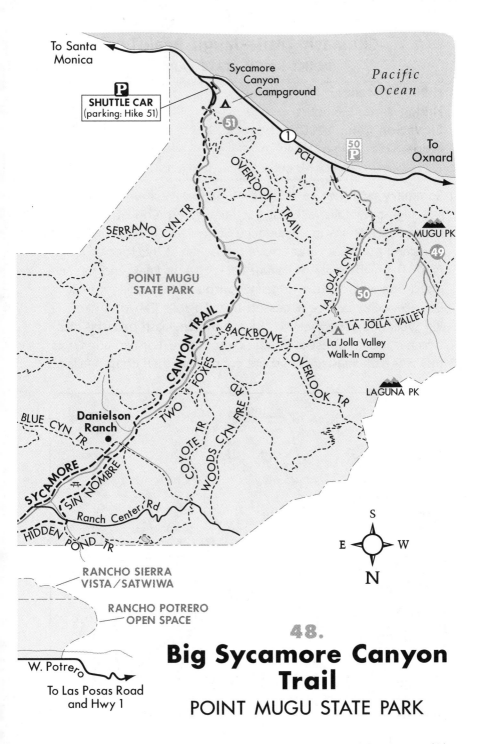

To Santa Monica

Pacific Ocean

Sycamore Canyon Campground

P
SHUTTLE CAR
(parking: Hike 51)

1 PCH

50 **P**

To Oxnard

OVERLOOK TRAIL

51

SERRANO CYN TR.

MUGU PK

49

POINT MUGU STATE PARK

LA JOLLA CYN

50

CANYON TRAIL

LA JOLLA VALLEY

La Jolla Valley Walk-In Camp

BACKBONE

LAGUNA PK

OVERLOOK TR

TWO FOXES TR

WOODS CYN FIRE RD

COYOTE TR

BLUE CYN TR

Danielson Ranch

SYCAMORE

SIN NOMBRE

Ranch Center Rd

HIDDEN POND TR

S
E ✦ W
N

RANCHO SIERRA VISTA/SATWIWA

RANCHO POTRERO OPEN SPACE

W. Potrero

To Las Posas Road and Hwy 1

48.
Big Sycamore Canyon Trail
POINT MUGU STATE PARK

49. Chumash Trail—Mugu Peak Loop
POINT MUGU STATE PARK

Hiking distance: 4.5-mile loop
Hiking time: 2.5 hours
Elevation gain: 1,100 feet
Maps: U.S.G.S. Point Mugu
      Santa Monica Mountains West Trail Map

map
page 144

Summary of hike: La Jolla Valley Natural Preserve is an expansive high-mountain valley at the far western end of the Santa Monica Mountains in Point Mugu State Park. The oak-studded grassland rests 800 feet above the ocean at the foot of Mugu Peak. The high ridges of Laguna Peak, La Jolla Peak, and the serrated Boney Mountain ridgeline surround the rolling meadow. La Jolla Valley can be accessed from La Jolla Canyon (Hike 50), Big Sycamore Canyon (Hike 48), and the Chumash Trail (this hike), which is the steepest and most direct route. For centuries, this trail was a Chumash Indian route connecting their coastal village

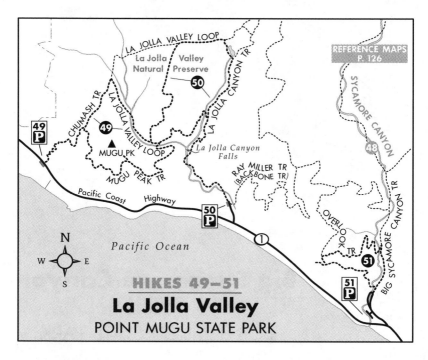

HIKES 49–51

La Jolla Valley
POINT MUGU STATE PARK

at Mugu Lagoon with La Jolla Valley. This hike steeply ascends the coastal slope on the west flank of Mugu Peak. The elevated Mugu Peak Trail circles the mountain slope below the twin peaks, offering sweeping mountain-to-coast vistas. A side path leads to the grassy summit

Driving directions: OXNARD. From the Pacific Coast Highway/Highway 1 and Las Posas Road in southeast Oxnard, drive 2.3 miles southbound on the PCH to the large parking pullout on the left, across from the Navy Rifle Range and Mugu Lagoon.

Heading northbound on the Pacific Coast Highway, the trailhead parking area is 16.8 miles past Malibu/Kanan Dume Road and 3.5 miles west of the well-marked Sycamore Canyon.

Hiking directions: Begin climbing up the hillside covered in chaparral and cactus, gaining elevation with every step. At a half mile, the trail temporarily levels out on a plateau with sweeping coastal views that include the Channel Islands. The steadily ascending trail gains 900 feet in 0.7 miles to a T-junction on a saddle. Begin the loop to the left, crossing over the saddle into the vast La Jolla Valley. The valley is surrounded by rounded mountain peaks, the jagged Boney Mountain ridge, and the surrealistic Navy radar towers by Laguna Peak. Cross the open expanse to a posted junction with the La Jolla Valley Loop Trail at 1.2 miles.

Take the right fork and head southeast across the meadow on a slight downward slope. Drop into an oak woodland and cross a stream. Parallel the stream through a small draw to another junction. Take the right fork 100 yards to a path on the right by an old circular metal tank. Bear right on the Mugu Peak Trail and cross the creek. Traverse the hillside to the west edge of La Jolla Canyon. Follow the ridge south on the oceanfront cliffs. Wind along the south flank of Mugu Peak, following the contours of the mountain to a trail split on a saddle between the mountain's double peaks. The right fork ascends the rounded grassy summit. Veer left, hiking along the steep hillside to the west side of the peak. Cross another saddle and complete the loop. Return down the mountain to the trailhead. ■

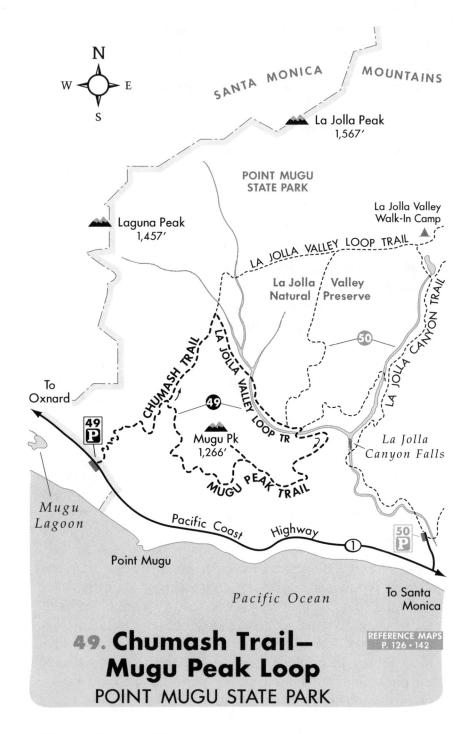

N
W E
S

SANTA MONICA MOUNTAINS

La Jolla Peak
1,567'

POINT MUGU
STATE PARK

La Jolla Valley
Walk-In Camp

Laguna Peak
1,457'

LA JOLLA VALLEY LOOP TRAIL

La Jolla Valley
Natural Preserve

CHUMASH TRAIL

LA JOLLA VALLEY LOOP TR

LA JOLLA CANYON TRAIL

50

To
Oxnard

49
P

49

Mugu Pk
1,266'

MUGU PEAK TRAIL

La Jolla
Canyon Falls

Mugu
Lagoon

Pacific Coast Highway

1

50
P

Point Mugu

To Santa
Monica

Pacific Ocean

49. Chumash Trail–
Mugu Peak Loop
POINT MUGU STATE PARK

REFERENCE MAPS
P. 126 • 142

50. La Jolla Valley Loop from La Jolla Canyon

POINT MUGU STATE PARK

Hiking distance: 6-mile loop
Hiking time: 3 hours
Elevation gain: 750 feet
Maps: U.S.G.S. Point Mugu
            Tom Harrison Maps: Point Mugu State Park Trail Map
            Santa Monica Mountains West Trail Map

map
page 146

Summary of hike: La Jolla Canyon is a steep, narrow gorge with a perennial stream and a 15-foot waterfall known as La Jolla Canyon Falls. The canyon leads up to La Jolla Valley Natural Preserve in Point Mugu State Park. The preserve sits at an 800-foot elevation in a broad valley with rolling grasslands at the west end of the Santa Monica Mountains. Mugu Peak, La Jolla Peak, and Laguna Peak surround the oak-dotted meadow. This hike climbs through the rock-walled canyon and loops around the meadow to a coastal overlook and a pond with a picnic area.

Driving directions: OXNARD. From the Pacific Coast Highway/ Highway 1 and Las Posas Road in southeast Oxnard, drive 4.2 miles southbound on the PCH to the posted La Jolla Canyon entrance on the left.

    Heading northbound on the Pacific Coast Highway, the trail-head parking area is 15 miles past Malibu/Kanan Dume Road and 1.6 miles west of the well-marked Sycamore Canyon..

Hiking directions: From the north end of the parking lot, at the Ray Miller Trailhead, take the La Jolla Canyon Trail north. Follow the wide path up the canyon, crossing the stream several times. The third crossing is just below La Jolla Canyon Falls, a beautiful 15-foot waterfall with a pool surrounded by large boulders. Natural rock steps lead to the top of the falls. Continue along the east side of the canyon, passing large sandstone rocks and caves. At a gorge, the trail sharply doubles back to the right, leading up the side of the canyon. At 1.2 miles, take the left fork towards Mugu Peak. Cross the stream and head southwest to a ridge above La Jolla Canyon and the ocean. The trail levels out and passes two trail junctions with the Hike 49 loop. Stay to the right both times, heading north across the rolling grassland. At 2.7 miles the trail joins the wide La Jolla Valley Loop Trail—head to the right. As you near the mountains of La Jolla Canyon, take the first cutoff trail to the right, leading past the pond and re-joining the La Jolla Canyon Trail. Head to the right, and go two miles down canyon, returning to the trailhead. ■

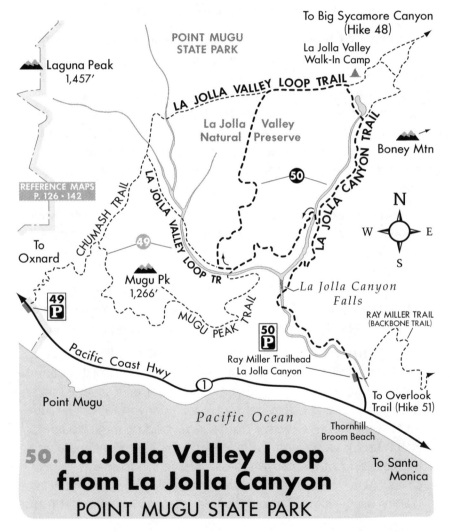

50. La Jolla Valley Loop from La Jolla Canyon
POINT MUGU STATE PARK

51. Scenic and Overlook Trails Loop
POINT MUGU STATE PARK

Hiking distance: 2-mile loop
Hiking time: 1 hour
Elevation gain: 900 feet
Maps: U.S.G.S. Point Mugu
Tom Harrison Maps: Point Mugu State Park Trail Map
Santa Monica Mountains West Trail Map

map
page 148

Summary of hike: The Scenic and Overlook Trails are located along the coastal frontage of Point Mugu State Park. The trail follows the ridge separating Big Sycamore Canyon from La Jolla Canyon. This short but beautiful hike climbs up the chaparral-covered ridge to several panoramic overlooks of the Pacific Ocean.

Driving directions: OXNARD. From the Pacific Coast Highway/Highway 1 and Las Posas Road in southeast Oxnard, drive 5.8 miles southbound on the PCH to the posted Big Sycamore Canyon entrance on the left. Turn left and park in the day-use pay parking lot 0.1 mile ahead on the left. (Parking is free in pull-outs along the PCH.)

Heading northbound on the Pacific Coast Highway, the trailhead parking entrance is on the right, 13.3 miles past Malibu/Kanan Dume Road and 5.3 miles west of the well-marked Leo Carrillo State Beach.

Hiking directions: From the parking area, walk up the road past the campground to the Big Sycamore Canyon trailhead gate. Continue up the unpaved road about 50 yards to the signed junction with the Scenic Trail. Take the trail to the left (west) across Big Sycamore Creek, and head up the wooden steps. The trail steadily gains elevation up an open, grassy hillside with views of Big Sycamore Canyon. At the saddle near the top of the hill is a trail split. The left fork leads a short distance to an ocean overlook. Continue up to several more viewpoints. Return back to the junction, and head north to a junction with the Overlook

Trail. Take this service road downhill to the right, winding 0.9 miles back to the Big Sycamore Canyon floor. Near the bottom, five gentle switchbacks lead to the junction across the creek. Take the canyon trail to the right, leading 0.4 miles back to the trailhead gate. ■

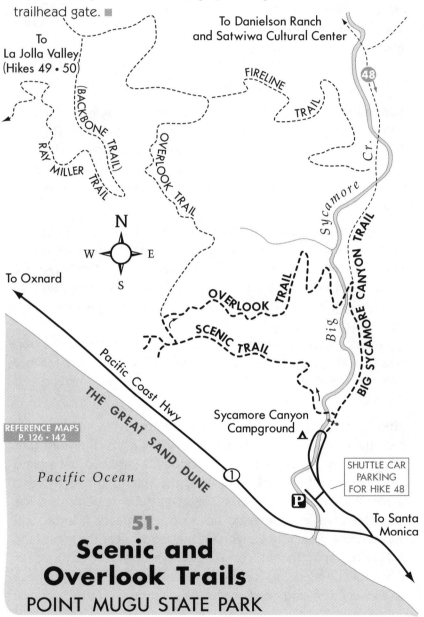

To Danielson Ranch
and Satwiwa Cultural Center

To
La Jolla Valley
(Hikes 49 • 50)

48

FIRELINE TRAIL

(BACKBONE TRAIL)

OVERLOOK TRAIL

RAY MILLER TRAIL

Sycamore Cr.

N
W   E
S

BIG SYCAMORE CANYON TRAIL

To Oxnard

OVERLOOK TRAIL

SCENIC TRAIL

Big

Pacific Coast Hwy

THE GREAT SAND DUNE

REFERENCE MAPS
P. 126 • 142

Pacific Ocean

1

Sycamore Canyon
Campground ▲

SHUTTLE CAR
PARKING
FOR HIKE 48

P

To Santa
Monica

51.
Scenic and
Overlook Trails
POINT MUGU STATE PARK

52. Grotto Trail
CIRCLE X RANCH

Hiking distance: 3.5 miles round trip
Hiking time: 2 hours
Elevation gain: 650 feet
Maps: U.S.G.S. Triunfo Pass

map
page 150

Tom Harrison Maps: Point Mugu State Park Trail Map
Santa Monica Mountains West Trail Map
N.P.S. Circle X Ranch Site

Summary of hike: The Grotto Trail is located in the 1,655-acre Circle X Ranch bordering Point Mugu State Park. Once a Boy Scout wilderness retreat, the Circle X Ranch is now a national park and recreation area. At the end of this trail is The Grotto, a maze of large, volcanic boulders in a sheer, narrow gorge formed from landslides. The natural rock garden contains numerous caves and pools. The West Fork of the Arroyo Sequit flows through the caves and caverns of The Grotto, creating cascades and pools.

Driving directions: OXNARD. From the Pacific Coast Highway/ Highway 1 and Las Posas Road in southeast Oxnard, drive 9 miles southbound to Yerba Buena Road, located 3.3 miles past Sycamore Canyon. Turn left and drive 5.3 winding miles up Yerba Buena Road to the Circle X Ranger Station on the right. Park by the ranger station, or drive 0.2 miles downhill to the day-use parking area, located just past the posted Grotto Trailhead.

Heading northbound on the Pacific Coast Highway, Yerba Buena Road is 2 miles past Leo Carrillo State Beach. Turn right on Yerba Buena Road, and follow the directions above.

Hiking directions: From the ranger station, walk 0.2 miles down the unpaved road to the posted Grotto Trailhead, just before reaching the lower parking area. Continue downhill, crossing the West Fork of Arroyo Sequit. At 0.4 miles, the trail passes the Canyon View Trail (Hike 53) and recrosses the creek at a 30-foot waterfall. After crossing, curve left, traversing a grassy ridge. Descend to the canyon floor where the trail joins the Happy Hollow Campground Road at 1.2 miles. Follow the road to the left into a primitive campground and cross the creek, picking up the posted Grotto Trail again. Head downstream to a bridge that crosses the creek into the Happy Hollow Campground. Instead of crossing the bridge, continue straight ahead and cross the creek by a pumphouse. Follow the creek a few hundred feet to The Grotto.

After exploring The Grotto, return to the bridge that accesses the campground. Walk through the campground to the road and bear to the right. Follow the winding road and rejoin the Grotto Trail on the left. Retrace your steps to the parking lot. ■

52. **Grotto Trail**
CIRCLE X RANCH

53. Canyon View —
Yerba Buena Road Loop
CIRCLE X RANCH

Hiking distance: 3.2-mile loop
Hiking time: 1.5 hours
Elevation gain: 500 feet

map
page 153

Maps: U.S.G.S. Triunfo Pass
      Tom Harrison Maps: Point Mugu State Park Trail Map
      Santa Monica Mountains West Trail Map
      N.P.S. Circle X Ranch Site

Summary of hike: Circle X Ranch, a former Boy Scout camp, sits below majestic Boney Mountain in the upper canyons of Arroyo Sequit. The Canyon View Trail traverses the brushy hillside of the deep, east-facing canyon. The panoramic views extend down the canyon to the Pacific Ocean. The northern views reach the jagged Boney Mountain ridge and the 3,111-foot Sandstone Peak, the highest peak in the Santa Monica Mountains. The trail connects the Grotto Trail (Hike 52) with the Sandstone Peak Trail (Hike 54).

Driving directions: OXNARD. From the Pacific Coast Highway/Highway 1 and Las Posas Road in southeast Oxnard, drive 9 miles southbound to Yerba Buena Road, located 3.3 miles past Sycamore Canyon. Turn left and drive 5.3 winding miles up Yerba Buena Road to the Circle X Ranger Station on the right. Park by the ranger station, or drive 0.2 miles downhill to the day-use parking area, located just past the posted Grotto Trailhead.
    Heading northbound on the Pacific Coast Highway, Yerba Buena Road is 2 miles past Leo Carrillo State Beach. Turn right on Yerba Buena Road, and follow the directions above.

Hiking directions: From the ranger station, walk 0.2 miles down the unpaved road to the posted Grotto Trailhead, just before reaching the lower parking area. Pass the trail gate and follow the dirt road past a picnic area to another trail sign. Take the footpath downhill and cross the West Fork Arroyo Sequit.

Parallel the east side of the creek to a signed junction. (Twenty yards to the right is a waterfall. Hike 52 continues down the trail to The Grotto.) Bear left on the Canyon View Trail, and traverse the canyon wall, following the contours of the mountain. Climb two switchbacks to a junction. For a shorter 1.5-mile loop, take the Connector Trail 100 yards to the left to Yerba Buena Road, and return 0.35 miles to the ranger station.

For this longer hike, stay to the right and cross a rocky wash. Head up the hillside to a south view that spans down canyon to the ocean and the Channel Islands and a north view of the Boney Mountain ridge. Continue to Yerba Buena Road, across from the Sandstone Peak Trail (Hike 54). For a loop hike, return to the left on Yerba Buena Road, and walk 1.1 mile back to the trailhead at the Circle X Ranger Station. ▨

54. Sandstone Peak
Mishe Mokwa — Sandstone Peak Loop
CIRCLE X RANCH

Hiking distance: 6-mile loop
Hiking time: 3 hours
Elevation gain: 1,100 feet

map page 155

Maps: U.S.G.S. Triunfo Pass and Newbury Park
Tom Harrison Maps: Point Mugu State Park Trail Map
Santa Monica Mountains West Trail Map
N.P.S. Circle X Ranch Site

Summary of hike: The Mishe Mokwa Trail in Circle X Ranch follows Carlisle Canyon along Boney Mountain past weathered red volcanic formations. There are views of the sculpted caves and crevices of Echo Cliffs and a forested streamside picnic area by a huge, split boulder known as Split Rock. The return route on the Sandstone Peak Trail (a section of the Backbone Trail) leads to Inspiration Point and Sandstone Peak, the highest point in the Santa Monica Mountains. Both points overlook the Pacific Ocean, the Channel Islands, and the surrounding mountains.

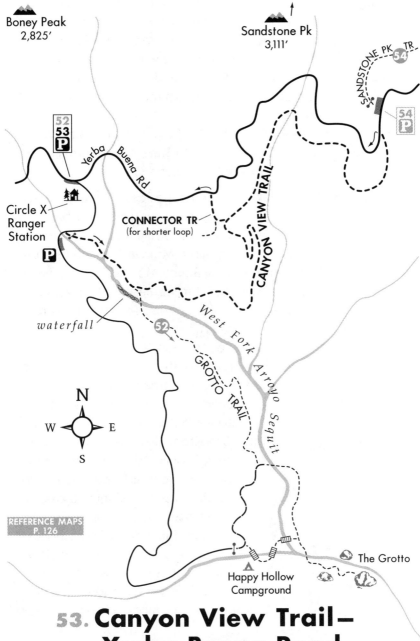

53. Canyon View Trail– Yerba Buena Road

CIRCLE X RANCH

Driving directions: OXNARD. From the Pacific Coast Highway/ Highway 1 and Las Posas Road in southeast Oxnard, drive 9 miles southbound to Yerba Buena Road, located 3.3 miles past Sycamore Canyon. Turn left and drive 5.3 winding miles up Yerba Buena Road to the Circle X Ranger Station on the right. From the ranger station, continue one mile to the Backbone Trailhead parking lot on the left.

Heading northbound on the Pacific Coast Highway, Yerba Buena Road is 2 miles past Leo Carrillo State Beach. Turn right on Yerba Buena Road, and follow the directions above.

Hiking directions: Take the Sandstone Peak Trail (a fire road) uphill to the north. At 0.3 miles, leave the road and take the signed Mishe Mokwa Connector Trail straight ahead. Continue 0.2 miles to a junction with the Mishe Mokwa Trail and take the left fork. The trail contours along Boney Mountain on the western edge of Carlisle Canyon. At 1.4 miles, Balanced Rock can be seen on the opposite side of the canyon. The enormous rock is precariously perched off a cliff balanced on a tiny pedestal. Descend into the canyon shaded by oaks, laurel, and sycamores to Split Rock and the picnic area. Take the trail across the stream, heading out of the canyon to another stream crossing by sculptured volcanic rocks. Parallel the stream to a signed junction. Take the left fork— the Sandstone Peak/Backbone Trail— curving uphill towards Inspiration Point. A short side path leads up to the overlook. Continue east on the main trail to another junction. This side trail switchbacks up to the 360-degree views at Sandstone Peak. From the junction, it is 0.8 miles downhill back to the Mishe Mokwa Connector Trail, completing the loop. ▪

Balanced Rock

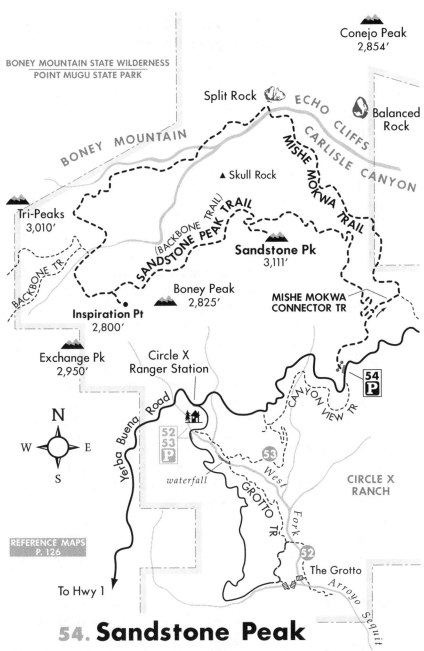

Conejo Peak
2,854'

BONEY MOUNTAIN STATE WILDERNESS
POINT MUGU STATE PARK

Split Rock

ECHO CLIFFS

Balanced
Rock

BONEY MOUNTAIN

CARLISLE CANYON

MISHE MOKWA TRAIL

▲ Skull Rock

Tri-Peaks
3,010'

(BACKBONE TRAIL)
SANDSTONE PEAK TRAIL

Sandstone Pk
3,111'

BACKBONE TR.

Boney Peak
2,825'

MISHE MOKWA
CONNECTOR TR

Inspiration Pt
2,800'

Exchange Pk
2,950'

Circle X
Ranger Station

54
P

Yerba Buena Road

52
53
P

53

CANYON VIEW TR

N
W · E
S

waterfall

West

GROTTO TR

CIRCLE X
RANCH

Fork

REFERENCE MAPS
P. 126

52

The Grotto

Arroyo Sequit

To Hwy 1

54. Sandstone Peak
Mishe Mokwa–Sandstone Peak Loop
CIRCLE X RANCH

55. Lower Arroyo Sequit Trail and Sequit Point

LEO CARRILLO STATE PARK

Hiking distance: 3 miles round trip
Hiking time: 1.5 hours
Elevation gain: 200 feet
Maps: U.S.G.S. Triunfo Pass
Tom Harrison Maps: Point Mugu State Park Trail Map
Leo Carrillo State Beach map

Summary of hike: Leo Carrillo State Park is a 2,000-acre haven with a 1.5-mile stretch of coastline, mountain canyons, and steep chaparral-covered hillsides. The area was once inhabited by the Chumash Indians. This hike is divided into two sections. At the north end of the campground, the Lower Arroyo Sequit Trail leads into a cool, stream-fed canyon shaded with willow, sycamore, oak, and bay trees. The path ends in the deep-walled canyon by large multicolored boulders and the trickling stream. At the south end of the park at the oceanfront, Sequit Point, a rocky bluff, juts out from the shoreline, dividing North Beach from South Beach. The weather-carved point has sea caves and coves, ocean-sculpted arches, tidepools, and pocket beaches.

Driving directions: OXNARD. From the Pacific Coast Highway/ Highway 1 and Las Posas Road in southeast Oxnard, drive 11.1 miles southbound on the PCH to the posted Leo Carrillo State Beach entrance and turn left. Park in the day-use parking lot. A parking fee is required.

Heading northbound on the Pacific Coast Highway, Leo Carrillo State Beach is on the right, 14 miles past Malibu Canyon Road and 8 miles past Kanan Dume Road.

Hiking directions: LOWER ARROYO SEQUIT TRAIL: Hike north through the campground on the road past mature sycamores and oaks. Pass the amphitheater on the right to a gated road. Continue past the gate, crossing over the seasonal Arroyo Sequit to the end of the paved road. Take the footpath a hundred yards, and rock hop over the creek by a small grotto. Follow the path upstream along the east side of the creek. Recross the creek to the trail's end in a steep-walled box canyon with pools and large boulders.

Retrace your steps to the amphitheater, and now bear left on the footpath. Cross to the east side of the creek and head through the forest canopy. Switchbacks and two sets of wooden steps lead to a flat above the canyon. Descend back to the campground road.

SEQUIT POINT: To reach Sequit Point, take the paved path under Highway 1 to the sandy beach. To the right (west), by the lifeguard station, are sandstone rock formations with caves, tunnels, a rock arch, tidepools, and a series of beach coves. ■

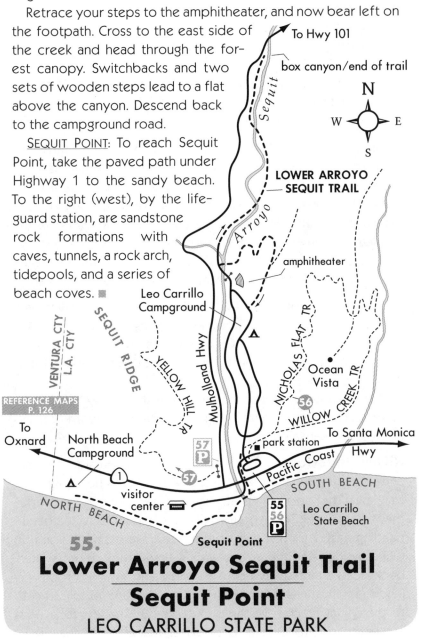

55.
Lower Arroyo Sequit Trail
Sequit Point
LEO CARRILLO STATE PARK

56. Nicholas Flat and Willow Creek Loop
LEO CARRILLO STATE PARK

Hiking distance: 2.5-mile loop
Hiking time: 1.3 hours
Elevation gain: 612 feet
Maps: U.S.G.S. Triunfo Pass
Tom Harrison Maps: Point Mugu State Park Trail Map
Santa Monica Mountains West Trail Map
Leo Carrillo State Beach map

Summary of hike: This loop hike in Leo Carrillo State Park leads to Ocean Vista, a 612-foot bald knoll with great views of the Malibu coastline and Point Dume. The Willow Creek Trail traverses the east-facing hillside up Willow Creek Canyon to Ocean Vista at the north end of the loop. En route to the overlook, the trail leads through native grasslands and coastal sage scrub. The hike returns along the Nicholas Flat Trail, one of the few trails connecting the Santa Monica Mountains to the Pacific Ocean.

Driving directions: OXNARD. From the Pacific Coast Highway/Highway 1 and Las Posas Road in southeast Oxnard, drive 11.1 miles southbound on the PCH to the posted Leo Carrillo State Beach entrance and turn left. Park in the day-use parking lot. A parking fee is required.

Heading northbound on the Pacific Coast Highway, Leo Carrillo State Beach is on the right, 14 miles past Malibu Canyon Road and 8 miles past Kanan Dume Road.

Hiking directions: The trailhead is 50 yards outside the park entrance station. Take the signed trail 100 yards northeast to a trail split. The loop begins at this junction. Take the right fork—the Willow Creek Trail—up the hillside and parallel to the ocean, heading east. At a half mile, curve north, traversing the hillside while overlooking the arroyo and Willow Creek. Three switchbacks lead aggressively up to a saddle and a signed four-way junction with the Nicholas Flat Trail, which leads 1.7 miles north to the upper reaches of the park (Hike 58). The left fork leads a quarter mile to Ocean Vista. After marveling at the views, return to the four-way junction and take the left (west) fork. Head downhill on the lower end of the Nicholas Flat Trail, returning to the trailhead along the grassy slopes above the park campground. ▤

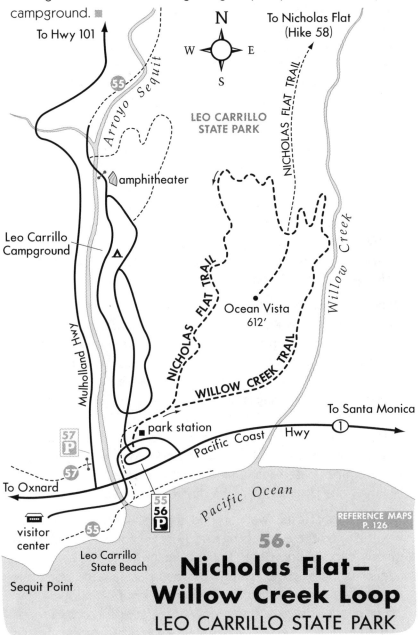

To Hwy 101

N
W · E
S

To Nicholas Flat
(Hike 58)

55

Arroyo Sequit

LEO CARRILLO
STATE PARK

NICHOLAS FLAT TRAIL

amphitheater

Leo Carrillo
Campground

Willow Creek

NICHOLAS FLAT TRAIL

Ocean Vista
612'

Mulholland Hwy

WILLOW CREEK TRAIL

To Santa Monica
1

park station

Pacific Coast Hwy

57
P

57

To Oxnard

Pacific Ocean

55
56
P

REFERENCE MAPS
P. 126

visitor
center

55

Leo Carrillo
State Beach

Sequit Point

56.
Nicholas Flat—
Willow Creek Loop
LEO CARRILLO STATE PARK

57. Yellow Hill Trail
LEO CARRILLO STATE PARK

Hiking distance: 5 miles round trip
Hiking time: 2.5 hours
Elevation gain: 1,300 feet
Maps: U.S.G.S. Triunfo Pass
       Tom Harrison Maps: Point Mugu State Park Trail Map
       Santa Monica Mountains West Trail Map
       Leo Carrillo State Beach map

Summary of hike: The Yellow Hill Trail is within Leo Carrillo State Park, a 3,000-acre park at the western tip of Los Angeles County. The trail steadily climbs 1,300 feet up a fire road on Sequit Ridge in the backcountry hills. The trailhead begins on the west side of Mulholland Highway in Los Angeles County and follows the mountain ridge, leaving the west side of the state park into Ventura County. En route are outstanding ocean views, including the four Channel Islands.

Driving directions: OXNARD. From the Pacific Coast Highway/ Highway 1 and Las Posas Road in southeast Oxnard, drive 10.8 miles southbound on the PCH to Mulholland Highway, just before the posted Leo Carrillo State Beach entrance. Turn left and go 100 yards to the gated fire road on the left. Park along the side of the road. Parking is also available in Leo Carrillo State Park off the PCH.

Heading northbound on the Pacific Coast Highway, Mulholland Highway is on the right, 14.3 miles past Malibu Canyon Road and 8.3 miles past Kanan Dume Road. Turn right on Mulholland Highway and proceed with the directions above.

Hiking directions: Walk around the trailhead gate, and follow the old dirt road, passing prickly pear cactus. Coastal views quickly expand, from Point Dume to Point Mugu and across the ocean to the Channel Islands. The trail parallels the coast for 0.3 miles, then curves inland. Climb steadily up the ridge. Cross over a minor side canyon to a view of the sculptured land forms in the interior of Leo Carrillo State Park and the Arroyo Sequit drainage. At 1.4 miles, the encroaching vegetation narrows the winding road to a single track trail. Cross the county line and walk around a gate, continuing 300 yards ahead to a Y-fork. The left fork descends to the PCH. Stay to the right, below a water tank on the right. At 2 miles the road/trail makes a left bend. On the bend is a footpath veering up the knoll to the right, our return route. Continue on the main trail, curving around the west flank of the knoll. Near the ridge, the uphill grade eases, reaching a trail sign. Continue to the ridge 150 yards ahead, with an outstanding view of the Boney Mountain ridgeline. Leave the road and return on the trail to the right, climbing up the north face of the knoll. Cross over the 1,366-foot summit, and descend along the ridge to the junction with the road at the water tank. Return along the same route. ∎

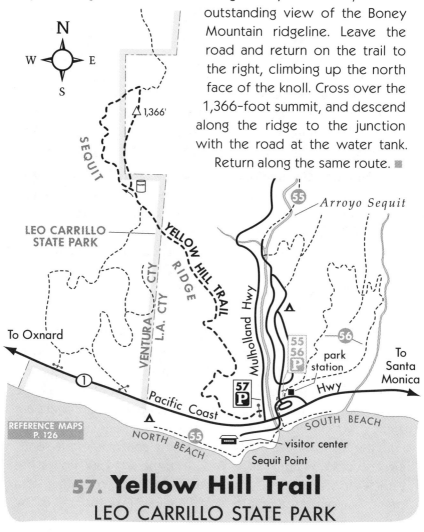

57. Yellow Hill Trail
LEO CARRILLO STATE PARK

58. Nicholas Flat
LEO CARRILLO STATE PARK

Hiking distance: 2.5-mile double loop
Hiking time: 1.3 hours
Elevation gain: 100 feet
Maps: U.S.G.S. Triunfo Pass
   Tom Harrison Maps: Point Mugu State Park Trail Map
   Santa Monica Mountains West Trail Map
   Leo Carrillo State Beach map

Summary of hike: Nicholas Flat, in the upper reaches of Leo Carrillo State Park, is a grassy highland meadow with large oak trees, an old cattle pond, and sandstone outcroppings that lie 1,700 feet above the sea. This hike skirts around Nicholas Flat, with spectacular views of the ocean, San Nicholas Canyon, and the surrounding mountains. The Nicholas Flat Trail may be hiked 3.5 miles downhill to the Pacific Ocean, connecting to Hike 56.

Driving directions: OXNARD. From the Pacific Coast Highway/ Highway 1 and Las Posas Road in southeast Oxnard, drive 13.3 miles southbound on the PCH to Decker Road and turn left. Continue 2.4 miles north to Decker School Road and turn left. Drive 1.5 miles to the road's end and park alongside the road.

Heading northbound on the Pacific Coast Highway, Decker Road is on the right, 11.8 miles past Malibu Canyon Road and 5.8 miles past Kanan Dume Road.

Hiking directions: Hike south past the gate and kiosk. Stay on the wide, oak-lined trail to a junction at 0.3 miles. Take the right fork, beginning the first loop. At 0.6 miles is another junction. Again take the right fork—the Meadows Trail. Continue past the Malibu Springs Trail on the right to Vista Point, where there are great views into the canyons. The trail curves south to a junction with the Nicholas Flat Trail, leading to the coastline at the southern end of Leo Carrillo State Park. Take the left fork around the perimeter of the flat. A trail on the right leads to another vista point. Complete the first loop at 1.8 miles. Take the trail to the right at two successive junctions to a pond. Follow along the pond through the meadow, completing the second loop. Return to the trailhead. ■

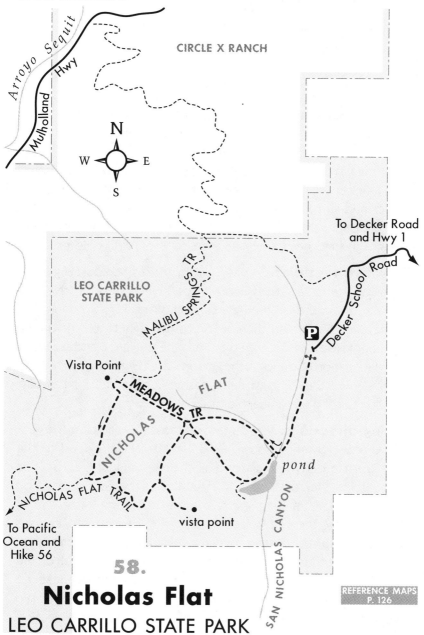

CIRCLE X RANCH

Arroyo Sequit

Mulholland Hwy

N
W   E
S

LEO CARRILLO
STATE PARK

MALIBU SPRINGS TR

To Decker Road
and Hwy 1

Decker School Road

P

Vista Point

MEADOWS TR

FLAT

NICHOLAS

pond

NICHOLAS FLAT TRAIL

vista point

SAN NICHOLAS CANYON

To Pacific
Ocean and
Hike 56

58.
Nicholas Flat
LEO CARRILLO STATE PARK

REFERENCE MAPS
P. 126

59. Arroyo Sequit Park

34138 Mulholland Highway · Malibu

Hiking distance: 2-mile loop
Hiking time: 1 hour
Elevation gain: 250 feet
Maps: U.S.G.S. Triunfo Pass
Santa Monica Mountains West Trail Map

Summary of hike: Arroyo Sequit Park was a ranch purchased by the Santa Monica Mountains Conservancy in 1985. Within the 155-acre park are open grassland meadows, picnic areas, and a small canyon cut by the East Fork Arroyo Sequit with oak groves and a waterfall. From the meadows are panoramic views of the ocean and surrounding mountains. This easy loop hike visits the diverse park habitats, crossing the meadows and dropping into the gorge that runs parallel to the East Fork Arroyo Sequit.

Driving directions: OXNARD. From the Pacific Coast Highway/ Highway 1 and Las Posas Road in southeast Oxnard, drive 10.8 miles southbound on the PCH to Mulholland Highway. Turn left and drive 5.5 miles up the canyon to the signed turnoff on the right at mailbox 34138. Turn right into the entrance and park.

Heading northbound on the Pacific Coast Highway, Mulholland Highway is 8.5 miles past Kanan Dume Road and 0.3 miles past the Leo Carrillo State Beach entrance.

Hiking directions: Head south on the park road past the gate, kiosk, and old ranch house. At 0.2 miles take the road to the left—past a barn, the astronomical observing site, and picnic area—to the footpath on the right. Leave the service road on the nature trail, heading south. The trail skirts the east edge of the meadow, then descends into a small canyon and crosses several seasonal tributaries of the Arroyo Sequit. Head west along the southern wall of the canyon, passing a waterfall on the left. Cross a wooden footbridge over the stream, and descend to the canyon floor. Continue west, cross the East Fork Arroyo Sequit, and begin the ascent out of the canyon to a junction.

Continue straight ahead up the hill. A series of switchbacks lead up the short but steep hill. Once at the top, cross the meadow to the road. Take the service road back to the parking area. ■

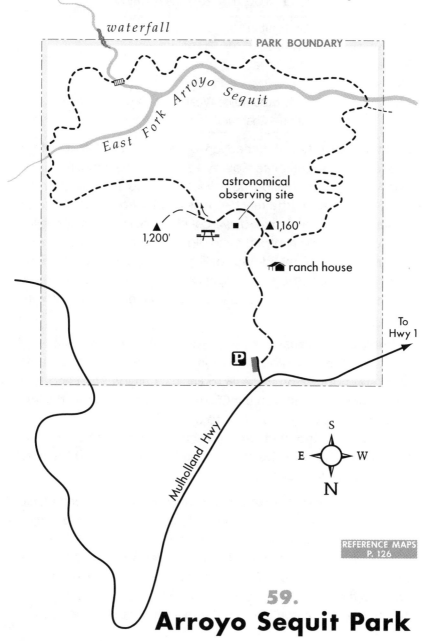

59.
Arroyo Sequit Park

60. Charmlee County Park

2577 S. Encinal Canyon Road · Malibu
Open 8:00 a.m. to sunset daily

Hiking distance: 3-mile loop
Hiking time: 1.5 hours
Elevation gain: 600 feet
Maps: U.S.G.S. Triunfo Pass
Santa Monica Mountains West Trail Map
City of Malibu—Charmlee Natural Area map

Summary of hike: Perched on oceanfront cliffs 1,300 feet above the sea, Charmlee County Park has a magnificent bird's-eye view of the Malibu coastline. The 460-acre wilderness park was once a cattle ranch. It was purchased by Los Angeles County in 1968 and opened as a county park in 1981. Eight miles of interconnecting footpaths and old ranch roads weave through expansive grassy meadows, oak and eucalyptus woodlands, mountain slopes, rocky ridges, and 1,250-foot bluffs overlooking the sea. The park has picnic areas and a nature center with plant exhibits.

Driving directions: OXNARD. From the Pacific Coast Highway/Highway 1 and Las Posas Road in southeast Oxnard, drive 14 miles southbound on the PCH to Encinal Canyon Road and turn left. Continue 3.7 miles to the Charmlee Park entrance on the left. Follow the park road 0.2 miles to the parking lot.

Heading northbound on the Pacific Coast Highway, Encinal Canyon Road is 11.2 miles past Malibu Canyon Road and 5.2 miles past Kanan Dume Road.

Hiking directions: Hike past the information board and picnic area on the wide trail. Pass a second picnic area on the left in an oak grove, and continue uphill to a three-way trail split. The middle trail is a short detour leading to an overlook set among rock formations and an old house foundation. Take the main trail to the left into the large grassy meadow. Two trails cross the meadow and rejoin at the south end—the main trail heads through the meadow while the right fork skirts the meadow's western edge. At the far end is an ocean overlook and a trail fork.

Bear left past an old ranch reservoir, and pass two junctions to a 1,200-foot overlook on the right. Continue downhill, curving north through an oak grove to the unsigned Botany Trail, a narrow footpath on the right. The Botany Trail winds back to the picnic area and the trailhead. ■

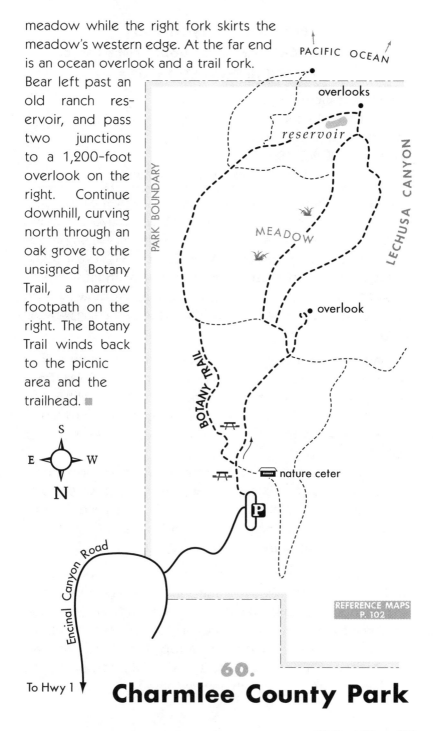

Charmlee County Park

60.

To Hwy 1

61. Newton Canyon Falls
ZUMA/TRANCAS CANYONS: Upper Zuma Canyon
NATIONAL RECREATION AREA

Hiking distance: 1.5 miles round trip
Hiking time: 1 hour
Elevation gain: 200 feet
Maps: U.S.G.S. Point Dume
      Santa Monica Mountains West Trail Map

Summary of hike: The Upper Zuma Canyon Trail is located in Newton Canyon in the Zuma/Trancas Canyons National Recreation Area. The trail leads a short distance along a portion of the Backbone Trail to Newton Canyon Falls, a year-round, 30-foot waterfall in a lush, forested grotto with mossy rocks, sandstone caves, and a tangle of vines. There are large, shaded boulders to sit on while enjoying the falls by cascading Newton Creek.

Driving directions: AGOURA HILLS. From the Ventura Freeway/Highway 101 in Agoura Hills, exit on Kanan Road. Drive 7.9 miles south to the trailhead parking lot on the right (west). The parking lot is located just before entering the third tunnel (T-1). (Kanan Road becomes Kanan Dume Road after it crosses Mulholland Highway.)

    SANTA MONICA. From Santa Monica, drive 18 miles northbound on the Pacific Coast Highway/Highway 1 to Kanan Dume Road, 5.8 miles past Malibu Canyon Road. Turn right and drive 4.4 miles north to the trailhead parking lot on the left (west). The parking lot is located just after the first tunnel (T-1).

Hiking directions: Hike west, away from Kanan Dume Road, on the signed Backbone Trail. The trail immediately begins its descent from the open chaparral into the shady canyon. After crossing the trickling Newton Creek, a side trail on the left leads 20 yards to sandstone rocks at the top of the falls. The main trail continues 100 yards downhill to a second cutoff trail on the left. Take this steep side path downhill through a forest of oaks, sycamores, and bay laurels to the creek, bearing to the left on the descent. Once at the creek, hike upstream along the path. Fifty yards up the narrow, limestone canyon is a lush grotto at the base of Newton Canyon Falls. The main Backbone Trail continues 1.9 miles northwest to the Zuma Ridge Trail, entering the rugged Zuma Canyon with its steep volcanic cliffs. Return by retracing your steps. ∎

To Zuma Ridge
Trail and Encinal
Canyon Road

To Hwy 101

UPPER ZUMA CYN TR (BACKBONE TRAIL)

Kanan Dume Road

ZUMA CANYON

Newton
Canyon
Falls

NEWTON CANYON

Newton Creek

Zuma Creek

PRIVATE DRIVE

61
62
P

N
W — E
S

62

BACKBONE TR

T-1 Tunnel

REFERENCE MAPS
P. 102

To
Hwy 1

61.
Newton Canyon Falls
ZUMA/TRANCAS CANYONS:
Upper Zuma Canyon

62. Newton Canyon
ZUMA/TRANCAS CANYONS • CASTRO CREST N.P.S.

Hiking distance: 4.6 miles round trip
Hiking time: 2.5 hours
Elevation gain: 300 feet
Maps: U.S.G.S. Point Dume
      Santa Monica Mountains West Trail Map

Summary of hike: This hike parallels Newton Canyon along a 2.3-mile section of the Backbone Trail between Kanan Dume Road and Latigo Canyon Road. The trail runs through the Castro Crest National Park Service corridor, which connects Zuma/ Trancas Canyons to Malibu Creek State Park. The forested trail winds along the south ridge of the dense oak-filled canyon with ocean views and seasonal stream crossings.

Driving directions: AGOURA HILLS. From the Ventura Free- way/Highway 101 in Agoura Hills, exit on Kanan Road. Drive 7.9 miles south to the trailhead parking lot on the right (west). The parking lot is located just before entering the third tunnel (T-1). (Kanan Road becomes Kanan Dume Road after it crosses Mulholland Highway.)

    SANTA MONICA. From Santa Monica, drive 18 miles north- bound on the Pacific Coast Highway/Highway 1 to Kanan Dume Road, 5.8 miles past Malibu Canyon Road. Turn right and drive 4.4 miles north to the trailhead parking lot on the left (west). The parking lot is located just after the first tunnel (T-1).

Hiking directions: The signed trail begins by Kanan Dume Road and heads south towards the ocean. The trail, an old fire road, climbs up to the tunnel and crosses over Kanan Dume Road. After crossing, the road narrows to a footpath and enters a for- ested canopy, slowly descending into Newton Canyon. The trail crosses a paved driveway, then enters the park and climbs to various overlooks. Continue along the winding mountainside above Newton Canyon. Near the end of the trail, maze-like switchbacks lead to Latigo Canyon Road, the turn-around spot.

    To hike farther, cross the road to the trailhead parking area, and continue on the Castro Crest Trail, a section of the Backbone Trail. The trail leads another 1.4 miles to Newton Motorway, 4.2 miles to Corral Canyon Road, and connects to Malibu Creek State Park. Return to the trailhead on the same trail. ▪

CASTRO
CREST TRAIL

Latigo Canyon Rd

CASTRO CREST
NAT'L. PARK SERVICE

BACKBONE TRAIL

E
N ✧ S
W

NEWTON CANYON

Newton Creek

PRIVATE DRIVE

To
Hwy 1

Newton Canyon
Falls

T-1 Tunnel

To Hwy 101

61

62
P

61

Kanan Dume Road

BACKBONE TR

ZUMA/TRANCAS
CANYONS

Zuma Creek

REFERENCE MAPS
P. 102

62. Newton Canyon
ZUMA/TRANCAS CANYONS

63. Rocky Oaks Park

Hiking distance: 2-mile loop
Hiking time: 1 hour
Elevation gain: 200 feet
Maps: U.S.G.S. Point Dume
Santa Monica Mountains West Trail Map
N.P.S. Rocky Oaks Site

Summary of hike: Rocky Oaks Park was once a working cattle ranch resting at the head of Zuma Canyon. The pastoral 200-acre ranch was purchased by the National Park Service in 1981. The park includes oak savannahs, rolling grasslands, chaparral-covered hills, volcanic rock formations, scenic overlooks, picnic areas, and a pond in the grassy meadow. This easy loop hike meanders through the park, visiting each of these diverse ecological communities.

Driving directions: AGOURA HILLS. From the Ventura Freeway/Highway 101 in Agoura Hills, exit on Kanan Road. Drive 6.1 miles south to Mulholland Highway. Turn right and a quick right again into the Rocky Oaks Park entrance and parking lot.

SANTA MONICA. From Santa Monica, drive 18 miles northbound on the Pacific Coast Highway/Highway 1 to Kanan Dume Road, 5.8 miles past Malibu Canyon Road. Turn right and drive 6.2 miles north to Mulholland Highway. Turn left, then quickly turn right into the park entrance.

Hiking directions: Hike north past the rail fence to the Rocky Oaks Loop Trail, which heads in both directions. Take the left fork a short distance to a 4-way junction. Continue straight ahead on the middle path towards the Overlook Trail. Ascend the hillside overlooking the pond, and take the horseshoe bend to the left. Beyond the bend is the Overlook Trail. This is a short detour on the left to a scenic overlook with panoramic views. Back on the main trail, continue northeast around the ridge, slowly descending to the valley floor near Kanan Road. Bear sharply to the right, heading south to the Pond Trail junction. Both the left and right forks loop around the pond and rejoin at the south end. At the junction, go south and back to the Rocky Oaks Loop, then retrace your steps back to the trailhead. ▪

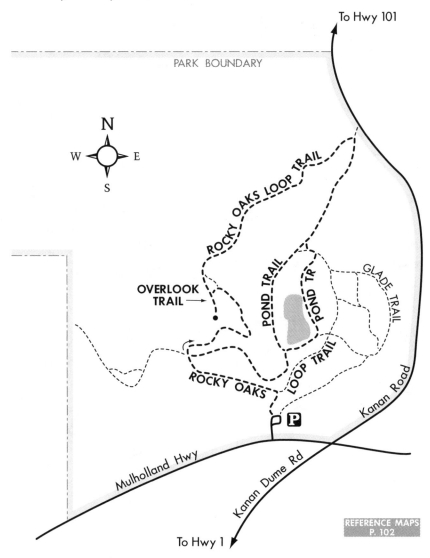

63.
Rocky Oaks Park

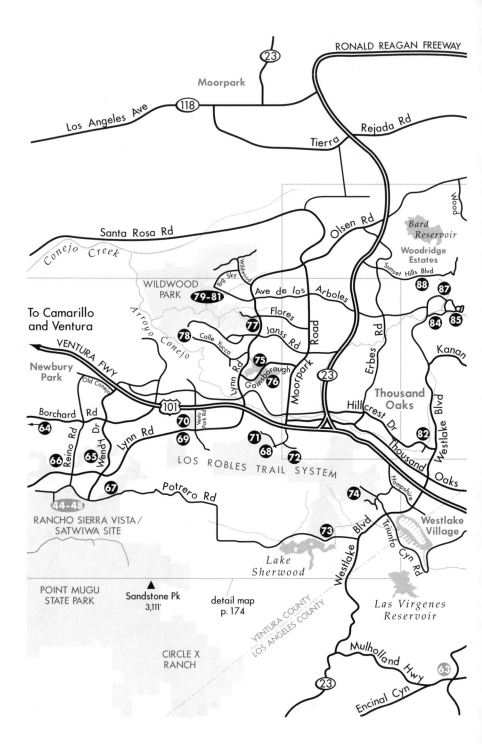

RONALD REAGAN FREEWAY

23

Moorpark

118

Los Angeles Ave

Rejada Rd

Tierra

Olsen Rd

Wood

Bard Reservoir

Santa Rosa Rd

Conejo Creek

Woodridge Estates

Sunset Hills Blvd

Wildwood

Big Sky

WILDWOOD PARK

79-81

Ave de los Arboles

88

87

To Camarillo and Ventura

Arroyo Conejo

78

Calle Yucca

Flores

77

Janss Rd

Road

Erbes Rd

84

85

Kanan

VENTURA FWY

75

Gainsborough

76

Moorpark

23

Thousand Oaks

Newbury Park

Old Conejo

Lynn Rd

Hillcrest Dr

Westlake Blvd

Borchard Rd

101

Ventura Park Rd

82

64

Wendy Dr

70

71

68

72

Thousand Oaks

66

65

Reino Rd

Lynn Rd

69

LOS ROBLES TRAIL SYSTEM

Hampshire

67

Potrero Rd

74

44-48

73

Westlake Blvd

Triunfo Cyn Rd

Westlake Village

RANCHO SIERRA VISTA / SATWIWA SITE

Lake Sherwood

Las Virgenes Reservoir

POINT MUGU STATE PARK

▲ Sandstone Pk 3,111'

detail map p. 174

VENTURA COUNTY
LOS ANGELES COUNTY

CIRCLE X RANCH

Mulholland Hwy

63

23

Encinal Cyn

Thousand Oaks area
NEWBURY PARK to SIMI HILLS

HIKES 64–103

118

114

Madera Rd

1st St

Sinaloa

Simi Valley

detail map p. 220

Highland

Valley Gate

Bluegate

Ranch

Canyon View

Cyn Rd

Long

91

92

93

Challenger Park

90

89

SIMI HILLS

detail map p. 258

Valley Circle Blvd

86

CHEESEBORO / PALO COMADO CANYONS SITE

Simi Pk ▲
2,403'

China Flat

EL ESCORPIAN PARK

Bell Cyn Rd

Rd

Falling Star

83

96

Oak Canyon Comm. Park

PALO COMADO CYN

CHEESEBORO CYN

LAS VIRGENES CYN

UPPER LAS VIRGENES CANYON OPEN SPACE PRESERVE

103 Vanowen

Lindero Cyn Rd

Doubletree Rd

94

95

97

Sunnycrest

Smoketree

Medea Creek Park

Kanan Rd

Medea

Laskey Mesa

102 Victory Blvd

West Hills

Oak Park

101

Long Valley Rd

Blvd

Agoura Hills

98–100

Crummer Cyn

To Los Angeles

VENTURA FREEWAY

Canwood

Rd

Palo Comado Canyon Road

Mureau Rd

Woodland Hills

Kanan Rd

Cornell Rd

Chesebro

101

Calabasas

Triunfo

Creek

Las Virgenes Rd

PARAMOUNT RANCH

Mulholland Hwy

Malibu

Creek

MALIBU CREEK STATE PARK

3 MILES

5 KILOMETERS

N W E S

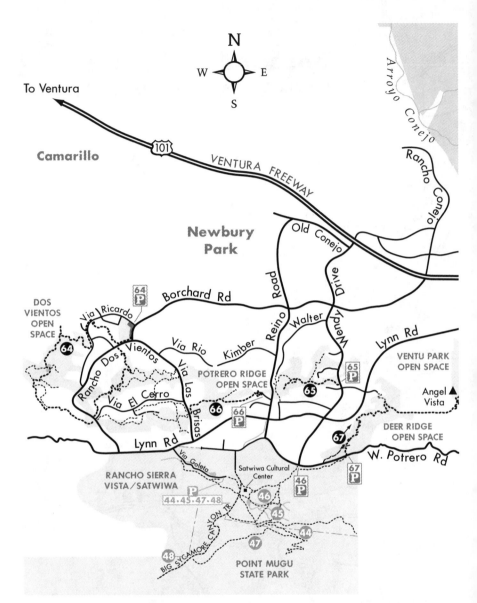

HIKES 64–74
Newbury Park–Thousand Oaks
Open Space Trail System
POTRERO RIDGE • LOS ROBLES TRAIL

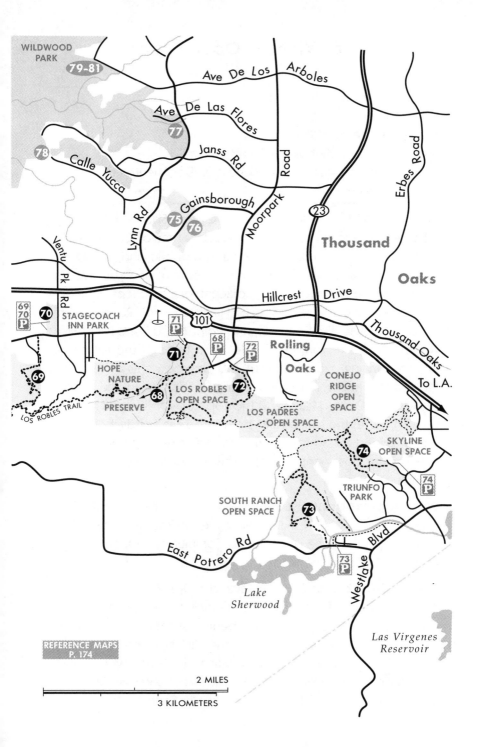

64. Dos Vientos Open Space

4801 Borchard Road · Newbury Park

Hiking distance: 5-mile loop
Hiking time: 2.5 hours
Elevation gain: 800 feet
Maps: U.S.G.S. Newbury Park and Camarillo
  Conejo Open Space Foundation Dos Vientos Open
    Space map

Summary of hike: Dos Vientos Open Space is a large, 1,216-acre preserve on the southwest corner of Conejo Valley by the Dos Vientos residential area. The public land, dominated by chaparral and coastal sage scrub, contains an extensive trail system which connects with adjacent open spaces, including the Potrero Ridge Open Space (Hikes 65—66), Rancho Sierra Vista/Satwiwa (Hikes 44—45), and Point Mugu State Park (Hikes 46—51). This hike forms a 5-mile loop through the rolling terrain to stunning overlooks with 360-degree vistas of the Santa Monica Mountains, Boney Ridge, the Pacific Ocean, the Channel Islands, the Oxnard Plain, and the Topatopa Mountains north of Ojai. En route, the trail passes between Twin Ponds, built in the 1920s as part of an irrigation system for ranching and agriculture for the Dos Vientos Ranch. The trail begins at Dos Vientos Community Park.

Driving directions: NEWBURY PARK. From the Ventura Freeway/Highway 101 in Newbury Park, exit on Borchard Road. Drive 3.5 miles south to the Dos Vientos Community Park on the right. Turn right and park in the lot.

Hiking directions: From the far end of Dos Vientos Community Park, follow the fence-lined path along the edge of the park. Just before reaching Via Rincon, begin the loop to the right by an opening in the fence. Follow the dirt path up a knoll that overlooks the park and the surrounding hills. Cross over the knoll and descend to Via Ricardo. Cross the street and bear left along the sidewalk. Walk 0.1 mile, crossing Via Sandra, to a distinct

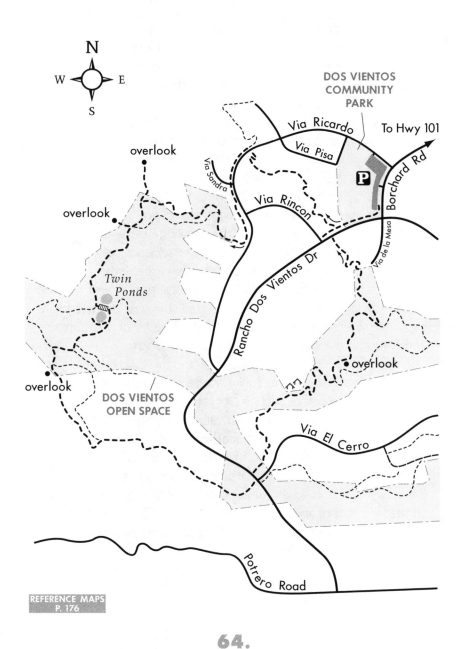

64.
Dos Vientos
Open Space

dirt footpath on the right. Veer right and climb the chaparral-covered hillside above and parallel to Via Ricardo. Curve right, away from the road and into the rolling hills to a Y-fork. Both routes meet up ahead, but to include a great overlook, take the right fork. Weave through the hills to a junction. Detour 200 yards to the right (north), and loop around a hill to the power lines at a spectacular overlook of Camarillo, the Oxnard Plain, the Pacific Ocean, the Channel Islands, and the Topatopa Mountains.

Return to the junction and head downhill, where the two paths rejoin. On the right, a side path leads a short distance to another overlook. Continue straight and curve around the first of the Twin Ponds on the left. Cross a bridge between the two ponds, and loop clockwise around the second pond. The secluded ponds, a designated conservation area, offer a respite for ducks and migrating waterfowl. Ascend the hill and top the slope, staying to the right past two trail splits. At the third fork, bear left to another great view of the Santa Monica Mountains, Boney Ridge, the ocean, and the Channel Islands.

Traverse the ocean-facing slope, then curve left, leaving the coastal views. Follow the rolling ridge to Rancho Dos Vientos Drive. Cross the street and go 20 yards to the left to the footpath on the right. Bear right and walk through the chaparral and coastal sage scrub slope with scattered eucalyptus. Skirt past a couple of homes on the left, then ascend the final hill. Near the top, stay left at a signed trail split to another great overlook. Gradually descend to a U-shaped left bend. Take the footpath on the left, and drop down the hill to Rancho Dos Vientos Drive. Cross the road and reenter Dos Vientos Community Park on Via Rincon, completing the loop. ▪

65. Potrero Ridge Trail
—Wendy Drive to Reino Road—

Hiking distance: 1.4 miles round trip
Hiking time: 40 minutes
Elevation gain: 200 feet
Maps: U.S.G.S. Newbury Park

map
page 183

Summary of hike: Potrero Ridge Open Space encompasses 207 acres in Newbury Park. The low-lying ridge runs east and west between residential neighborhoods. The undeveloped area offers hiking, biking, and equestrian use through the hills among coastal sage scrub, open grassland, and oak woodlands. This hike begins from Wendy Drive and leads to scenic overlooks of Rancho Sierra Vista/Satwiwa, Point Mugu State Park, and Boney Mountain. Sweeping vistas span across Thousand Oaks to the Santa Susana Mountains by Simi Valley and the Topatopa Mountains by Ojai.

Driving directions: NEWBURY PARK. From the Ventura Freeway/Highway 101 in Newbury Park, exit on Wendy Drive. Drive 1.7 miles south to trailhead parking lot on the right (west).

Hiking directions: Pass the trailhead sign and head up the sloping dirt road. Pass a vehicle gate to far-reaching vistas across Newbury Park, the Los Padres National Forest, and the Santa Susana Mountains. Traverse the north slope, skirting the ridge to views of the Santa Monica Mountains above Rancho Sierra Vista/Satwiwa. Just before reaching the prominent water tank on the right, a side path on the left leads to an overlook by a bench with south-facing views across Point Mugu State Park and Boney Mountain. Continue 0.1 mile to a knoll at the end of the spur trail, with additional sweeping, 360-degree panoramas.

Return to the main trail and continue west, passing the water tank. Curve left by an unsigned fork. The right fork descends the hillside and leads to Reino Road and a trail access at the end of Walter Avenue. Straight ahead, the main path gently descends along the west flank of the hill to the gated end of the trail. Return by retracing your steps. ■

Potrero Ridge Trail

HIKE 65: Wendy Drive to Reino Road
HIKE 66: Reino Road to Via Las Brisas

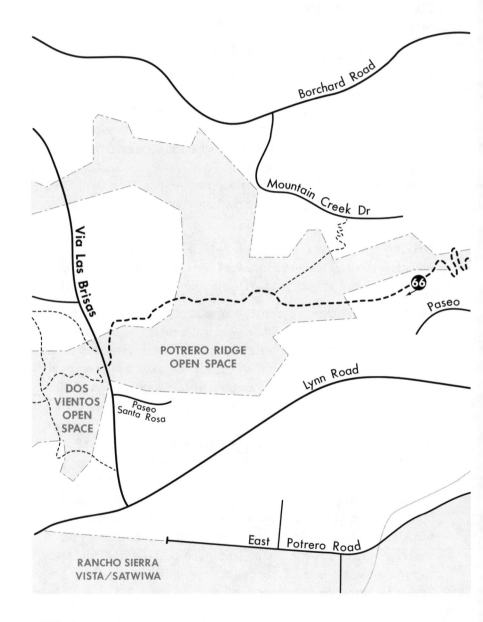

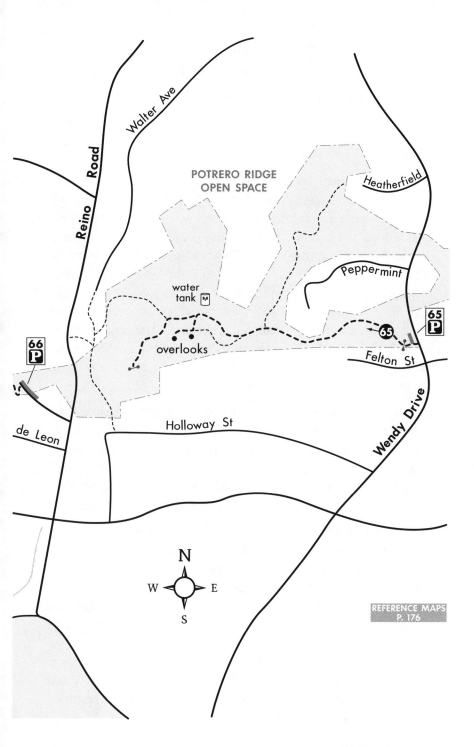

POTRERO RIDGE
OPEN SPACE

Walter Ave

Reino Road

Heatherfield

Peppermint

water
tank

overlooks

Felton St

66 P

65 P

65

de Leon

Holloway St

Wendy Drive

N
W ⊕ E
S

REFERENCE MAPS
P. 176

66. Potrero Ridge Trail
—Reino Road to Via Las Brisas—

Hiking distance: 2.8 miles round trip

Hiking time: 1.5 hours

Elevation gain: 300 feet

Maps: U.S.G.S. Newbury Park

map
page 182

Summary of hike: Potrero Ridge Open Space is a 207-acre dedicated public open space in Newbury Park. The hiking, biking, and equestrian trail climbs to the low ridge dominated by coastal sage scrub and chaparral. The route offers spectacular 360-degree views of the surrounding terrain, including the Pacific Ocean, the Channel Islands, Point Mugu State Park, and Thousand Oaks. This hike begins from the Reino Road trailhead and heads west. To the west, the path connects with Dos Vientos Open Space at Via Las Brisas (Hike 64). This larger preserve encompasses more than 1,200 acres in the southwest corner of the Conejo Valley. To the east, the trail continues through another section of the Potrero Ridge Open Space (Hike 65).

Driving directions: NEWBURY PARK. From the Ventura Freeway/Highway 101 in Newbury Park, exit on Wendy Drive. Drive 2.2 miles south to Lynn Road. Turn right and continue 0.6 miles to Reino Road. Turn right and go 0.2 miles to the trailhead turnoff on the left, located just after Paseo De Leon. Turn left and drive 0.1 mile to the trailhead parking lot at the end of the road.

Hiking directions: Walk past the trailhead kiosk, and ascend the chaparral-cloaked hillside dotted with a few oaks. Switchback up the hill to the ridge. Traverse the ridge while overlooking Point Mugu State Park, Boney Mountain, and the cities of Newbury Park and Thousand Oaks. Steadily follow the ridge on an upward slope. At the far west end, veer right, staying atop the ridge to the highest point on the trail at 1,100 feet. The vistas extend from Thousand Oaks to the Santa Susana Mountains and from Camarillo to the Topatopa Mountains by Ojai. Slowly descend to the end of the trail at Via Las Brisas, 100 yards north of Paseo Santa Rosa. Return by retracing your steps. ▪

67. Los Robles Trail

WESTERN SEGMENT:

Potrero Gate to Angel Vista

Hiking distance: 5 miles round trip
Hiking time: 2.5 hours
Elevation gain: 500 feet
Maps: U.S.G.S. Newbury Park
     Santa Monica Mountains West Trail Map
     Los Robles Trail to Lake Sherwood map

map page 188

Summary of hike: The Los Robles Trail System is a well-planned network of trails weaving through the growing residential communities of Westlake Village, Thousand Oaks, and Newbury Park. The 25 miles of multi-use trails link the designated open spaces of the Conejo Valley with Point Mugu State Park and the ocean-front Santa Monica Mountains. This is an important wildlife corridor that connects the Santa Monica range with the Simi Hills.

The hike from Potrero Gate follows an east-west ridge beginning at the 188-acre Deer Ridge Open Space in Newbury Park. The open space is dominated by ridges and canyons dense with chaparral and pockets of oak woodlands. The Los Robles Trail traverses the length of Deer Ridge Open Space to Angel Vista, a 1,600-foot overlook in the Ventu Park Open Space. From the overlook are bird's-eye views of the Conejo Valley, Hidden Valley, and the surrounding mountains to the sea. This hike may be combined with Hike 68 for a 6-mile, one-way shuttle hike.

Driving directions: NEWBURY PARK. From the Ventura Freeway/Highway 101 in Newbury Park, exit on Wendy Drive. Drive 2.7 miles south to Potrero Road. Turn left (east) and go 0.5 miles to the posted trailhead parking area on the left.

Hiking directions: Walk up the hill past the trailhead kiosk to a paved, private road. Cross the road and curve right 100 yards to a Y-fork. Veer left and drop down the hill, curving to the right. Follow the undulating path parallel to Lynn Road on the open rolling hills. The trail slowly descends to the open space boundary behind homes fronting Lynn Road. Curve away from civilization, returning to the tall brush and rolling hills. Continue to a posted junction on a saddle at 1.2 miles. The left fork descends to Felton Street off of Lynn Road. Bear right and climb just shy of the ridge. Follow the rail fence through a private property easement, passing horse stables and corrals on the left. Cross the saddle and drop into the adjacent draw to the east. Four switchbacks zigzag up the hillside to a Y-junction at 2.5 miles. The right fork—the Los Robles Trail—descends 3.5 miles to Moorpark Road (for a 6-mile, one-way shuttle with Hike 68).

For this hike, take the Rosewood Trail to the left, quickly reaching another fork. To the right, the Rosewood Trail (Hike 69) continues 1.8 miles downhill to Lynn Road near the Stagecoach Inn Museum. Instead, bear left 0.1 mile to Angel Vista, an overlook and picnic bench at the summit. Return by retracing your route. ■

68. Los Robles Trail

CENTRAL SEGMENT:

Moorpark Gate to Angel Vista

Hiking distance: 7.2 miles round trip
Hiking time: 3.5 hours
Elevation gain: 700 feet
Maps: U.S.G.S. Newbury Park
       Santa Monica Mountains West Trail Map
       Los Robles Trail to Lake Sherwood map

map
page 189

Summary of hike: The Los Robles Trail System, encompassing nearly 2,000 acres, flanks the southern end of Conejo Valley. The trail system traverses a network of open space areas, including Los Robles, Conejo Ridge, Deer Ridge, Hope Nature Preserve, Los Padres, Los Vientos, Old Conejo, Rancho Potrero, and Ventu Park. Neighborhood connector trails link the trail system with the communities of Westlake Village, Thousand Oaks, and Newbury Park. The multi-use trails are thoughtfully blended with the encroaching residential areas, linking several inland valleys and undeveloped tracts of land with the Santa Monica Mountains at Point Mugu State Park.

This hike begins in the Los Robles Open Space and heads west on the central segment of the trail. The trail traverses the chaparral-covered slopes and the flat, grassy potreros from Moorpark Gate, entering the 359-acre Hope Nature Preserve, a gift from comedian Bob Hope. The hike ends at Angel Vista, a 1,600-foot overlook with 360-degree vistas in the Ventu Park Open Space. Throughout the hike are far-reaching vistas that span across the valleys and mountains to the Channel Islands. This hike may be combined with Hike 67 for a 6-mile shuttle.

Driving directions: THOUSAND OAKS. From the Ventura Freeway/Highway 101 in Thousand Oaks, exit on Moorpark Road. Drive 0.5 miles south to Greenmeadow Avenue. Cross through the intersection and park on the right in the posted trailhead parking area.

Hiking directions: Walk past the trailhead gate to a trail fork at 100 yards. Stay to the right and pass the Oak Creek Canyon Trail on the right (Hike 71). At 0.4 miles is a trail split, where the Los Robles Trail heads south, then east. Again, stay to the right on the Los Robles Trail heading west. Shortly after, pass a junction with the Spring Canyon Trail on the right. Cross the rolling terrain through chaparral to the base of the hills. Short, steep switchbacks climb from the lower reaches of the hillside to the ridge. At 2 miles, cross a saddle and follow the contours of the hillside, dipping into the canyon while overlooking the landscape of Thousand Oaks and Newbury Park. Zigzag down two switchbacks on the brush-shaded path to an unpaved, private extension of Ventu Park Road at just under 3 miles.

Carefully cross the road and climb again, skirting the edge of a ranch. Continue through the tall brush to a posted junction with the Rosewood Trail at 3.5 miles. The left fork descends 2.5 miles to Potrero Road, across from the Rancho Sierra Vista/Satwiwa site (Hike 67). Take the Rosewood Trail to the right, quickly reaching another fork. To the right, the Rosewood Trail continues 1.8 miles downhill to Lynn Road (Hike 69). Instead, bear left 0.1 mile to Angel Vista, an overlook and picnic bench at the summit. After enjoying the vistas, return by retracing your steps. ▪

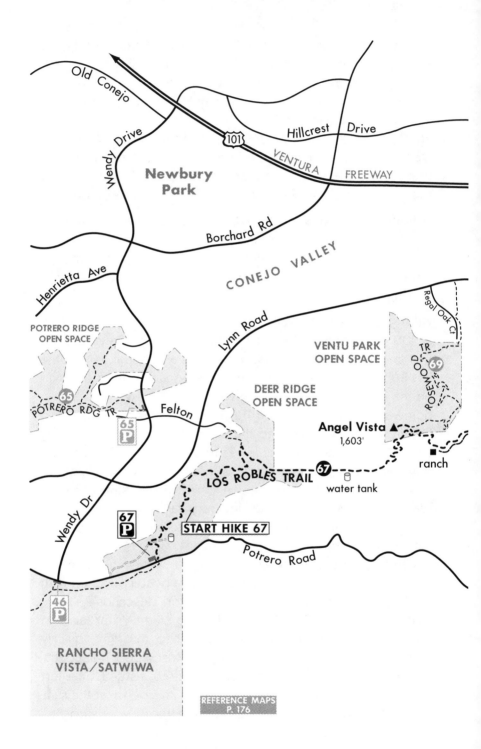

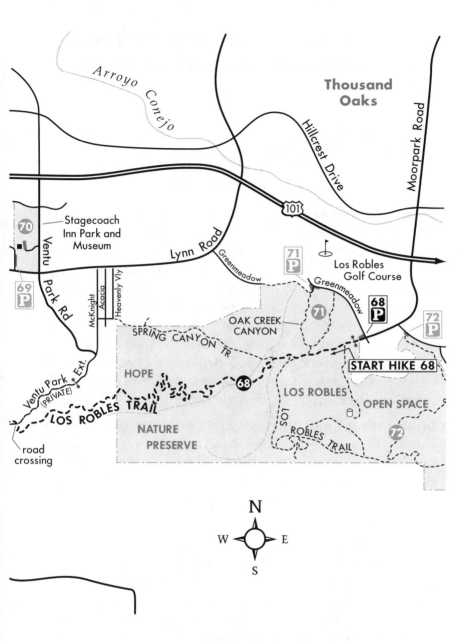

Los Robles Trail

HIKE 67: Potrero Gate to Angel Vista
HIKE 68: Moorpark Gate to Angel Vista

69. Rosewood Trail to Angel Vista Point

VENTU PARK OPEN SPACE • LOS ROBLES TRAIL SYSTEM

Hiking distance: 3.5 miles round trip
Hiking time: 1.5 hours
Elevation gain: 700 feet
Maps: U.S.G.S. Newbury Park
  Santa Monica Mountains West Trail Map
  Los Robles Trail to Lake Sherman map

Summary of hike: The Ventu Park Open Space encompasses 141 acres and connects the community of Ventu Park with the Los Robles Trail System along the ridge to its south. The open space covers a sloping, chaparral-covered hillside dotted with coastal live oaks. The Rosewood Trail begins on the Conejo Valley floor and climbs the north-facing slope through an oak woodland, then up the open, rolling chaparral to Angel Vista on the 1,600-foot ridge. The vista point is located on a flat knoll with a picnic table. From the overlook are 360-degree views across Conejo Valley, Hidden Valley, the Santa Susana Mountains, Point Mugu State Park, the Oxnard Plain, and the Pacific Ocean.

Driving directions: NEWBURY PARK. From the Ventura Freeway/Highway 101 in Newbury Park, exit on Ventu Park Road. Drive 0.6 miles south to Lynn Road, just past the Stagecoach Inn Museum. Turn right and drive one block to Susan Drive on the right. Turn right and park in the paved parking spaces on the right at the Stagecoach Inn Park.

Hiking directions: Cautiously cross Lynn Road, and walk 160 yards west (right) to the trailhead on the left. Bear left on the forested footpath, and follow the north edge of a stream, passing a few homes. Cross the stream amid mature oak and bay trees towards the mountains. Leave the development behind, and begin climbing on the serpentine path through chaparral and oaks. Views quickly open up of Newbury Park, Thousand Oaks, and the surrounding mountains, including Montclef Ridge in Wildwood Park (Hike 81) and Dawn's Peak (Hike 75). Weave up the mountain at a moderate grade on the wide footpath among

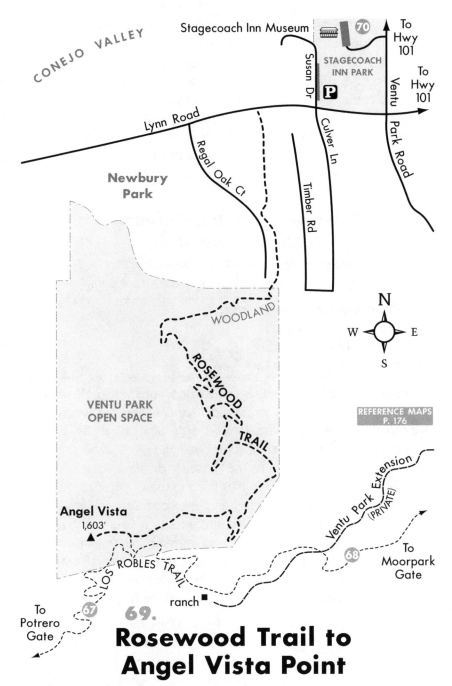

CONEJO VALLEY

Stagecoach Inn Museum

STAGECOACH INN PARK

To Hwy 101

To Hwy 101

Susan Dr

Lynn Road

Regal Oak Ct

Culver Ln

Timber Rd

Ventu Park Road

Newbury Park

WOODLAND

N
W E
S

ROSEWOOD TRAIL

VENTU PARK OPEN SPACE

REFERENCE MAPS P. 176

Ventu Park Extension (PRIVATE)

Angel Vista
1,603'

68

To Moorpark Gate

LOS ROBLES TRAIL

ranch

To Potrero Gate

37

69.

Rosewood Trail to Angel Vista Point

VENTU PARK OPEN SPACE • LOS ROBLES TRAIL SYSTEM

the tall chaparral, passing a one-mile marker. As you near the summit, the Los Robles Trail comes into view along with Point Mugu State Park and the jagged Boney Ridge. Continue up to a Y-fork on the ridge. The left fork descends a short distance to the Los Robles Trail, which leads west to the trailhead at Potrero Road (Hike 67) and east to Moorpark Avenue (Hike 68). For this hike, take the right fork and follow the ridge 100 yards to a pic-nic bench atop the knoll at Angel Vista Point. After enjoying the gorgeous 360-degree views, return along the same route. ■

70. Stagecoach Inn Museum and Nature Trail
51 South Ventu Park Road · Newbury Park
Open Wednesday—Sunday · 1 p.m. to 4 p.m.

Hiking distance: 0.5-mile loop
Hiking time: 30 minutes
Elevation gain: 30 feet
Maps: U.S.G.S. Newbury Park

Summary of hike: The Stagecoach Inn, located in Newbury Park, opened in 1876 as a rest stop for travelers between Los Angeles and Santa Barbara. (It was originally called the Grand Union Hotel.) The Monterey-style building with a wrap-around balcony is now a museum. The museum displays local history and highlights three cultures that lived in the Conejo Valley: the Chumash Indians, the Spanish and Mexican settlers, and the American pioneers. Among the artifacts is a Chumash hut, an outdoor beehive oven, a restored carriage house, an adobe house, a pioneer house, a windmill, and a display of antique ranch equipment and carriages. This easy loop meanders along a stream-fed oak glen and returns through the historic displays.

Driving directions: NEWBURY PARK. From the Ventura Free-way/Highway 101 in Newbury Park, exit on Ventu Park Road. Drive 0.5 miles south to the posted Stagecoach Inn Museum and turn right. Park in the lot on the right, by the museum entrance.

Hiking directions: Follow the paved path to the rear of the Stagecoach Inn Museum. Descend the steps to the posted nature trail. Cross a wooden footbridge over the stream, and wind along the oak-shaded dirt path to a junction. The lower path crosses over the stream on two bridges. The upper path climbs the hill-side and rejoins the canyon bottom path. Follow the waterway downstream, and make a final stream crossing. Ascend steps to an old Spanish adobe and a beehive oven. Stroll among the numerous historic artifacts and educational displays. Return to the parking area through the rose garden. ■

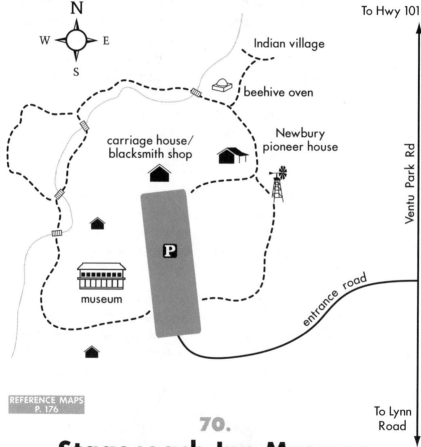

70.

Stagecoach Inn Museum
AND NATURE TRAIL

71. Oak Creek Canyon
LOS ROBLES TRAIL SYSTEM

Hiking distance: 0.8-mile loop
Hiking time: 45 minutes
Elevation gain: 100 feet
Maps: U.S.G.S. Newbury Park
Santa Monica Mountains West Trail Map
Los Robles Trail to Lake Sherwood map

Summary of hike: The Oak Creek Canyon Trail is a short hike through a beautiful oak woodland just minutes from the heart of Thousand Oaks. The forested pathway links to the extensive Los Robles Trail System. The first quarter mile of the hike meanders through the Oak Creek Canyon Whole Access Trail, an interpretive trail with learning stations and a guide wire to assist the blind. The text at each station is written in English and Braille, describing the immediate surroundings through touch, smell, and sound. The trail continues on the Oak Creek Canyon Loop through chaparral-covered hills, looping back to Greenmeadow Avenue.

Driving directions: THOUSAND OAKS. From the Ventura Freeway/Highway 101 in Thousand Oaks, exit on Moorpark Road. Drive 0.5 miles south to Greenmeadow Avenue and turn right. Continue 0.4 miles to the road's end and the trailhead parking lot at the Arts Council Center.

Hiking directions: From the parking lot, walk to the left (south) past the kiosk and restrooms. The trail begins in the forested canopy along a wooden fence. At the end of the quarter-mile Whole Access Trail, pass through the fence to the Oak Creek Canyon Loop. A short distance ahead is a junction. The right fork connects to the Los Robles Trail (Hikes 67—68). Instead, take the left fork, looping back to the north. At 0.3 miles, the trail connects with Greenmeadow Avenue. The parking lot is a short distance along the road to the left. Return on the road for a 0.8-mile loop. ▩

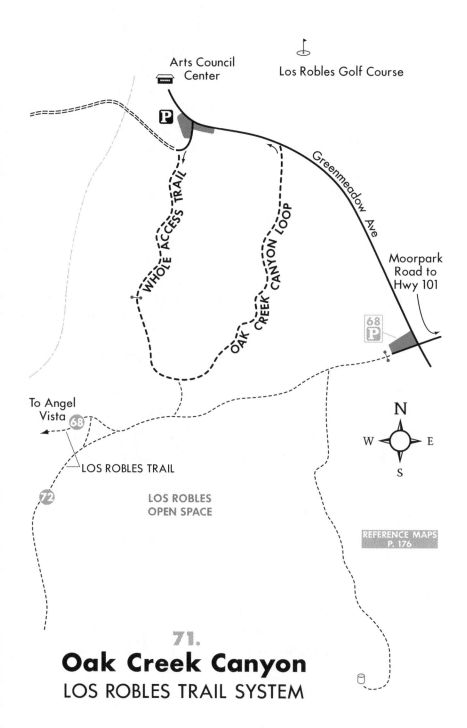

Arts Council Center

Los Robles Golf Course

P

WHOLE ACCESS TRAIL

OAK CREEK CANYON LOOP

Greenmeadow Ave

Moorpark Road to Hwy 101

68 P

To Angel Vista 68

LOS ROBLES TRAIL

72

LOS ROBLES OPEN SPACE

N
W E
S

REFERENCE MAPS
P. 176

71.
Oak Creek Canyon
LOS ROBLES TRAIL SYSTEM

72. Los Padres—Los Robles Loop

LOS PADRES OPEN SPACE · LOS ROBLES OPEN SPACE
LOS ROBLES TRAIL SYSTEM

Hiking distance: 3.5 mile loop
Hiking time: 1.5 hours
Elevation gain: 400 feet
Maps: U.S.G.S. Newbury Park
Santa Monica Mountains West Trail Map
Los Robles Trail to Lake Sherwood map

Summary of hike: This is a loop hike within the expansive open space to the south of Thousand Oaks, looping through two preserves and up along the open ridgeline. The Los Padres Open Space encompasses 187 acres near the southern end of Moorpark Road. The preserve contains chaparral-covered hillsides and gorgeous groves of coastal live oaks. The Los Padres Trail winds through an oak woodland with a seasonal stream, then joins the main Los Robles Trail on a ridge. The hike follows the ridge across an open highland meadow with unobstructed views overlooking Hidden Valley and Conejo Valley. The hike returns through a draw back down to Moorpark Road.

Driving directions: THOUSAND OAKS. From the Ventura Freeway/Highway 101 in Thousand Oaks, exit on Moorpark Road. Drive 0.4 miles south to Los Padres Drive and turn left. Continue 100 yards and park by the trailhead gate on the right, located across the street from Woodlet Way.

Hiking directions: Take the trail south past the Los Padres Trailhead sign and gate. Walk through the oak forest, parallel to a seasonal stream. Cross the stream and begin a gradual but steady ascent, zigzagging from the canyon floor to a junction. Take the wide, signed trail to the right, staying on the Los Padres Trail, and continue uphill to a junction at the top of the hill by a bench above the valley. Bear to the right and head west on the Los Robles Trail. In a quarter mile is a junction with the Scenic Overlook Loop on the right. Take this short trail through the open meadow, overlooking Thousand Oaks and the Conejo Valley. After rejoining the Los Robles Trail, take the path downhill to the right. At the bottom are two trail splits. Bear to the right each time, following the signs to Moorpark Road. Pass the trails on the left to Angel Vista (Hike 68) and Oak Creek Canyon (Hike 71). The trail exits at Moorpark Road. Walk one block and turn right at Los Padres Drive, returning to the trailhead. ■

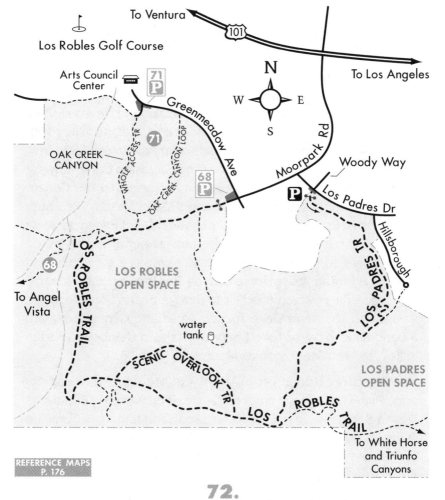

72.
Los Padres–Los Robles Loop
LOS ROBLES TRAIL SYSTEM

73. White Horse Canyon Trail

SOUTH RANCH OPEN SPACE
LOS ROBLES TRAIL SYSTEM

Hiking distance: 3.5-mile loop
Hiking time: 1.5 hours
Elevation gain: 500 feet
Maps: U.S.G.S. Thousand Oaks
　　　　Santa Monica Mountains West Trail Map
　　　　Los Robles Trail to Lake Sherwood map

Summary of hike: The Los Robles Trail System is a well-planned network of trails weaving through the growing residential communities of Westlake Village, Thousand Oaks, and Newbury Park. The multi-use trails link the open spaces of the inland valley with the oceanfront Santa Monica Mountains at Point Mugu State Park. The South Ranch Open Space covers 662 acres on the southwest corner of the Los Robles Trail System, adjacent to the Conejo Ridge Open Space and the Los Padres Open Space. The South Ranch Open Space has a variety of habitats, including coast live oak woodlands, coastal sage scrub, and chaparral. It is an important wildlife corridor between the Santa Monica Mountains and the Simi Hills. The White Horse Canyon Trail loops around the rolling, chaparral-covered foothills to a ridge overlooking Westlake Village and Thousand Oaks. There is an additional overlook with a panoramic view of Lake Sherwood, the cliffs above Hidden Valley, and the Santa Monica Mountains.

Driving directions: THOUSAND OAKS. From the Ventura Freeway/Highway 101 in Thousand Oaks, exit on Westlake Boulevard. Drive 1.8 miles south to East Potrero Road and turn right. Continue 0.4 miles and turn right on Trafalger Place, then an immediate left on Potrero Road, a frontage road. Drive one block to Margate Place. Park along the curb.

Hiking directions: Take the paved walking path west towards seasonal Potrero Valley Creek. To the right, the paved path follows the south side of the creek to Westlake Boulevard. Go to the left and cross the East Potrero Road bridge over the creek

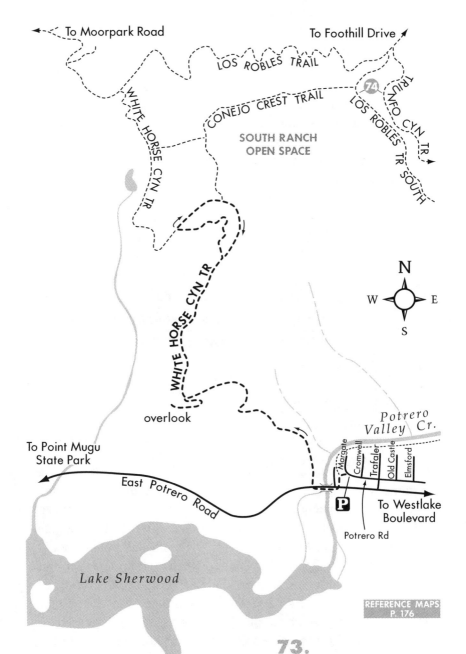

To Moorpark Road

To Foothill Drive

LOS ROBLES TRAIL

CONEJO CREST TRAIL

WHITE HORSE CYN TR

LOS ROBLES TR SOUTH

INFO CYN TR

74

SOUTH RANCH
OPEN SPACE

WHITE HORSE CYN TR

N

W ● E

S

overlook

Potrero
Valley Cr.

To Point Mugu
State Park

Margate
Cromwell
Trafalar
Old Castle
Elmsford

East Potrero Road

P

To Westlake
Boulevard

Potrero Rd

Lake Sherwood

REFERENCE MAPS
P. 176

73.

White Horse Canyon Trail
LOS ROBLES TRAIL SYSTEM

to the trailhead on the right. Descend on the footpath to the trailhead kiosk. Head up the hill and pass the homes on the right to a fire road. The dirt road leads up to a junction. The left fork is a short side trip to a scenic overlook of Lake Sherwood.

Back at the junction, take the north fork a half mile to another junction. The main White Horse Canyon Trail goes right. Begin the loop by taking the footpath on the left, curving around the back side of the canyon before rejoining the fire road. Take the road to the right a short distance to a junction with the Conejo Crest Trail on the left. The Conejo Crest Trail heads west to Triunfo Park (Hike 74). Instead, go to the right. Stay on the fire road and complete the loop. Retrace your steps down the slope and back to the trailhead. ■

74. Triunfo Canyon Trail
CONEJO RIDGE OPEN SPACE
LOS ROBLES TRAIL SYSTEM

Hiking distance: 2.5-mile loop
Hiking time: 1 hour
Elevation gain: 400 feet
Maps: U.S.G.S. Thousand Oaks
　　　　Santa Monica Mountains West Trail Map
　　　　Los Robles Trail to Lake Sherwood map

Summary of hike: The Los Robles Trail System is a large network of paths linking the Conejo and Russell Valleys by Westlake Village, Thousand Oaks, and Newbury Park with the Santa Monica Mountains at Point Mugu State Park. The multi-use trails connect numerous open spaces that are thoughtfully blended with the encroaching residential areas. The Triunfo Canyon Trail is part of the Conejo Ridge Open Space near Westlake Village. The hike follows Triunfo Canyon to rolling grasslands on the ridge, where it connects with the Los Robles Trail atop the ridge. From the ridge are sweeping vistas of Westlake Village, Thousand Oaks, the Conejo Valley, and the Santa Monica Mountains. The trail returns through an adjacent residential area.

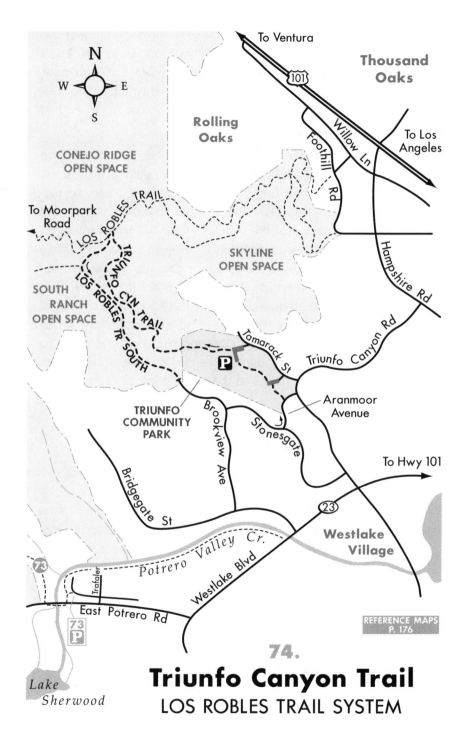

N
W   E
S

To Ventura

Thousand Oaks

101

Willow Ln

To Los Angeles

Rolling Oaks

CONEJO RIDGE OPEN SPACE

Foothill Rd

To Moorpark Road

LOS ROBLES TRAIL

Hampshire Rd

SKYLINE OPEN SPACE

TRIUNFO CYN TRAIL

LOS ROBLES TR SOUTH

SOUTH RANCH OPEN SPACE

Tamarack St

Triunfo Canyon Rd

P

Aranmoor Avenue

TRIUNFO COMMUNITY PARK

Brookview Ave

Stonesgate

To Hwy 101

Bridgegate St

23

Westlake Village

Potrero Valley Cr.

73

Trafalgar

Westlake Blvd

East Potrero Rd

73 P

REFERENCE MAPS P. 176

Lake Sherwood

74.
Triunfo Canyon Trail
LOS ROBLES TRAIL SYSTEM

Driving directions: THOUSAND OAKS. From the Ventura Freeway/Highway 101 in Thousand Oaks, exit on Hampshire Road. Drive 0.6 miles south to Triunfo Canyon Road and turn right. Continue 0.5 miles to Tamarack Street and turn right. The trailhead is 0.2 miles ahead in the parking lot at the north end of Triunfo Community Park.

Hiking directions: From the parking lot, head northwest on the signed trail past the kiosk. The trail gradually climbs along the contours of Triunfo Canyon to the ridgeline. Near the top, a short series of steep switchbacks lead to a bench. From the bench are great views of the valley below. The trail then levels out to a junction with the Los Robles Trail—go to the left. Thirty feet ahead is a ridge with views of the mountains and another junction. Take the signed Los Robles Trail South to the left to a third trail split. Proceed downhill on the left fork. The trail ends at Brookview Avenue. Walk through the neighborhood one block to Stonesgate Street. Go to the left and proceed one block to Aranmoor Avenue. Go left again, returning to the park. The park path heads left, leading back to the parking lot. ■

75. Dawn's Peak

Hiking distance: 1 mile round trip
Hiking time: 30 minutes
Elevation gain: 250 feet
Maps: U.S.G.S. Newbury Park

Summary of hike: Dawn's Peak (also known as Tarantula Hill) is a 400-foot rounded mound in the heart of Thousand Oaks. It lies directly across from the Conejo Valley Botanic Garden and Community Park (Hike 76). The trail spirals up the mound in the 45-acre Conejo Open Space. From the 1,057-foot summit are 360-degree panoramic vistas of Thousand Oaks and the surrounding mountains.

Driving directions: THOUSAND OAKS. From the Ventura Freeway/Highway 101 in Thousand Oaks, exit on Lynn Road and drive 0.6 miles north to Gainsborough Road. Turn right and continue

0.5 miles to the posted Conejo Valley Botanic Garden entrance. (Dawn's Peak is the rounded mound on the left.) Turn right and park in the botanic garden lot on the left, 0.2 miles ahead.

Hiking directions: Walk a quarter mile up the entrance road back to Gainsborough Road. Cross the street to the dirt path. Walk up the path to the southern base of Dawn's Peak. Take the paved, vehicle-restricted service road to the left. The road immediately loops back to the right, spiraling in a counter-clockwise direction. The road corkscrews up the hill, gaining elevation with every step while the views continuously change. At the summit is a fenced waterworks facility. A footpath circles the peak, with a south-facing bench to enjoy the great views of Thousand Oaks, the Santa Monica Mountains, Wildwood Park, and the Simi Hills. Return by retracing your steps.

To extend the hike, continue through the Conejo Valley Botanic Garden (Hike 76). ▨

Lynn Road

To Hwy 101

Dawn's Peak
1,057'

bench

N
W — E
S

75
76
P

CONEJO
OPEN SPACE

76

Conejo Valley
Botanic Garden

Gainsborough Road

CONEJO
COMMUNITY
PARK

REFERENCE MAPS
P. 176

75.
Dawn's Peak

76. Conejo Valley Botanic Garden

350 West Gainsborough Road · Thousand Oaks
www.conejogarden.org

Hiking distance: 1.5 miles round trip
Hiking time: 1 hour
Elevation gain: 100 feet
Maps: U.S.G.S. Newbury Park
Conejo Valley Botanic Garden map

Summary of hike: The Conejo Valley Botanic Garden, in the heart of Thousand Oaks, encompasses 33 acres within Conejo Community Park. The garden's meandering paths lead past native plants and fruit trees, with sections of desert, Mediterranean, herb, and butterfly gardens. From the gardens, a nature trail follows a creek in a natural canyon filled with oaks and willows.

Driving directions: THOUSAND OAKS. From the Ventura Freeway/Highway 101 in Thousand Oaks, exit on Lynn Road. Drive 0.6 miles north to Gainsborough Road and turn right. Continue 0.5 miles to the Conejo Valley Botanic Garden entrance and turn right. The parking lot is 0.2 miles ahead on the left.

Hiking directions: From the parking lot, walk to the end of the road to the botanic garden entrance. Hike up the pathway into Conejo Community Park. A sign directs you to the right into the garden to an information kiosk and trail junction. Take the left fork on the upper trail to another junction. Steps lead straight ahead to benches and overlooks. Many interconnecting trails lead to various overlooks. There are numerous garden paths. The nature trail descends into a forested canyon to a junction by the creek. The left (south) fork leads deeper into the canyon and crosses a wooden bridge over the creek. The right fork crosses the creek. In both cases, reverse the route to return. After enjoying the gardens and various paths, return to the parking lot. ■

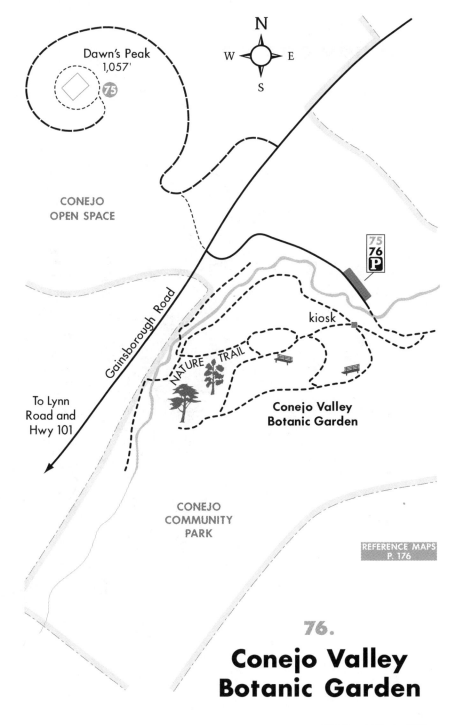

N
W — E
S

Dawn's Peak
1,057'
75

CONEJO
OPEN SPACE

Gainsborough Road

75
76
P

kiosk

NATURE TRAIL

To Lynn
Road and
Hwy 101

Conejo Valley
Botanic Garden

CONEJO
COMMUNITY
PARK

REFERENCE MAPS
P. 176

76.
Conejo Valley
Botanic Garden

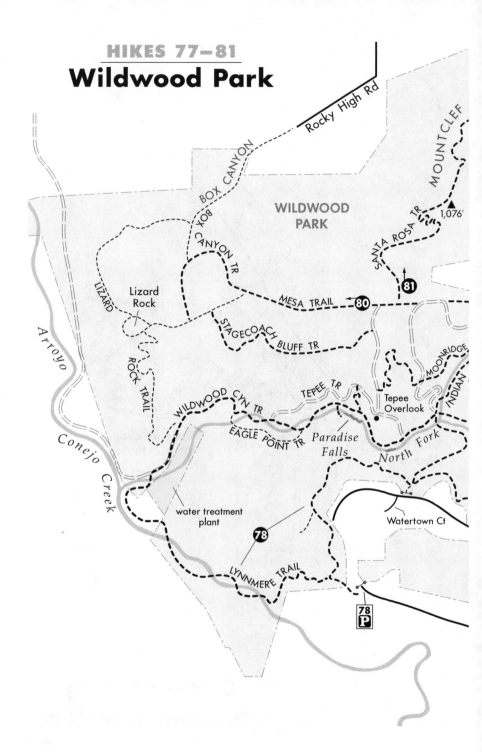

HIKES 77-81
Wildwood Park

Rocky High Rd

MOUNTCLEF

BOX CANYON

WILDWOOD PARK

BOX CANYON TR

SANTA ROSA TR

▲ 1,076'

81

Lizard Rock

LIZARD

MESA TRAIL **80**

STAGECOACH BLUFF TR

ROCK TRAIL

Arroyo

WILDWOOD CYN TR

TEPEE TR

Tepee Overlook

MOONRIDGE

INDIAN

EAGLE POINT TR

Paradise Falls

North Fork

Conejo Creek

water treatment plant

78

Watertown Ct

LYNNMERE TRAIL

78 P

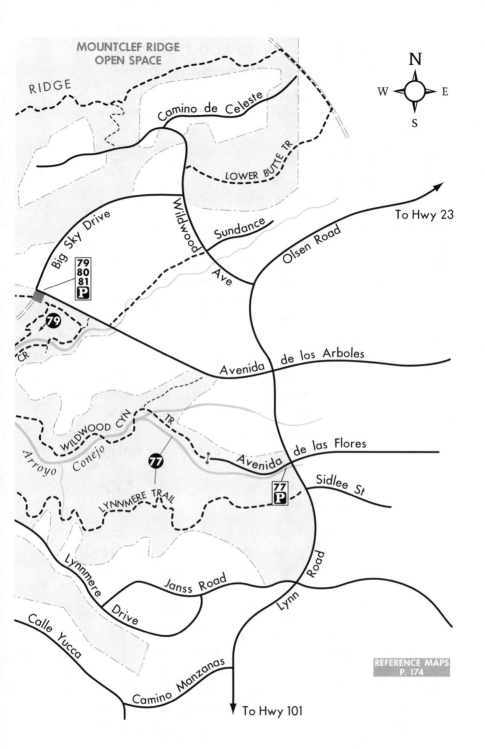

77. Lynnmere—Wildwood Canyon: East Loop

WILDWOOD PARK

Hiking distance: 4-mile loop
Hiking time: 2 hours
Elevation gain: 500 feet
Maps: U.S.G.S. Newbury Park
　　　　Wildwood Park Trail Guide

Summary of hike: Wildwood Park in Thousand Oaks is an immense 1,700-acre park with 27 miles of hiking trails. The diverse terrain includes volcanic rock formations, several canyons with riparian and oak-shaded woodlands, two year-round streams, and two waterfalls. The Lynnmere Trail and Wildwood Canyon Trail form a large loop that crosses from the east side of Wildwood Park to the west side. The Lynnmere Trail is a hillside path that follows the rolling terrain above Wildwood Canyon. The Wildwood Canyon Trail travels along the canyon bottom of Arroyo Conejo Creek and the North Fork of the Arroyo Conejo.

This hike explores the east end of the Lynnmere—Wildwood loop. The east loop trail traverses the chaparral-covered ridge and lush gullies, then returns along the North Fork through a deep rock canyon.

To hike the entire 8-mile Lynnmere—Wildwood Canyon Loop, combine Hikes 77 and 78.

Driving directions: THOUSAND OAKS. From the Ventura Freeway/Highway 101 in Thousand Oaks, exit on Lynn Road and drive 2.2 miles north to Avenida de las Flores. Turn left and park along the street.

Hiking directions: Walk back to Lynn Road, and go to the right (south) 0.2 miles to a footpath on the right, across from Sidlee Street. Bear right and ascend the knoll, traversing the chaparral-covered ridge. Gradually descend to the canyon floor, and cross the stream to an unmarked junction. Stay on the main trail, heading up the hill. The undulating path climbs over

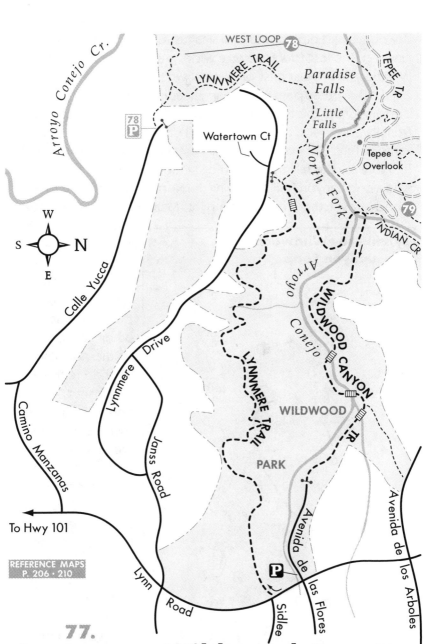

WEST LOOP 78

LYNNMERE TRAIL

Paradise Falls

TEPEE TR

Little Falls

78 P

Watertown Ct

North Fork

Tepee Overlook

79

INDIAN CR

W

S — N

E

Calle Yucca

Arroyo Conejo Cr.

Arroyo

Conejo

WILDWOOD CANYON

LYNNMERE TRAIL

WILDWOOD

WILDWOOD TR

Lynnmere Drive

Janss Road

PARK

Camino Manzanas

To Hwy 101

REFERENCE MAPS
P. 206 · 210

Lynn Road

Sidlee

P

Avenida de las Flores

Avenida de los Arboles

77.
Lynnmere–Wildwood Canyon:
East Loop
WILDWOOD PARK

dry ridges and dips into lush drainages. Cross a footbridge to a junction. The left fork follows a wide, grassy draw 150 yards to Lynnmere Drive, just east of Watertown Court.

Take the grassy path to the right, heading down to the canyon bottom. Cross the North Fork Arroyo Conejo Creek, upstream from Paradise Falls, to the Wildwood Canyon Trail. To the left is Paradise Falls. (For a side trip, walk west on the Wildwood Canyon Trail to view the falls.) Back at the junction, continue east on the Wildwood Canyon Trail, following the North Fork upstream. Cross a bridge over the creek on the right. Meander along the creek through a shady canyon lined with rock walls, passing sculpted rock formations and pools. Cross another footbridge to the north side of the creek and a posted junction. Stay to the right and cross the creek again. Ascend the wide, eroded path, and traverse the hill along the park boundary to the entrance gate at Avenida de las Flores. Continue along the road for two blocks, completing the loop. ∎

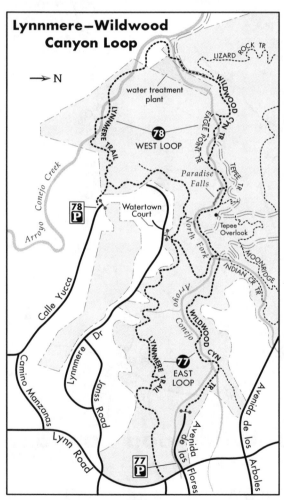

78. Lynnmere–Wildwood Canyon: West Loop

WILDWOOD PARK

Hiking distance: 4.5-mile loop
Hiking time: 2.5 hours
Elevation gain: 500 feet
Maps: U.S.G.S. Newbury Park
　　　Wildwood Park Trail Guide

map
page 213

Summary of hike: Wildwood Park in Thousand Oaks is an immense 1,700-acre park with 27 miles of hiking trails. The diverse terrain includes volcanic rock formations, several canyons with riparian and oak-shaded woodlands, two year-round streams, and two waterfalls. The Lynnmere Trail and Wildwood Canyon Trail form a large loop that crosses from the east side of Wildwood Park to the west side. The Lynnmere Trail is a hillside path that follows the rolling terrain above Wildwood Canyon. The Wildwood Canyon Trail travels along the canyon bottom of Arroyo Conejo Creek and the North Fork of the Arroyo Conejo.

This hike explores the west end of the Lynnmere–Wildwood loop. The hike begins from the trailhead off of Calle Yucca. Hiking clockwise, the trail descends into lush Arroyo Conejo Canyon under the shade of coastal live oaks. The path follows Arroyo Conejo Creek and returns along the North Fork in Wildwood Canyon, skirting the water treatment plant at the loop's west end. A highlight of the hike is Paradise Falls. The waterfall plunges 50 feet over a wall of volcanic rock into a large pool.

To hike the entire 8-mile Lynnmere–Wildwood Canyon Loop, combine Hikes 77 and 78.

Driving directions: THOUSAND OAKS. From the Ventura Freeway/Highway 101 in Thousand Oaks, exit on Lynn Road and drive 1.3 miles north to Camino Manzanas. Turn left and continue 0.4 miles to Calle Yucca. Turn right and go 1.1 mile to the gate at the end of the street and park. The trailhead is on the left.

Hiking directions: Take the distinct trail a short distance west to a trail split. The right fork is our return route. Cross the concrete water channel and veer to the left. A long, steady descent leads to an attractive grove of coastal live oaks at the canyon floor. Under the shaded canopy, curve right and follow Arroyo Conejo Creek downstream. Cross to the west bank of the stream, and follow the unpaved road lined with stately oaks. Rock hop over the creek two more times to the water treatment plant. Cross the creek and skirt around the left side of the facility on a dirt road. At the north end of the industrial mecca, watch for the first footpath on the right.

Take this path, walk parallel to the fenceline, and cross the bridge over the North Fork of Arroyo Conejo Creek. Reenter the beautiful canyon along the north bank of the creek on the Wildwood Canyon Trail. Pass a junction with the Eagle Point Trail (an alternative trail which crosses the creek to the Skunk Hollow Picnic Area). Make two consecutive creek crossings to a junction with the Tepee Trail on the left. Stay to the right towards Paradise Falls, crossing to the south side of the creek. Stroll through an oak grove, and cross to the north side of the creek as Paradise Falls comes into view. Steps to the right lead down to the falls and pool.

On the main trail, steps lead up to the brink of the falls, then the trail parallels the cascading creek upstream to a 4-way junction with the Tepee and Lynnmere Trails. Bear right, crossing the creek on the Lynnmere Trail, and ascend the south canyon wall. Forty yards before reaching the Lynnmere Drive trailhead gate, bear right and traverse the hillside along the south park boundary. Follow the ridge and descend to a junction. Bear left into a draw. Climb up the hill and follow the fenceline to the right, completing the loop. ■

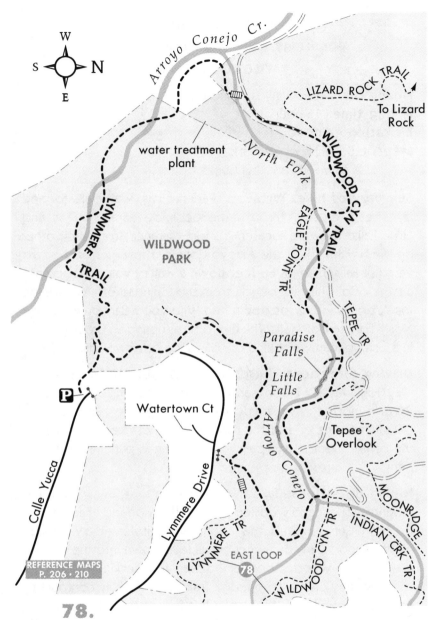

78.
Lynnmere–Wildwood Canyon:
West Loop
WILDWOOD PARK

79. Paradise Falls
Moonridge Trail—Indian Creek Canyon
WILDWOOD PARK

Hiking distance: 3 miles round trip
Hiking time: 1.5 hours
Elevation gain: 400 feet
Maps: U.S.G.S. Newbury Park
       Wildwood Park Trail Guide

Summary of hike: Wildwood Park has two waterfalls formed by stream erosion through the bedrock—Paradise Falls and Little Falls. They are located a short distance from each other on the North Fork of the Arroyo Conejo. The larger of the two, Paradise Falls, plunges 50 feet down a wall of volcanic rock into a large pool. This hike begins from the trailhead off Avenida de los Arboles and loops down into Wildwood Canyon along the North Fork to both falls. The hike returns up Indian Creek Canyon in a lush riparian woodland of oaks and cottonwoods.

Driving directions: THOUSAND OAKS. From the Ventura Freeway/Highway 101 in Thousand Oaks, exit on Lynn Road and drive 2.5 miles north to Avenida de los Arboles. Turn left and continue 0.9 miles to the end of the road at Big Sky Drive. Loop around the center median, and park in the trailhead parking lot on the right.

Hiking directions: Take the trail to the east, away from the mountains. Descend wooden steps to the Moonridge and Indian Creek Trail junction. Take the Moonridge Trail along the west side of Wildwood Canyon. Switchbacks lead down into the canyon and across a wooden bridge. Proceed to a service road. After crossing, stay on the Moonridge Trail along the hilly contours to another junction. Take the signed left fork towards Paradise Falls, crossing a small ravine to the Tepee Overlook Trail, a service road. Head left to Tepee Overlook. Proceed along the road for about 100 yards into the canyon to a junction. Take the signed left trail down the steps to Paradise Falls and to the pool at its base.

After exploring the area around the falls and pool, return up the steps. Take the Wildwood Canyon Trail to the right, past the brink of the falls. Pass Little Falls and a picnic area. As the trail parallels Indian Creek, cross the creek on a wooden bridge, and take the signed Indian Creek Trail up the canyon to the left. Cross the creek again and ascend the hill to the top. The left fork leads back to the parking lot. ▪

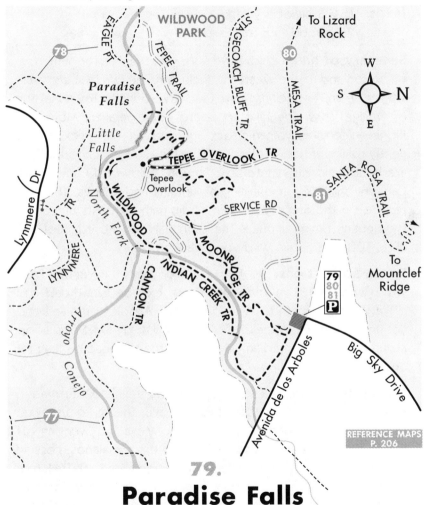

79.
Paradise Falls
Moonridge Trail—Indian Creek Canyon
WILDWOOD PARK

80. Lizard Rock
Mesa Trail—Stagecoach Bluff Loop
WILDWOOD PARK

Hiking distance: 3 miles round trip
Hiking time: 1.5 hours
Elevation gain: 150 feet
Maps: U.S.G.S. Newbury Park
Wildwood Park Trail Guide

Summary of hike: Wildwood Park was the site for numerous television and movie westerns, including *The Rifleman, Bonanza, Wagon Train,* and *Gunsmoke* (and the original town setting of Dodge City). The hike to Lizard Rock parallels Mountclef Ridge—a serrated volcanic rock outcropping—on an expansive, gently rolling grassland plateau. From the Lizard Rock formations are panoramic views into Box Canyon, Wildwood Canyon, Hill Canyon, and the surrounding mountains and valleys. The hike returns on the Stagecoach Bluff Trail, named for its numerous stagecoach racing scenes. The path follows the edge of the cliffs 400 feet above Wildwood Canyon.

Driving directions: THOUSAND OAKS. From the Ventura Free-way/Highway 101 in Thousand Oaks, exit on Lynn Road and drive 2.5 miles north to Avenida De Los Arboles. Turn left and continue 0.9 miles to the end of the road at Big Sky Drive. Loop around the center median, and park in the trailhead parking lot on the right.

Hiking directions: Head west past the trailhead information board and up a short hill. Drop down over the hill to a service road. Follow the road 70 yards to the Mesa Trail, veering off to the right. Take the Mesa Trail across the grasslands, passing the Santa Rosa Trail (Hike 81) and the Tepee Overlook Trail, to a posted trail split. Take the right fork—the Box Canyon Trail—to a knoll. From the knoll, take the left path to the Lizard Rock Trail. Continue along the Lizard Rock Trail to the right. Ascend a short, steep hill to the top of the rock. The trail loops around and re-joins the trail coming up.

Retrace your steps to the signed Stagecoach Bluff Trail. Take this trail to the right (east) along the cliff edge overlooking Wildwood Canyon. The trail ends at a junction with the Tepee Overlook Trail. Turn left, rejoining the Mesa Trail 100 yards ahead. Return to the trailhead on the right. ▪

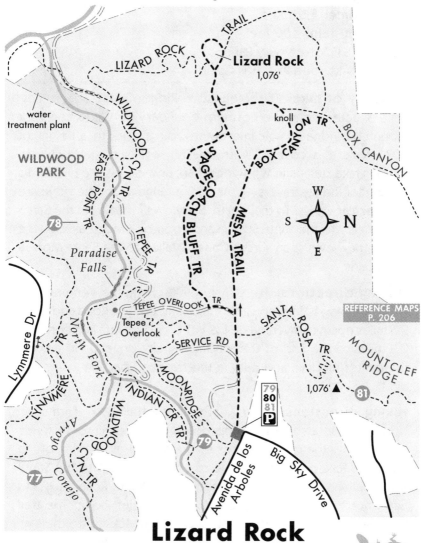

Lizard Rock
80. Mesa Trail–Stagecoach Bluff Loop
WILDWOOD PARK

81. Mountclef Ridge
Santa Rosa Trail—Lower Butte Loop
MOUNTCLEF RIDGE OPEN SPACE • WILDWOOD PARK

Hiking distance: 5-mile loop
Hiking time: 2.5 hours
Elevation gain: 400 feet
Maps: U.S.G.S. Newbury Park
Wildwood Park Trail Guide

Summary of hike: The Mountclef Ridge Open Space covers 212 acres along the northern boundary of Wildwood Park. Mountclef Ridge, a volcanic outcropping, rises to a height of 1,076 feet. It is covered with coastal sage scrub and chaparral. This hike begins in Wildwood Park and climbs the hillside to Mountclef Ridge, traversing the rocky range. From the ridge are spectacular views. To the north, the views range from the Santa Rosa Valley to the Santa Susana and Topatopa Mountains. To the south, the views span across Conejo Valley to the Santa Monica Mountains.

Driving directions: THOUSAND OAKS. From the Ventura Freeway/Highway 101 in Thousand Oaks, exit on Lynn Road and drive 2.5 miles north to Avenida de los Arboles. Turn left and continue 0.9 miles to the end of the road at Big Sky Drive. Loop around the center median, and park in the trailhead parking lot on the right.

Hiking directions: Head west past the trailhead information board and up a short hill. Drop down over the hill to a service road. Follow the road 70 yards to the Mesa Trail, veering off to the right. Take the Mesa Trail across the grasslands to the Santa Rosa Trail on the right. Bear right on the Santa Rosa Trail, and head north towards the prominent Mountclef Ridge. The trail traverses the hillside to the east and switchbacks up to the saddle of the Mountclef Ridge summit. Topping the slope, curve right along the contour of the cliff's ridge. The ridge overlooks Wildwood Mesa and Wildwood Canyon, with far-reaching vistas across Conejo Valley and Santa Rosa Valley.

A short distance ahead, the trail drops down along the northern slope. Continue east, past the junction with the Wildwood Avenue access trail, to a service road. Take the road to the right to a residential area. Cross the road and continue straight ahead on the signed Lower Butte Trail. Watch for a footpath on the right that leads up to a saddle and over the ridge to the trail's end at Wildwood Avenue. Go left and walk 0.4 miles downhill on the sidewalk to a footpath on the right, across from Sundance Street. Take the path and follow a canal into Wildflower Playfield Park to Avenida de los Arboles. Complete the loop, returning to the parking lot on the right. ■

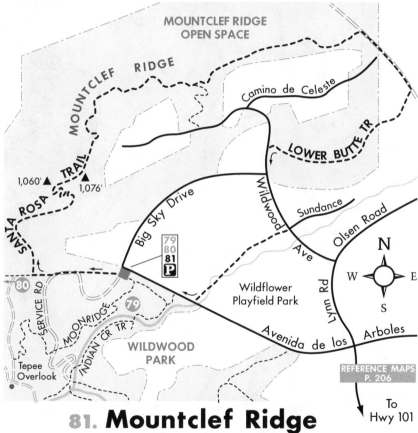

81. **Mountclef Ridge**
Santa Rosa Trail–Lower Butte Loop
WILDWOOD PARK

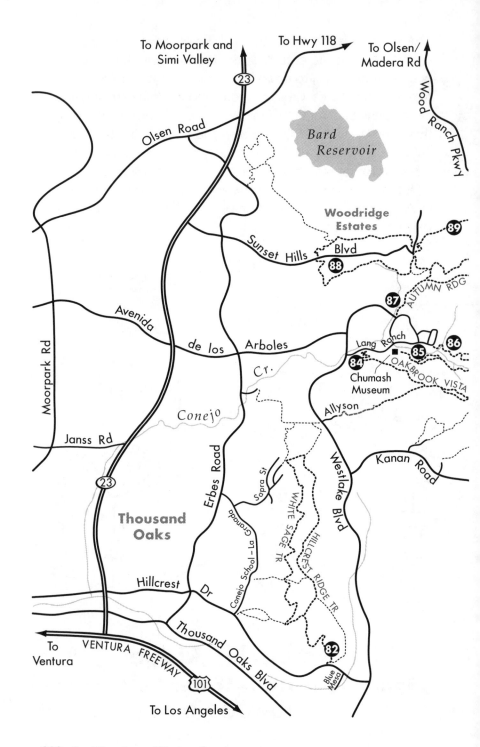

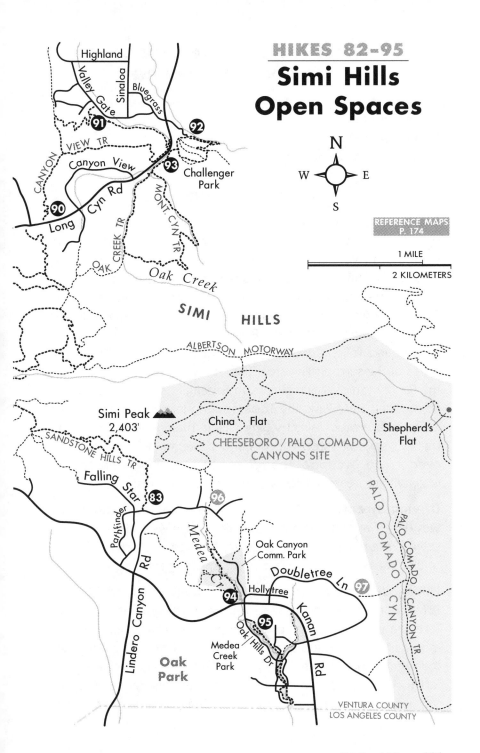

HIKES 82-95
Simi Hills
Open Spaces

N
W ⊕ E
S

REFERENCE MAPS
P. 174

1 MILE
2 KILOMETERS

Highland
Valley Gate
Sinaloa
Bluegrass
91
92
CANYON VIEW TR
Canyon View
93
Challenger Park
Long
Cyn Rd
90
OAK CREEK TR
MONT CYN TR
Oak Creek

SIMI HILLS

ALBERTSON MOTORWAY

Simi Peak
2,403'
China Flat
Shepherd's Flat
SANDSTONE HILLS TR
CHEESEBORO/PALO COMADO
CANYONS SITE
Falling Star
83
96
Pathfinder
Medea Cr
Oak Canyon Comm. Park
Doubletree Ln
97
Hollytree
94
Kanan Rd
Lindero Canyon Rd
Oak Park
Oak/Hills Dr
95
Medea Creek Park
PALO COMADO CANYON
PALO COMADO CANYON TR
VENTURA COUNTY
LOS ANGELES COUNTY

82. Hillcrest Ridge—White Sage Loop
HILLCREST OPEN SPACE PRESERVE

Hiking distance: 5.6-mile loop
Hiking time: 3 hours
Elevation gain: 1,000 feet
Maps: U.S.G.S. Thousand Oaks
Trails of the Simi Hills
Conejo Open Space Foundation map

Summary of hike: The Hillcrest Open Space Preserve is an undiscovered gem in the heart of Thousand Oaks. The preserve encompasses two canyons. A series of scenic knolls lies along the ridge separating the two canyons. Two main trails form a loop through the coastal sage-covered hills with spectacular views. This hike begins from the south end of the preserve on Hillcrest Drive, just west of Westlake Boulevard. The trail climbs up the canyon and follows the ridge to four knolls with 360-degree vistas of the surrounding area. The views include the ridgeline of the Santa Monica Mountains from Topanga Canyon State Park to Point Mugu State Park, the Topatopa Mountains at Ojai, and the Santa Susana Mountains by Simi Valley. The undulating ridgetop trail has several steep ascents and descents as it winds from overlook to overlook. The return route traverses the canyon wall, with more great views to the south and west.

Driving directions: THOUSAND OAKS. From the Ventura Freeway/Highway 101 in Thousand Oaks, exit on Westlake Boulevard. Drive 1 mile north to Hillcrest Drive. Turn left and drive 0.2 miles to Blue Mesa Street. Turn left and park along the street.

Hiking directions: Walk 0.2 miles west (left) on Hillcrest Drive to the posted trailhead on the north side of the street. Take the path 20 yards to a junction. Both routes lead up the mountain to a junction atop a knoll at 1,581 feet. The right fork follows the ridge with a very steep ascent. This hike takes the left fork straight ahead on the path of least resistance. Head up the west canyon slope. A few sweeping curves lead up to the

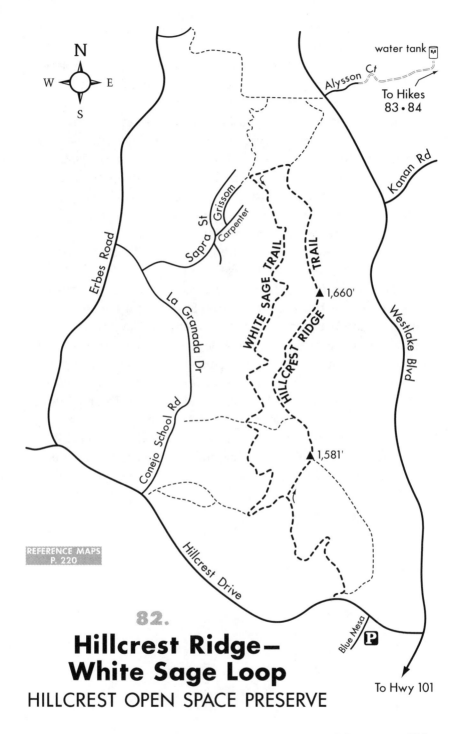

water tank

Alysson Ct

To Hikes
83 • 84

Kanan Rd

N
W — E
S

Sapra St

Grissom

Carpenter

Erbes Road

La Granada Dr

WHITE SAGE TRAIL

HILLCREST RIDGE TRAIL

▲ 1,660'

Westlake Blvd

Conejo School Rd

▲ 1,581'

REFERENCE MAPS
P. 220

Hillcrest Drive

Blue Mesa

P

To Hwy 101

82.
Hillcrest Ridge–
White Sage Loop
HILLCREST OPEN SPACE PRESERVE

ridge, where there is a panoramic view of the surrounding terrain. Follow the undulating ridge to a junction at 0.8 miles.

Begin the loop on the right fork, and climb the ridge to the flat 1,581-foot knoll at one mile, where the two trails from the trailhead merge. For a shorter 1.8-mile loop, bear right and return down the ridge to the trailhead on the steep path. To continue, veer slightly left on the Hillcrest Ridge Trail and descend the slope, with a view of the next peak on the descent. Climb the steep slope to the exposed 1,660-foot summit, where you are rewarded with amazing vistas of the surrounding topography. After marveling at the views, steeply descend to a saddle, then ascend the third peak and a junction at 2.4 miles. The right fork leads to Westlake Boulevard and connects with the Oakbrook Vista-Sandstone Hills Trail (Hikes 83 and 84).

Bear left and follow the ridge across the head of the canyon to a junction at the end of Grissom Street by the water tanks. Bear left and head south down the canyon. Traverse the east-facing canyon wall on the White Sage Trail, a narrow fire road. Follow the contours of the hills on a gradual downhill slope to an unsigned 4-way junction by a power pole at 4 miles. The left fork climbs back up to the Hillcrest Ridge Trail. The right fork descends to Conejo School Road. Continue straight, weaving down the canyon to an overlook by a U-shaped left bend. Bear left and climb the hill, completing the loop. Go to the right and return 0.8 miles to the trailhead. ▪

83. Sandstone Hills—
Oakbrook Vista Trail
NORTH RANCH OPEN SPACE

Hiking distance: 7 miles round trip
Hiking time: 3.5 hours
Elevation gain: 600 feet

map page 227

Maps: U.S.G.S. Thousand Oaks
Trails of the Simi Hills
Lang Ranch/Woodridge Open Space map

Summary of hike: The North Ranch Open Space encompasses 2,614 acres in the Simi Hills above the North Ranch neighborhoods north of Kanan Road and Lindero Canyon Road. An extensive trail system weaves through the protected area. The diverse habitats include sandstone cliffs, black walnut groves, coastal live oak woodlands, grasslands, and coastal sage scrub. The trails connect with Oakbrook Regional Park, Lang Ranch Open Space, and Hillcrest Open Space (Hikes 82—87). This trail winds through the hills among sculpted sandstone formations and follows a ridge with spectacular 360-degree panoramas.

Driving directions: WESTLAKE VILLAGE. From the Ventura Freeway/Highway 101 in Westlake Village, exit on Lindero Canyon Road. Drive 2.9 miles north to Kanan Road. Turn left to the first street, Falling Star Avenue, and turn right. Continue 0.5 miles to Pathfinder Avenue and turn right. Drive one block to the hilltop at the posted Sandstone Hills Trail on the left. Park along the street.

Hiking directions: Walk past the trail gate, and climb a short hill through the open space, passing private residences. Head north towards the jagged sandstone formations below Simi Peak. Ascend a second hill before dropping into an arroyo. At the uppermost hillside home, curve left. Climb wood steps to a power pole and a view across Westwood Village, Agoura Hills, and the Santa Monica Mountains. Traverse the hillside to the west, parallel to Conejo Ridge. Walk around a chainlink fence to an unpaved fire road. The winding road—the Sandstone Hills Trail—heads westward beneath magnificent sandstone formations and caves. At 1.4 miles, the Edison Road branches right. Detour to the right 0.6 miles uphill, passing outcroppings and caves to Vista Point, a 1,904-foot knoll at the end of the trail. From this spot are phenomenal views to the north, west and south, including 2,403-foot Simi Peak and the Santa Monica Mountain Range.

Back on the Sandstone Hills Trail, descend through a garden of sandstone formations to a junction on the left at 1.9 miles. The left fork descends a half mile on the Yerba Santa Trail to Kanan Road; the Hidden Meadows Trail drops 0.7 miles to the trailhead off of Falling Star Avenue. For this hike, stay atop the ridge and continue strolling among the beautiful sandstone outcrops. At 2.2 miles is another junction. The Sandstone Hills Trail veers left and descends 0.9 miles to Rayburn Street by Kanan Road.

Take the Oakbrook Vista Trail, and pass a short but steep footpath that climbs to a 1,765-foot peak. The main trail follows the ridge to a Y-fork, overlooking Oakbrook Regional Park, Lang Ranch Open Space, and the Albertson Motorway. At the Y-fork, the right branch zigzags down the hill into Oakbrook Regional Park. Take the left fork and cross the rolling grassy hills to a huge water tank on the right and a paved utility road at 3.5 miles, just shy of Westlake Boulevard. This is the turn-around spot. Return by retracing your steps. ■

84. Oakbrook Vista— Sandstone Hills Trail
OAKBROOK REGIONAL PARK to VISTA POINT
Lang Ranch Parkway · Thousand Oaks

Hiking distance: 5.4 miles round trip
Hiking time: 3 hours
Elevation gain: 860 feet
Maps: U.S.G.S. Thousand Oaks
Trails of the Simi Hills
Lang Ranch/Woodridge Open Space map

map
page 229

Summary of hike: The Oakbrook Vista and Sandstone Hills Trails weave along a ridge through spectacular sandstone rock

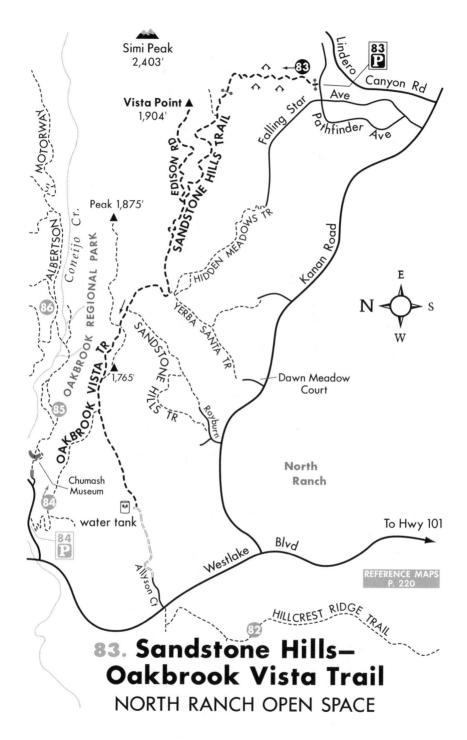

Simi Peak
2,403'

Vista Point ▲
1,904'

83 P

Lindero

Canyon Rd

Falling Star

Pathfinder Ave

Ave

EDISON RD

SANDSTONE HILLS TRAIL

Peak 1,875'
▲

HIDDEN MEADOWS TR

Coneijo Cr.

OAKBROOK REGIONAL PARK

MOTORWAY

ALBERTSON

86

YERBA SANTA TR

Kanan Road

85

SANDSTONE VISTA TR

OAKBROOK

1,765'
▲

SANDSTONE HILLS TR

Royburn

N
E
S
W

Dawn Meadow
Court

Chumash
Museum

84

water tank

North
Ranch

To Hwy 101

84 P

Allyson Ct

Westlake   Blvd

REFERENCE MAPS
P. 220

82   HILLCREST RIDGE TRAIL

83. Sandstone Hills–
Oakbrook Vista Trail
NORTH RANCH OPEN SPACE

formations to 1,904-foot Vista Point. The overlook, directly across from Simi Peak, has incredible 360-degree panoramas. This hike begins in Oakbrook Regional Park and climbs to the ridge 600 feet above the grassy park floor. Throughout the hike are overlooks of Lang Ranch Open Space, Thousand Oaks, North Ranch, Oak Park, and the Santa Monica Mountain Range.

Driving directions: THOUSAND OAKS/HIGHWAY 23. From the Ventura Freeway/Highway 101 in Thousand Oaks, take Highway 23 north 2.5 miles to the Avenida de los Arboles exit. Turn right and drive 1.6 miles to Westlake Boulevard. Turn right and go 0.2 miles to Lang Ranch Parkway. Turn left and continue 0.2 miles to the trailhead on the right. Park along the curb.

THOUSAND OAKS/WESTLAKE BLVD. From the Ventura Freeway/Highway 101 and Westlake Boulevard in Thousand Oaks, drive 4.2 miles north to Lang Ranch Parkway. Turn right and continue 0.2 miles to the trailhead on the right. Park along the curb.

Hiking directions: From the trailhead, head up the south slope of Oakbrook Regional Park. Zigzag up the hill on five switchbacks through chaparral and pockets of oaks. At the fifth switchback is an overlook with a bench, offering views across Thousand Oaks to the Los Padres National Forest, lying beyond Fillmore and the Topatopa Mountains north of Ojai. A short distance ahead, as the trail temporarily levels out, a side path on the right drops down the slope. Continue straight ahead to the east while overlooking Oakbrook Regional Park. Steadily climb along the ridge, gaining 600 feet in the first mile, to a T-junction. The right fork descends one mile to Westlake Boulevard and Allyson Court by the Hillcrest Open Space.

Go to the left, staying atop the ridge 0.1 mile to a Y-fork. The right fork steeply climbs to a 1,765-foot peak, then returns to the main trail. The left fork skirts the peak and is the easier route. At 1.3 miles, the two trails merge, where a spur trail on the left climbs 0.4 miles to Peak 1,875. The Oakbrook Vista Trail ends at 1.4 miles at a junction with the Sandstone Hills Trail. The right branch descends one mile to Kanan Road at North Ranch. Take the left fork and stroll among beautiful sandstone outcrops. Make a hairpin left bend to an unsigned junction at 1.7 miles. The

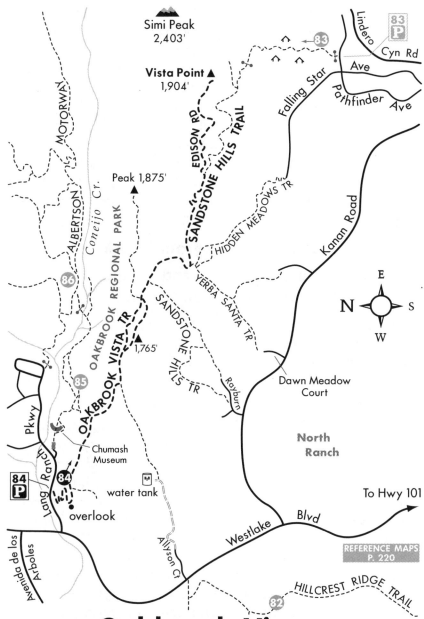

84. Oakbrook Vista–
Sandstone Hills Trail
OAKBROOK REGIONAL PARK to VISTA POINT

right fork descends a half mile on the Yerba Santa Trail to Kanan Road; the Hidden Meadows Trail drops 0.7 miles to the trailhead off of Falling Star Avenue, both in North Ranch.

For this hike, stay atop the flat and continue east. Climb through a garden of sandstone formations to a well-defined road split at 2.2 miles. The right fork drops 1.4 miles to Pathfinder Avenue (Hike 83). Take the left fork on Edison Road, and climb along the rocky bluffs to the trail's end at Vista Point. The overlook sits on the edge of a knoll by an electrical tower. The phenomenal views span to the north, west and south, including 2,403-foot Simi Peak and the Santa Monica Mountain Range. After savoring the views, along along the same route. ■

85. Oakbrook Regional Park
Chumash Museum and Village
3290 Lang Ranch Parkway · Thousand Oaks

Hiking distance: 1.5 miles round trip
Hiking time: 45 minutes
Elevation gain: 100 feet
Maps: U.S.G.S. Thousand Oaks
Trails of the Simi Hills
Chumash Indian Museum trail map

Summary of hike: Oakbrook Regional Park encompasses 436 acres on the east side of Westlake Boulevard adjacent to the Lang Ranch Open Space in Thousand Oaks. For thousands of years, this site was occupied by the Chumash people. The park features the Chumash Indian Museum, a historical site and living history museum. The interpretive center is dedicated to protecting the cultural resources and to preserving the historical culture and present-day influence of the Chumash people. Behind the museum is a 25-acre preserve in the canyon along Conejo Creek. A tree-shaded trail weaves up the canyon through groves of old-growth oaks dating back 200–300 years. The trail passes through lush overgrown meadows and dramatic rock formations with mortar holes made by the Chumash while processing food. Under a canopy of oaks is a reconstructed Chumash village .

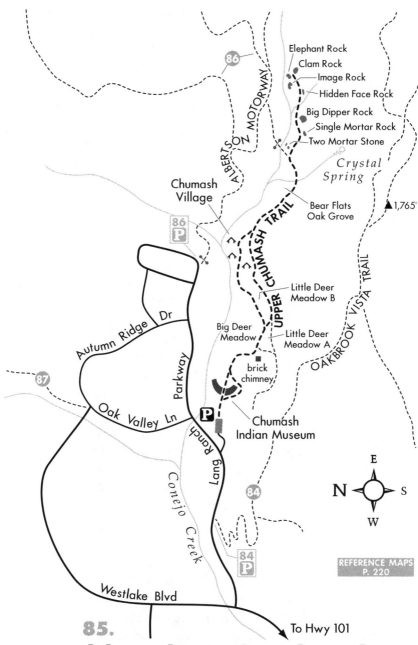

Elephant Rock
Clam Rock
Image Rock
Hidden Face Rock
Big Dipper Rock
Single Mortar Rock
Two Mortar Stone

Crystal Spring

Chumash Village

Bear Flats Oak Grove

▲1,765'

UPPER CHUMASH TRAIL

OAKBROOK VISTA TRAIL

Little Deer Meadow B

Autumn Ridge Dr

Big Deer Meadow

Little Deer Meadow A

Parkway

brick chimney

Chumash Indian Museum

Oak Valley Ln

Lang Ranch

Conejo Creek

E
N — S
W

REFERENCE MAPS
P. 220

Westlake Blvd

To Hwy 101

85.

Oakbrook Regional Park
CHUMASH MUSEUM and VILLAGE

Driving directions: THOUSAND OAKS/HIGHWAY 23. From the Ventura Freeway/Highway 101 in Thousand Oaks, take Highway 23 north 2.5 miles to the Avenida de los Arboles exit. Turn right and drive 1.6 miles to Westlake Boulevard. Turn right and go 0.2 miles to Lang Ranch Parkway. Turn left and continue 0.4 miles to the signed Oakbrook Regional Park Museum on the right. Turn right and park in the Chumash Indian Museum parking lot.

THOUSAND OAKS/WESTLAKE BLVD. From the Ventura Freeway/Highway 101 and Westlake Boulevard in Thousand Oaks, drive 4.2 miles north to Lang Ranch Parkway. Turn right and continue 0.4 miles to signed Oakbrook Regional Park Museum on the right. Turn right and park in the Chumash Indian Museum parking lot.

Hiking directions: From the parking lot, loop around the right side of the museum to the trailhead by the large tree stump, or visit the museum and go out the back door to the trailhead. Walk a couple hundred yards to the remains of a home and brick chimney. This was the site of the Lang Ranch caretaker's home dating back to the early 1900s. Continue straight to a Y-fork and veer right on the Upper Chumash Trail, a dirt path. Pass the replica of a Chumash village while walking under an oak canopy on the south edge of the canyon floor. Pass Bear Flats Oak Grove on the left, then cross over Crystal Spring. Stay to the right, parallel to the south bank of Conejo Creek, and pass mortar holes in the rocks. The path curves around the rocks and the canyon narrows. Pass caves on the south hill, with a short, steep side path leading up to the caves. Continue past a series of weather-carved sandstone formations. The formations include Image Rock on the north hillside, resembling a head profile; Elephant Rock, a finely etched rock with a trunk; and Clam Rock, in the shape of a partially opened clam. The trail ends by Clam Rock.

Return along the same route. Just before reaching the Chumash village, veer right and walk through the village. Pass the dome houses built of willow sticks, and rejoin the main trail at the Y-fork. North of the village, across Conejo Creek, are the remains of the Lang Ranch House. From the Y-fork, return back to the museum and parking lot. ▪

86. Lang Ranch Loop
from Lang Ranch Parkway
LANG RANCH OPEN SPACE

Hiking distance: 3.8-mile loop
Hiking time: 2 hours
Elevation gain: 500 feet
Maps: U.S.G.S. Thousand Oaks
Trails of the Simi Hills
Lang Ranch/Woodridge Open Space map

map
page 235

Summary of hike: The Lang Ranch Open Space lies in northeast Thousand Oaks along the north side of Oakbrook Regional Park. The picturesque 901-acre open space (composed of several open spaces) includes oak woodlands, riparian corridors, and rolling grasslands. The trail system links up with many other trails through the public lands, including China Flats, Cheeseboro/Palo Comado Canyons, North Ranch Open Space, and Wood Ranch Open Space in Simi Valley.

The main access into Lang Ranch Open Space is from the east end of Lang Ranch Parkway, where this hike begins. The hike forms a loop using fire roads and single track trails. The diverse route weaves through oak groves, chaparral-clad hillsides, and jagged sandstone formations while climbing to a ridge overlooking the Simi Hills, Simi Valley, Santa Susana Mountains, Thousand Oaks, and the Santa Monica Mountains.

Driving directions: THOUSAND OAKS/HIGHWAY 23. From the Ventura Freeway/Highway 101 in Thousand Oaks, take Highway 23 north 2.5 miles to the Avenida de los Arboles exit. Turn right and drive 1.6 miles to Westlake Boulevard. Turn right and go 0.2 miles to Lang Ranch Parkway. Turn left and continue 0.8 miles to the gated trailhead where Lang Ranch Parkway makes a 90-degree left bend. Park alongside the road.

THOUSAND OAKS/WESTLAKE BLVD. From the Ventura Freeway/Highway 101 and Westlake Boulevard in Thousand Oaks, drive 4.2 miles north to Lang Ranch Parkway. Turn right and continue 0.8

miles to the gated trailhead where Lang Ranch Parkway makes a 90-degree left bend. Park alongside the road.

Hiking directions: Pass the trailhead gate and descend into the oak-filled canyon. The trail overlooks the replica of a Chumash village below (Hike 85). Skirting the north rim of the oak-cloaked canyon, pass a historic rock-walled foundation on the left. Weave along the Albertson Motorway, a dirt fire road, between the chaparral-covered hillside on the left and the oak-rich canyon on the right.

Reach a junction at 0.4 miles, the beginning of the loop. Leave the motorway and bear left on the narrower path. Head up the slope, overlooking several canyons, the surrounding peaks, the rocky canyon walls, and sections of the loop trail yet to come. Steadily climb, gaining 500 feet in just under one mile, to views across Thousand Oaks to the Santa Monica Mountains and across Simi Valley to the Santa Susana Mountains. At 1.3 miles is a Y-split at the base of a hill. The left fork leads to the Sunrise Trail and connects with the Long Canyon Trail in Wood Ranch (Hikes 87 and 89).

For this hike, go right and traverse the contours of the hills on a downward slope. Snake down into a ravine, and walk through an oak grove to a T-junction with a dirt road at 2 miles—the Meadow Vista Trail. The left fork climbs back up to the ridge. Bear right to a junction with the Albertson Motorway at 2.3 miles. The left fork leads 1.5 miles to China Flat, Hike 96. Instead, go right and continue downhill. Veer right on the signed public trail by the gated road. Stroll under a gorgeous oak canopy, and climb back to the open chaparral and expansive views. Pass a faint path on the right that leads to the top of Knoll 1,606. Reconnect with the Albertson Motorway, completing the loop at 3.4 miles. Return to the trailhead on the right. ▪

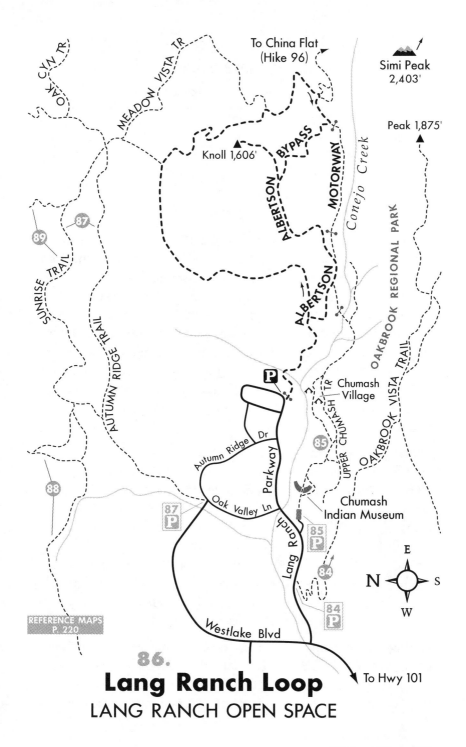

OAK CYN TR

MEADOW VISTA TR

To China Flat
(Hike 96)

Simi Peak
2,403'

Peak 1,875'

Knoll 1,606'

ALBERTSON BYPASS

MOTORWAY

Conejo Creek

ALBERTSON

OAKBROOK REGIONAL PARK

SUNRISE TRAIL

87

89

AUTUMN RIDGE TRAIL

P

OAKBROOK VISTA TRAIL

Chumash
Village

UPPER CHUMASH TR

CHUMASH TR

85

Autumn Ridge Dr

Parkway

Oak Valley Ln

88

87
P

Lang Ranch

Chumash
Indian Museum

85
P

84

N

E

S

W

84
P

REFERENCE MAPS
P. 220

Westlake Blvd

To Hwy 101

86.
Lang Ranch Loop
LANG RANCH OPEN SPACE

87. Sunrise—Autumn Ridge Loop
from Westlake Boulevard
LANG RANCH OPEN SPACE

Hiking distance: 2.9-mile loop
Hiking time: 1.5 hours
Elevation gain: 450 feet
Maps: U.S.G.S. Thousand Oaks
Trails of the Simi Hills
Lang Ranch/Woodridge Open Space map

Summary of hike: The Sunrise Trail and Autumn Ridge Trail form a loop along the northern end of the 901-acre Lang Ranch Open Space. The trails are adjacent to, and connect with, the Rancho Simi Open Space (Hikes 89–91). The Sunrise Trail follows a ridge and weaves past naturally-carved sandstone formations while overlooking Simi Valley, Tierra Rejada Valley, and the 231-acre Bard Reservoir (Lake Bard). The return on the Autumn Ridge Trail traverses the open hillside with great views across Thousand Oaks to the Santa Monica Mountains. The hike loops through coastal sage scrub, open grasslands, and weathered sandstone outcroppings.

Driving directions: THOUSAND OAKS/HIGHWAY 23. From the Ventura Freeway/Highway 101 in Thousand Oaks, take Highway 23 north 2.5 miles to the Avenida de los Arboles exit. Turn right and drive 1.6 miles to Westlake Boulevard. Turn left and go 0.6 miles to the end of Westlake Boulevard at the junction with Autumn Ridge Drive. Park along the curb.

THOUSAND OAKS/WESTLAKE BLVD. From the Ventura Freeway/Highway 101 and Westlake Boulevard in Thousand Oaks, drive 5 miles north to the end of Westlake Boulevard at the junction with Autumn Ridge Drive. Park along the curb.

Hiking directions: At the northeast corner of Autumn Ridge Drive and Westlake Boulevard, take the posted trail north. Pass an information kiosk and walk through the open, rolling hills on the Autumn Ridge Trail to a junction at a half mile at the base of

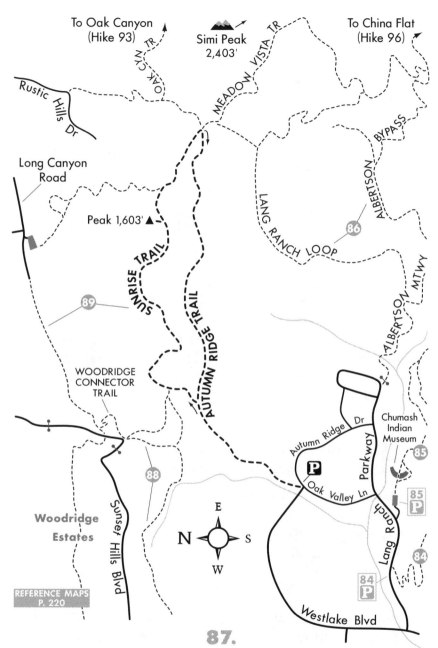

To Oak Canyon
(Hike 93)

Simi Peak
2,403'

To China Flat
(Hike 96)

OAK CYN TR

MEADOW VISTA TR

Rustic Hills Dr

BYPASS

Long Canyon
Road

ALBERTSON

Peak 1,603' ▲

LANG RANCH LOOP

86

SUNRISE TRAIL

ALBERTSON MTWY

89

AUTUMN RIDGE TRAIL

WOODRIDGE
CONNECTOR
TRAIL

Autumn Ridge Dr

Chumash
Indian
Museum

85

88

P

Parkway

Oak Valley Ln

85
P

Woodridge
Estates

Sunset Hills Blvd

E

Lang Ranch

84

N — S

W

84
P

REFERENCE MAPS
P. 220

Westlake Blvd

87.
Sunrise–Autumn Ridge Loop
LANG RANCH OPEN SPACE

multiple peaks. The right fork, the Autumn Ridge Trail, is our return route. (It is locally known as One Tree Trail, named for the single mature oak rising from the barren hillside.)

Begin the loop to the left, and head to a junction 0.1 mile ahead. The left fork connects with the Sunset Hills-Woodridge Loop (Hike 88). Veer right and wind up the south canyon wall, passing caves in the weather-sculpted sandstone formations. Climb the hillside to far-reaching vistas across Thousand Oaks. Top the slope and bend left, following a near-level grade east. The views stretch across Simi Valley and Tierra Rejada Valley to the Santa Susana Mountains. Loop around a knoll and walk uphill again. Top the second slope, skirting Peak 1,603. A short path on the left ascends the peak. Drop down to a posted junction with the Long Canyon Trail on the left. Continue straight, walking amidst the multi-colored rock formations to a 4-way junction. The left fork leads to Oak Canyon (Hike 93), and the middle fork leads to the Lang Ranch Loop (Hike 86). Take the sharp right fork on the Autumn Ridge Trail. Continue west on a long, meandering downward slope. At 2.3 miles, descend another 0.2 miles, completing the loop. Bear left and return a half mile to the trailhead. ▪

88. Sunset Hills—Woodridge Loop
WOODRIDGE ESTATES • SUNSET HILLS OPEN SPACE

Hiking distance: 2.7-mile loop
Hiking time: 1.5 hours
Elevation gain: 200 feet
Maps: U.S.G.S. Thousand Oaks
      Trails of the Simi Hills
      Lang Ranch/Woodridge Open Space map

Summary of hike: Sunset Hills Open Space covers 410 acres of undeveloped rolling hills in northeast Thousand Oaks. The open space is tucked between the Bard Reservoir, the 608-acre Woodridge Open Space, and Lang Ranch Open Space. The habitat is varied with oak woodlands, coastal sage scrub, non-

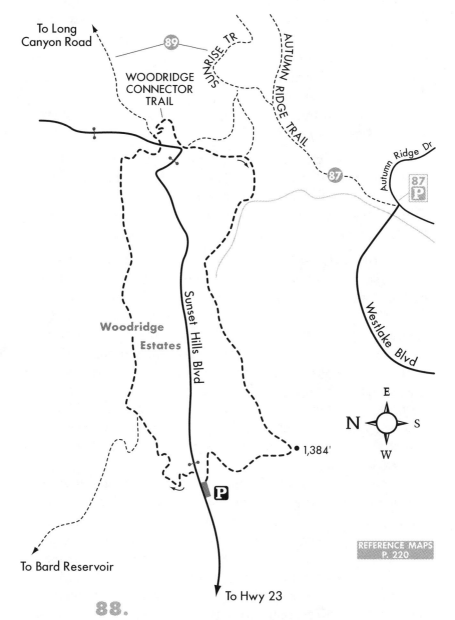

To Long Canyon Road

89

WOODRIDGE CONNECTOR TRAIL

SUNRISE TR

AUTUMN RIDGE TRAIL

Autumn Ridge Dr

87

87 P

Woodridge Estates

Sunset Hills Blvd

Westlake Blvd

E
N ✦ S
W

• 1,384'

P

REFERENCE MAPS
P. 220

To Bard Reservoir

To Hwy 23

88.
Sunset Hills—Woodridge Loop
WOODRIDGE ESTATES
SUNSET HILLS OPEN SPACE

native grasslands and weathered sandstone outcroppings. This hike weaves through the open space while circling Woodridge Estates, a gated community. The trail passes gorgeous sandstone outcroppings and includes views of the 231-acre Bard Reservoir, Simi Valley, Thousand Oaks, and the Tierra Rejada Valley. The loop connects with a myriad of trails in the Lang Ranch trail system and Wood Ranch Open Space.

Driving directions: THOUSAND OAKS. From the Ventura Freeway/Highway 101 in Thousand Oaks, take H-23 north 3.5 miles to the Sunset Hills Boulevard exit. Turn right and drive one mile to the trailhead parking lot on the right. It is located just before the gated entrance to the Woodridge Estates subdivision.

Hiking directions: The loop begins at the trailhead. The return can be seen at the southeast corner of the parking lot. To begin, cross Sunset Hills Boulevard and walk 50 yards to the right to the trailhead, located just before reaching the Woodridge Estates entrance gate. Bear left on the footpath, passing sandstone boulders. Views quickly open up across Thousand Oaks to Dawn's Peak (Hike 75) and the Santa Monica Mountains. Gently gain elevation through the coastal sage scrub as the serpentine path traverses the hillside. Follow the ridge east, overlooking Woodridge Estates. Cross the length of a saddle to views of Bard Reservoir, the Rancho Simi Open Space, Simi Valley, and the Tierra Rejada Valley.

At the east end of Woodridge Estates, descend into the canyon amidst tilted sandstone formations with small caves. Cross a utility road and ascend the south canyon wall to a junction. Stay to the right past three junctions that lead into the extensive Lang Ranch trail system. At the cement water channel, veer right on the narrow paved road, and skirt the edge of Woodridge Estates, parallel to a small stream. Cross a private road and continue on the dirt footpath. Crest the 1,384-foot hill and make a U-shaped right bend. Walk across the flat hilltop and descend to the trailhead parking lot. ■

89. Long Canyon—Sunrise Loop
WOOD RANCH OPEN SPACE

Hiking distance: 2.8-mile loop
Hiking time: 1.5 hours
Elevation gain: 450 feet
Maps: U.S.G.S. Thousand Oaks
Trails of the Simi Hills
Lang Ranch/Woodridge Open Space map

map
page 243

Summary of hike: Hundreds of acres of open space are located in the rolling hills and canyons between Thousand Oaks and Simi Valley. This hike makes a loop through the Wood Ranch, Rancho Simi, and Lang Ranch Open Spaces. The Long Canyon Trail climbs past beautiful sandstone outcroppings to a ridge with continuous vistas. The views overlook Simi Valley, Tierra Rejada Valley, the Santa Susana Mountains, and across Thousand Oaks to the Santa Monica Mountains. The Sunrise Trail continues along the ridge past additional naturally carved sandstone formations.

Driving directions: THOUSAND OAKS/HIGHWAY 23. From the Ventura Freeway/Highway 101 in Thousand Oaks, take Highway 23 north 4.5 miles to the Olsen Road exit. Turn right and drive 1.9 miles to Wood Ranch Parkway. Turn right and drive 1.9 miles to a T-junction at Long Canyon Road. Turn right and a quick left into the Wood Ranch trailhead parking lot.

SIMI VALLEY. From Highway 118/Ronald Reagan Freeway in Simi Valley, exit on Madera Road South. Drive 3 miles south to Wood Ranch Parkway. Turn left and drive 1.9 miles to a T-junction at Long Canyon Road. Turn right and a quick left into the Wood Ranch trailhead parking lot.

Hiking directions: From the far end of the parking lot, pass the trailhead kiosk and head up the slope. Climb the canyon's east slope to a fork by gorgeous sandstone formations. Stay left to overlooks of Simi Valley and the Bard Reservoir, built in 1965 to supply the cities of Camarillo, Moorpark, Oxnard, Simi Valley, and Thousand Oaks with water. Weave up the hillside, passing more weather-carved rock outcroppings as the views expand with every step. Steadily gain elevation to a posted T-junction with the Sunrise Trail at 0.7 miles. The left fork connects with the Autumn Ridge Trail (Hike 87) and the Lang Ranch Loop (Hike 86).

For this hike go to the right and follow the crest, passing sandstone formations with caves and enjoying the great vistas across Simi Valley and Tierra Rejada Valley. Weave down the hill to a junction at 1.6 miles. The left fork connects with Sunset Hills-Woodridge Loop (Hike 88). Take the right fork and loop to the right around the hill. Follow the contours of the hillside at a near-level grade to a paved utility road by Woodridge Estates, the gated community to the west. Veer right on the Woodridge Connector Trail, staying on the footpath. Gently descend to the east through the chaparral. Pass a few more sandstone outcrops, and skirt the back yards of homes in Wood Ranch to the west end of Long Canyon Road. Walk 125 yards along the road to the trailhead. ■

90. Canyon View Trail

Hiking distance: 3.1-mile loop
Hiking time: 1.5 hours
Elevation gain: 200 feet
Maps: U.S.G.S. Thousand Oaks
      Trails of the Simi Hills
      Rancho Simi Trail Blazers Canyon View Trail Map

map
page 245

Summary of hike: The Canyon View Trail follows a minor 1,200-foot ridge in the Simi Hills at the north end of the Wood Ranch Open Space. The trail climbs the brushy slope above the community of Wood Ranch. The undeveloped open area is covered with coastal sage scrub, chaparral, and tilted sandstone formations. The trail follows the grassy ridge, with vistas across Simi Valley and Wood Ranch to the Santa Susana Mountains.

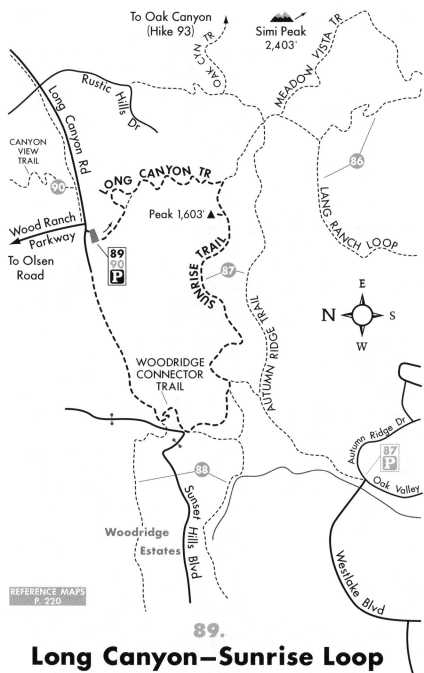

To Oak Canyon (Hike 93)

Simi Peak 2,403'

OAK CYN TR

MEADOW VISTA TR

Rustic Hills Dr

Long Canyon Rd

CANYON VIEW TRAIL

LONG CANYON TR

Peak 1,603' ▲

86

LANG RANCH LOOP

90

Wood Ranch Parkway

To Olsen Road

89
90
P

SUNRISE TRAIL

87

AUTUMN RIDGE TRAIL

N E S W

WOODRIDGE CONNECTOR TRAIL

Autumn Ridge Dr

87
P

Oak Valley

88

Woodridge Estates

Sunset Hills Blvd

Westlake Blvd

REFERENCE MAPS P. 220

89.
Long Canyon–Sunrise Loop
WOOD RANCH OPEN SPACE

Driving directions: THOUSAND OAKS. From the Ventura Free-way/Highway 101 in Thousand Oaks, take Highway 23 north 4.5 miles to the Olsen Road exit. Turn right and drive 1.9 miles to Wood Ranch Parkway. Turn right and drive 1.9 miles to a T-junction at Long Canyon Road. Turn right and a quick left into the Wood Ranch trailhead parking lot.

SIMI VALLEY. From Highway 118/Ronald Reagan Freeway in Simi Valley, exit on Madera Road South. Drive 3 miles south to Wood Ranch Parkway. Turn left and drive 1.9 miles to a T-junction at Long Canyon Road. Turn right and a quick left into the Wood Ranch trailhead parking lot.

Hiking directions: Return to the intersection of Long Canyon Road and Wood Ranch Parkway. Walk 175 yards east on Long Canyon Road to the trailhead on the left by the flashing yellow traffic light. Take the dirt path up the slope among picturesque sandstone outcroppings. Weave up the chaparral-clad hillside to views of the surrounding Simi Hills. At the ridge are great views of 231-acre Bard Reservoir (also referred to as Lake Bard) and Simi Valley to the Santa Susana Mountains. Follow the roll-ing ridge north along the long, sweeping dips and rises. Make a short but steep ascent to a junction at 0.8 miles. The Wood Ranch Trail goes left, descending to Humboldt Street and the trailhead at Coyote Hills Park (Hike 91).

For this hike, continue straight, staying on the undulating path with 360-degree vistas. At the east end of the ridge, high above Long Canyon Road/1st Street, leave the ridge and wind down the hill, reaching Long Canyon Road at 2 miles. Bear right and return 1.3 miles on the wide, landscaped sidewalk back to the trailhead. ▪

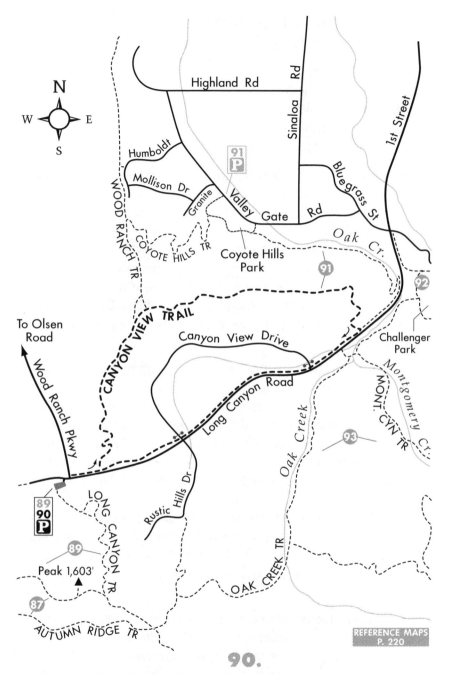

90.
Canyon View Trail

91. Coyote Hills—Wood Ranch Loop

275 Valley Gate Road · Simi Valley

Hiking distance: 3-mile loop
Hiking time: 1.5 hours
Elevation gain: 400 feet
Maps: U.S.G.S. Thousand Oaks
Trails of the Simi Hills

Summary of hike: Wood Ranch Open Space Park is located in the rolling hills and canyons adjacent to the community of Wood Ranch in Simi Valley. This hike begins at Coyote Hills Park on the north end of the open space. The trail winds up the north-facing slope through coastal sage scrub, chaparral, and pockets of oaks to a 1,200-foot ridge. From the ridge are great views across the Simi Hills, the Simi Valley to the Santa Susana Mountains, and southward to the Conejo Open Space and the Santa Monica Mountains. The return trail parallels Oak Creek through the riparian vegetation.

Driving directions: THOUSAND OAKS. From the Ventura Freeway/Highway 101 in Thousand Oaks, take Highway 23 north 4.5 miles to the Olsen Road exit. Turn right and drive 1.9 miles to Wood Ranch Parkway. Turn right and drive 1.9 miles to a T-junction at Long Canyon Road. Turn left and continue 1.7 miles to Bluegrass Street. Turn left and drive 0.1 miles to Valley Gate Road. Turn left and go a half mile to Coyote Hills Park on the left. Park along the curb.

SIMI VALLEY. From Highway 118/Ronald Reagan Freeway in Simi Valley, exit on 1st Street. Drive 2.7 miles south to Bluegrass Street. Turn right and drive 0.1 miles to Valley Gate Road. Turn left and go a half mile to Coyote Hills Park on the left. Park along the curb.

Hiking directions: Walk across grassy Coyote Hills Park to the base of the chaparral-covered hill and a bridle trail. Pass through an opening in the fence and follow the paved path 40 yards to where the asphalt ends. Continue on the natural path—the

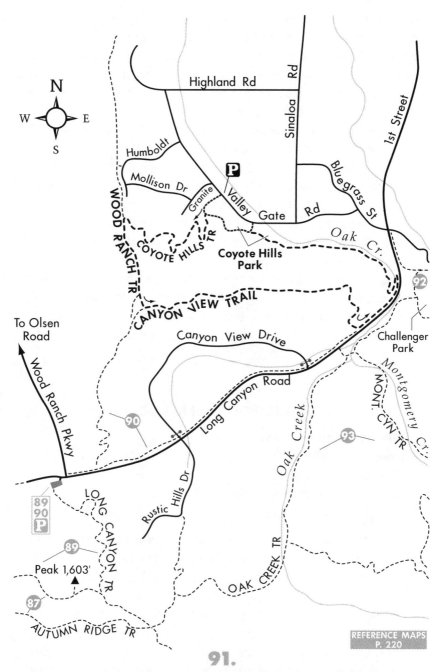

91.
Coyote Hills–Wood Ranch Loop

Coyote Hills Trail. Head up the hill at an easy grade on the long switchbacks. Weave in and out of a side canyon under a shady pocket of oak trees. Follow the contours of the hill to a T-junction with the Wood Ranch Trail at 0.7 miles. The right fork descends to the residential area at Humboldt Street off of Valley Gate Road. Go left and climb 0.4 miles, with two steep sections, to the ridge and a junction with the Canyon View Trail (Hike 90). The right fork leads to the Long Canyon Trailhead by the intersection of Long Canyon Road and Wood Ranch Parkway.

For this hike, bear left and follow the rolling ridge while enjoying the spectacular 360-degree vistas. At 1.7 miles, on the east end of the ridge, leave the ridge and wind down the hill to Long Canyon Road. Bear left on the bridle trail. Parallel Long Canyon Road for 0.3 miles to the traffic signal, just shy of Bluegrass Street. Before the signal, switchback to the left on the trail, and descend to the base of the hill. Curve right and follow the wide path between the mountain and the lush, vegetated corridor of Oak Creek. Continue a half mile, completing the loop at Coyote Hills Park. ▦

92. Challenger Park Loop

Hiking distance: 1.4 miles round trip
Hiking time: 45 minutes
Elevation gain: 250 feet
Maps: U.S.G.S. Thousand Oaks
　　　　Trails of the Simi Hills

Summary of hike: Challenger Park is a 208-acre community park in Simi Valley. The diverse park contains canyons with a year-round creek; shady oak, willow, and sycamore groves; and hillsides covered with coastal sage scrub chaparral. More than two miles of hiking trails weave through the park, exploring the various habitats. This short, easy hike forms a loop, passing through two riparian canyons and traversing open hillsides. The trail leads up to a ridge with great vistas of the surrounding terrain.

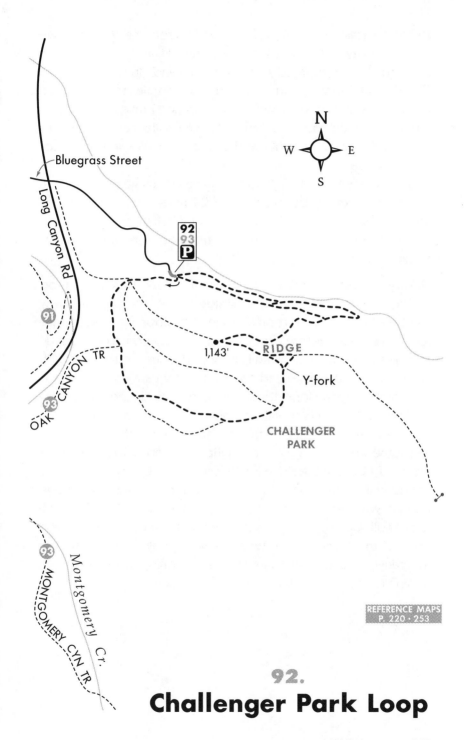

Bluegrass Street

Long Canyon Rd

92
93
P

91

OAK CANYON TR

93

RIDGE

1,143'

Y-fork

CHALLENGER PARK

N
W E
S

Montgomery Cr.

93

MONTGOMERY CYN TR

REFERENCE MAPS
P. 220 · 253

92.
Challenger Park Loop

Driving directions: THOUSAND OAKS. From the Ventura Freeway/Highway 101 in Thousand Oaks, take Highway 23 north 4.5 miles to the Olsen Road exit. Turn right and drive 1.9 miles to Wood Ranch Parkway. Turn right and drive 1.9 miles to a T-junction at Long Canyon Road. Turn left and continue 1.7 miles to Bluegrass Street. Turn right and go 0.3 miles on the Challenger Park road to the posted trailhead at the end of the road. Park in the spaces along the road.

SIMI VALLEY. From Highway 118/Ronald Reagan Freeway in Simi Valley, exit on 1st Street. Drive 2.7 miles south to Bluegrass Street. Turn left and go 0.3 miles on the Challenger Park road to the posted trailhead at the end of the road. Park in the spaces along the road.

Hiking directions: From the trailhead kiosk, begin the loop on the right fork. Head up the hillside to the ridge and a 5-way junction. Veer gently left on a downward slope into the stream-fed canyon. Just before dropping into the canyon, a path on the right leads to Oak Canyon (Hike 92). Continue on the left path, and drop into the oak-filled drainage to the canyon floor. Climb the south canyon slope to the rim and an unsigned junction at a half mile. Continue straight ahead on the left fork and slowly descend. Cross the canyon bottom and head up the slope again to another trail fork. Stay to the right and climb to the 1,100-foot ridge. Just before the ridge is a Y-fork, where both paths lead to the ridge. From the summit, bear left and follow the rolling ridge 0.1 mile west to a trail on the right, located just shy of a 1,143-foot knoll. Go right and descend a quarter mile to the canyon floor of the main canyon. Two near-level, parallel paths follow the canyon bottom through oaks, sycamores, and willows, returning to the trailhead. ▨

93. Montgomery Canyon—
Oak Canyon Loop

Hiking distance: 4.3-mile loop
Hiking time: 2 hours
Elevation gain: 600 feet
Maps: U.S.G.S. Thousand Oaks
Trails of the Simi Hills

map
page 253

Summary of hike: Montgomery Canyon and Oak Canyon sit on the east section of Wood Ranch Open Space in Simi Valley. Both scenic canyons are stream-fed drainages filled with majestic oaks. This hike begins in Challenger Park and climbs Montgomery Canyon to spectacular vistas from overlooks as high as 1,562 feet. The path weaves along the ridgeline of the Simi Hills, then descends back down through an oak canopy parallel to the creek in Oak Canyon. Connecting trails lead into the adjacent Lang Ranch Open Space and Woodridge Open Space.

Driving directions: THOUSAND OAKS. From the Ventura Freeway/Highway 101 in Thousand Oaks, take Highway 23 north 4.5 miles to the Olsen Road exit. Turn right and drive 1.9 miles to Wood Ranch Parkway. Turn right and drive 1.9 miles to a T-junction at Long Canyon Road. Turn left and continue 1.7 miles to Bluegrass Street. Turn right and go 0.3 miles on the Challenger Park road to the posted trailhead at the end of the road. Park in the spaces along the road.

SIMI VALLEY. From Highway 118/Ronald Reagan Freeway in Simi Valley, exit on 1st Street. Drive 2.7 miles south to Bluegrass Street. Turn left and go 0.3 miles on the Challenger Park road to the posted trailhead at the end of the road. Park in the spaces along the road.

Hiking directions: From the trailhead kiosk, bear right and head up the hillside to the ridge and a 5-way junction. Veer gently left on a downward slope, and curve left along the base of the knoll. Just before dropping into the canyon, take the path on the right, then curve left and cross the drainage. Head south down Oak Canyon, sheltered from Long Canyon Road by the dense riparian vegetation. At 0.7 miles, the streamside path reaches a junction at the mouth of Montgomery Canyon.

Begin the loop to the left on the Montgomery Canyon Trail. Follow the east wall of the oak-filled canyon, parallel to the seasonal stream. Cross over to the west side of the drainage, passing through an open, grassy flat. Skirt a grove of mature oaks on the left. Recross the waterway and continue up canyon. As you approach a mountain bowl, make a horseshoe right bend. Climb the west canyon wall to the ridge, where there are far-reaching views across Montgomery Canyon to Simi Valley and the Santa Susana Mountains. Switchback to the left and follow the ridge uphill, crossing the head of Montgomery Canyon at the high point of the trail at 2.1 miles, just below Peak 1,923. Loop to the right and descend back into Oak Canyon. Pass a couple of sandstone formations while steadily losing elevation to a junction on the canyon floor under the shade of oaks at 2.8 miles. The left fork climbs to the Lang Ranch Open Space (Hike 86 and 87). Bear right and continue down canyon through the oak forest, staying on the east side of the creek. Complete the loop at 3.6 miles. Return 0.7 miles to the trailhead at Challenger Park. ▩

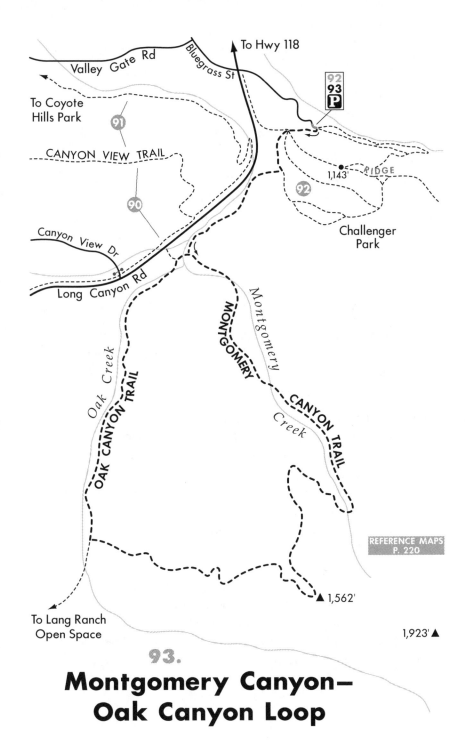

To Hwy 118

Valley Gate Rd

Bluegrass St

92
93
P

To Coyote
Hills Park

91

CANYON VIEW TRAIL

90

RIDGE

1,143'

92

Challenger
Park

Canyon View Dr

Long Canyon Rd

Oak Creek

OAK CANYON TRAIL

MONTGOMERY

Montgomery

MONTGOMERY

CANYON TRAIL

Creek

REFERENCE MAPS
P. 220

To Lang Ranch
Open Space

▲ 1,562'

1,923' ▲

93.

Montgomery Canyon–
Oak Canyon Loop

94. Oak Canyon Community Park

Hiking distance: 1.6 miles round trip
Hiking time: 45 minutes
Elevation gain: 100 feet
Maps: U.S.G.S. Thousand Oaks

Summary of hike: Oak Canyon Community Park is a beautiful 60-acre park with sandstone cliffs, a year-round creek, and a pond. Medea Creek flows through the length of the park from the south slope of Simi Peak in the Simi Hills. The creek descends from the Conejo Ridge and flows all year, eventually merging with Malibu Creek on its journey to the sea. A nature trail loops through an oak and willow forest with several crossings over Medea Creek. Near the trailhead is a beautiful man-made waterfall cascading into the pond. Walking paths circle the pond.

Driving directions: AGOURA HILLS. From the Ventura Freeway/Highway 101 in Agoura Hills, exit on Kanan Road. Head north 3 miles to Hollytree Drive and turn right. Turn left 70 yards ahead into the Oak Canyon Community Park parking lot.

Hiking directions: From the parking lot, take the paved walking path north past the restrooms, playground, and covered picnic area. Follow the curving bike/pedestrian path up canyon on the east side of Medea Creek and the park road. Various side trails lead down into the oak tree canopy to the willow-lined creek. The trail reaches nature trail station #8 at 0.4 miles. Take the footpath to the left, which leads into the forest to Medea Creek. The Medea Creek Trail begins down the canyon and crosses the creek three times. After the third crossing, by station #15, is a junction. The right fork is a quarter-mile side trip through chaparral to an archery range at the back of a small canyon. The left fork leads back to the pond and the trailhead. Several paths cross the creek to the parking lot, or you may circle around the pond and view the falls. ■

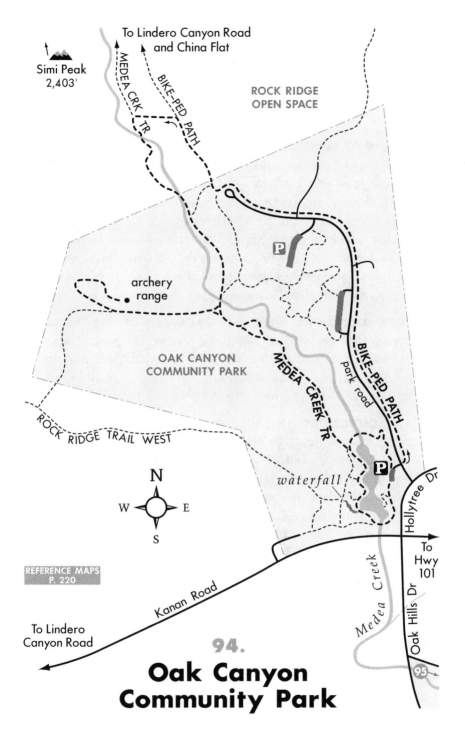

Simi Peak
2,403'

To Lindero Canyon Road
and China Flat

ROCK RIDGE
OPEN SPACE

MEDEA CRK TR

BIKE-PED PATH

archery
range

OAK CANYON
COMMUNITY PARK

MEDEA CREEK TR

BIKE-PED PATH

park road

ROCK RIDGE TRAIL WEST

N
W   E
S

waterfall

Hollytree Dr

REFERENCE MAPS
P. 220

Kanan Road

To Lindero
Canyon Road

Medea Creek

Oak Hills Dr

To
Hwy
101

95

94.
**Oak Canyon
Community Park**

95. Medea Creek Park

Hiking distance: 1.8 miles round trip
Hiking time: 1 hour
Elevation gain: Level
Maps: U.S.G.S. Thousand Oaks

Summary of hike: The Medea Creek Trail winds through Medea Creek Park, an oak-shaded suburban greenbelt in Oak Park. The long and narrow wetland winds through residential neighborhoods, creating a wildlife habitat and urban wilderness. Medea Creek forms on the south flank of Simi Peak in the Simi Hills. The creek descends from Conejo Ridge and flows year-round through Oak Canyon Community Park (Hike 94), Oak Park, Agoura Hills, and into the Santa Monica Mountains, merging with Malibu Creek at Malibu Lake.

Driving directions: WESTLAKE VILLAGE. From the Ventura Freeway/Highway 101 in Westlake Village, exit on Lindero Canyon Road, and drive 2.9 miles north to Kanan Road. Turn right and drive 1.2 miles to Oak Hills Drive. Turn right and continue 0.2 miles to Calle Rio Vista. Turn left and park in the cul-de-sac.

Hiking directions: Take the paved path southeast 40 yards, skirting the ball fields to a side path on the right. Both paths parallel the stream, but the right fork is a natural path that drops down to the creek, shaded with oaks and willows. Follow the creek downstream, rejoining the paved path. Cross Medea Creek Lane to a T-junction, 90 yards north of Oak Hills Drive. The left fork returns to Kanan Road.

Go to the right and cross Oak Hills Drive, just west of Park View Drive. Follow the watercourse. A footpath stays close to the creek bank, paralleling the paved path. Cross the cement spillway over Medea Creek, and walk through the creekside tunnel under Conifer Street. Cross a long footbridge over Medea Creek to the cul-de-sac on East Tamarind Street at the Los Angeles-Ventura county line. From the cul-de-sac, loop back along the east bank of the creek. It is easy to switch from the paved trail to the dirt footpaths and from one side of the creek to the other. Create your own route to return. ■

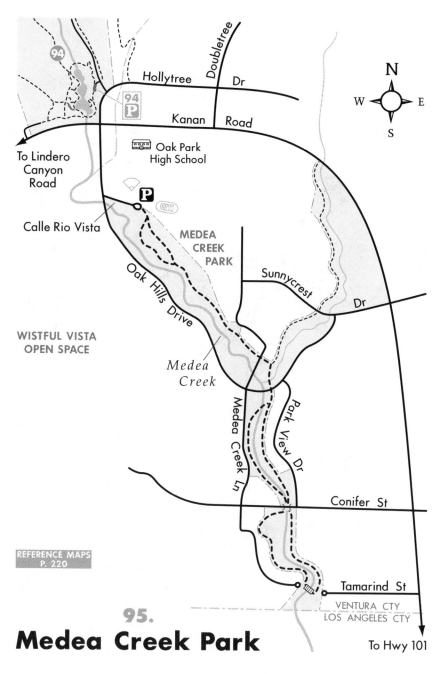

95.
Medea Creek Park

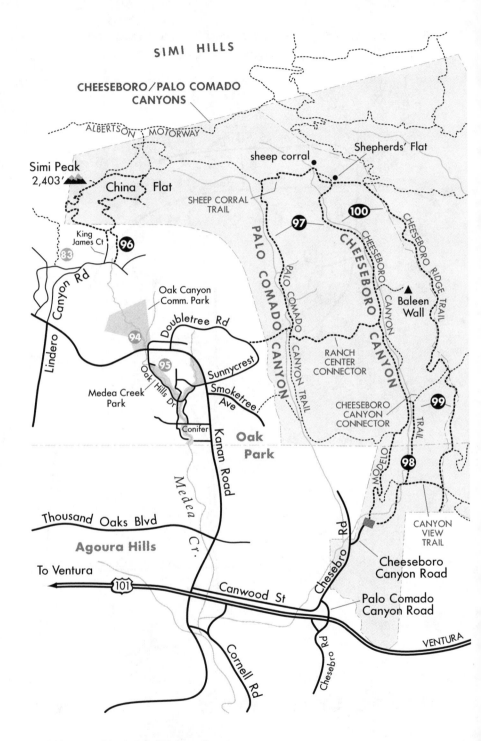

SIMI HILLS

CHEESEBORO/PALO COMADO
CANYONS

ALBERTSON MOTORWAY

Simi Peak
2,403'

China Flat

sheep corral

Shepherds' Flat

SHEEP CORRAL
TRAIL

97

100

King
James Ct

96

83

Oak Canyon
Comm. Park

Lindero Canyon Rd

Doubletree Rd

94

95

Oak Hills Dr

Sunnycrest

Medea Creek
Park

Smoketree
Ave

Conifer

Kanan Road

Oak
Park

PALO COMADO CANYON

CHEESEBORO CANYON

Cheeseboro Canyon

Cheeseboro Ridge Trail

Baleen
Wall

RANCH
CENTER
CONNECTOR

CHEESEBORO
CANYON
CONNECTOR

99

MODELO TRAIL

98

Medea Cr.

Thousand Oaks Blvd

Agoura Hills

To Ventura

101

Canwood St

Cornell Rd

Chesebro Rd

Chesebro Rd

CANYON
VIEW
TRAIL

Cheeseboro
Canyon Road

Palo Comado
Canyon Road

VENTURA

Simi Hills:
Cheeseboro/Palo Comado Canyons
Upper Las Virgenes Canyon

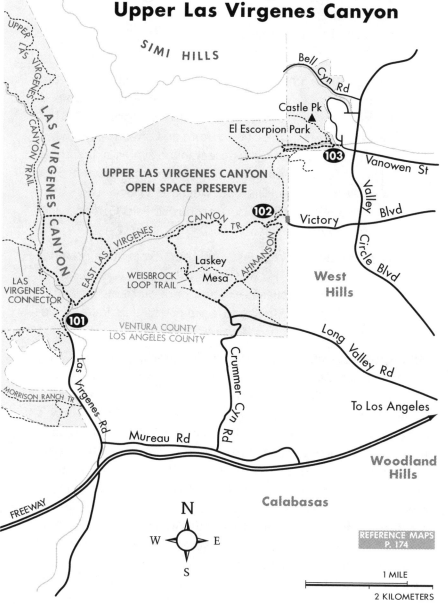

96. China Flat Trail
CHEESEBORO/PALO COMADO CANYONS

Hiking distance: 4-mile loop
Hiking time: 2 hours
Elevation gain: 1,000 feet
Maps: U.S.G.S. Thousand Oaks
      N.P.S. Cheeseboro/Palo Comado Canyons

Summary of hike: China Flat, a newer addition to the Cheeseboro/Palo Comado Canyons site, is a high, oak-dotted grassland meadow with sedimentary rock outcroppings. The flat is perched on the west side of Palo Comado Canyon beneath the shadows of Simi Peak, the highest peak in the Simi Hills. The China Flat Trail is a steep hike with awesome, panoramic views of Simi Valley, Oak Park, Agoura Hills, and Westlake Village. Connector trails link China Flat to the upper reaches of Palo Comado and Cheeseboro Canyons (Hikes 97—100).

Driving directions: WESTLAKE VILLAGE. From the Ventura Freeway/Highway 101 in Westlake Village, exit on Lindero Canyon Road. Drive 4 miles north and park on Lindero Canyon Road by the China Flat Trailhead on the left. It is located between King James Court and Wembly Avenue.

Hiking directions: Hike north past the trailhead sign towards the mountains. Climb the short, steep hill to where a trail from King James Court merges with the main trail. Continue around the east side of a large sandstone outcropping. The trail levels out and heads east, following the contour of the mountain base, to an unsigned junction. Take the left fork north, heading uphill towards the ridge. Once over the ridge, the trail meets another unsigned junction. Take the left fork and head west, with views overlooking the canyon. Proceed uphill along the ridgeline to a flat area and trail junction. The right fork leads back towards Palo Comado and Cheeseboro Canyons. Take the left fork and descend to another junction. Again, take the left fork, winding downhill to a gate at King James Court. Leave the trail and walk one block on the sidewalk to Lindero Canyon Road. The trail-head is on the left. ■

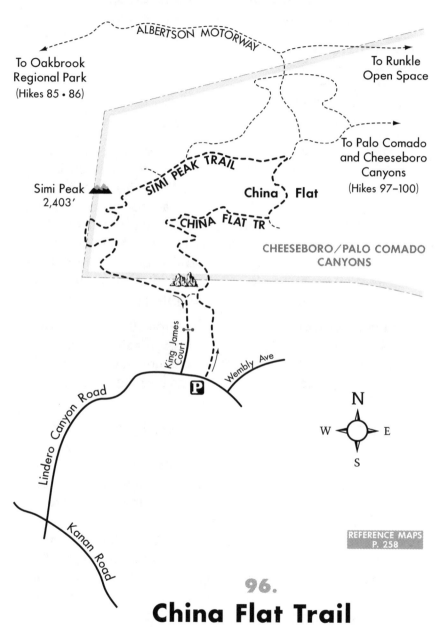

To Oakbrook
Regional Park
(Hikes 85 • 86)

ALBERTSON MOTORWAY

To Runkle
Open Space

To Palo Comado
and Cheeseboro
Canyons
(Hikes 97–100)

SIMI PEAK TRAIL

China Flat

Simi Peak
2,403'

CHINA FLAT TR

CHEESEBORO/PALO COMADO
CANYONS

King James Court

Wembly Ave

P

Lindero Canyon Road

Kanan Road

N

W ◯ E

S

REFERENCE MAPS
P. 258

96.

China Flat Trail
CHEESEBORO/PALO COMADO CANYONS

97. Palo Comado –
Cheeseboro Canyons Loop
CHEESEBORO/PALO COMADO CANYONS

Hiking distance: 5-mile loop
Hiking time: 2.5 hours
Elevation gain: 800 feet
Maps: U.S.G.S. Thousand Oaks and Calabasas
N.P.S. Cheeseboro/Palo Comado Canyons

Summary of hike: Palo Comado and Cheeseboro Canyons, in the Simi Hills near Agoura Hills, is a wildlife corridor connecting the Santa Monica Mountains with the Santa Susana Mountains. This north-south corridor allows animals to move between the two ranges. This loop hike heads up the undeveloped Palo Comado Canyon parallel to a stream and adjacent meadows. After crossing over into Cheeseboro Canyon, the hike follows the canyon floor on an old ranch road through grasslands with groves of stately valley oaks and twisted coast live oaks.

Driving directions: AGOURA HILLS. From the Ventura Freeway/Highway 101 in Agoura Hills, exit on Kanan Road. Head north 2.2 miles to Sunnycrest Drive and turn right. Continue 0.8 miles to the "Public Open Space" sign on the right. Park along the curb.

Hiking directions: From the trailhead, hike east past the gate and up a short hill on the Sunnycrest Connector Trail. As you top the hill, the trail descends into Palo Comado Canyon. Cross the stream at the canyon floor to a junction with the Palo Comado Canyon Trail, an old ranch road. Head left up the canyon through rolling grasslands with sycamore and oak groves. At one mile the trail begins to climb out of the canyon, winding along the contours of the mountain. Near the head of the canyon, the Palo Comado Canyon Trail curves left, heading to China Flat (Hike 96). There is an unmarked but distinct path leading sharply to the right at the beginning of this curve—the Old Sheep Corral Trail. Take this path uphill to a couple of ridges that overlook Cheeseboro

Canyon. Descend into the canyon a short distance to the corral and a junction at Shepherds' Flat. Straight ahead the trail climbs up to Cheeseboro Ridge. Take the right fork and follow Cheeseboro Canyon gently downhill. At Sulphur Springs, identified by its smell, walk beneath the white sedimentary cliffs of the Baleen Wall on the east canyon wall. Continue down canyon through oak groves to the posted Ranch Center Connector Trail, 1.3 miles down the canyon on the right. Bear right and wind 1.1 mile up and over the chaparral hillside from Cheeseboro Canyon back to Palo Comado Canyon. Bear right a short distance, completing the loop. Return to the left on the Sunnycrest Connector Trail. ■

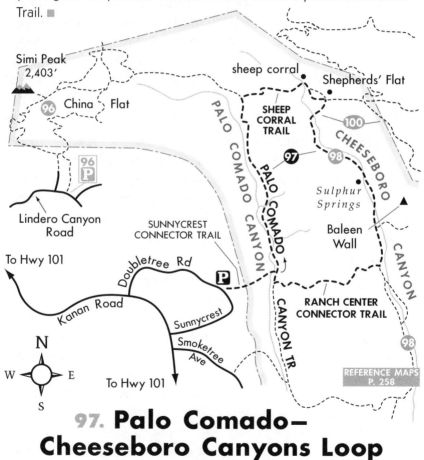

97. **Palo Comado–**
Cheeseboro Canyons Loop
CHEESEBORO/PALO COMADO CANYONS

98. Cheeseboro Canyon to Shepherds' Flat
CHEESEBORO/PALO COMADO CANYONS

Hiking distance: 8.6 miles round trip
Hiking time: 4 hours
Elevation gain: 600 feet
Maps: U.S.G.S. Calabasas
       N.P.S. Cheeseboro/Palo Comado Canyons

Summary of hike: Cheeseboro Canyon is a lush stream-fed canyon with large valley oaks, gnarled coast live oaks, and sycamores in the Cheeseboro/Palo Comado Canyons site. The hike follows an old abandoned ranch road on a gentle grade up the forested canyon floor, traveling from the south end of the park to the north. The trail passes fragrant Sulphur Springs as you pass beneath the Baleen Wall, a vertical rock formation on the east canyon wall. At the upper reaches of the canyon is Shepherds' Flat, a grassland flat and a sheep corral.

Driving directions: AGOURA HILLS. From the Ventura Freeway/Highway 101 in Agoura Hills, exit on Chesebro Road. Continue straight one block, past the stop sign, to Palo Comado Canyon Road and turn left. Drive 0.3 miles to Chesebro Road again and turn right. Continue 0.7 miles to Cheeseboro Canyon Road and turn right. The trailhead parking lot is 0.2 miles ahead.

Hiking directions: Take the service road east toward Cheeseboro Canyon to a road split. Bear left on the Cheeseboro Canyon Trail, heading into the canyon past the Modelo Trail and the Canyon View Trail. At 1.3 miles is a junction with the Cheeseboro Ridge Connector Trail (also known as the Baleen Wall Trail). Take the left fork towards Sulphur Springs to another junction with the Modelo Trail on the left. Proceed a short distance on the main trail to a junction. Take the left branch. As you near Sulphur Springs, the white, jagged cliffs of the Baleen Wall can be seen towering on the cliffs to the east. At 3.5 miles, the canyon and trail both narrow as the smell of sulphur becomes stronger. At the head of the canyon is a three-way junction at

Shepherds' Flat, the turn-around point.

To return, retrace your steps back on the Cheeseboro Canyon Trail to the Modelo Trail junction. Take the Modelo Trail along the western ridge of the canyon back to the trailhead. ■

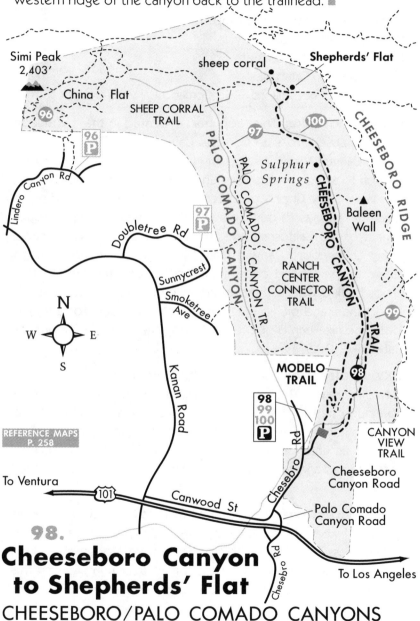

98.
Cheeseboro Canyon
to Shepherds' Flat
CHEESEBORO/PALO COMADO CANYONS

99. Canyon View—
Cheeseboro Canyon Loop
CHEESEBORO/PALO COMADO CANYONS

Hiking distance: 4-mile loop
Hiking time: 2 hours
Elevation gain: 500 feet
Maps: U.S.G.S. Calabasas
N.P.S. Cheeseboro/Palo Comado Canyons

Summary of hike: This loop trail is located in the lower end of the Cheeseboro/Palo Comado Canyons site. The hike begins on the Canyon View Trail, climbing the east wall of Cheeseboro Canyon to a knoll overlooking Cheeseboro Canyon and the Lost Hills landfill. The Cheeseboro Canyon Trail is an abandoned ranch road that passes through groves of 200-year-old valley oaks, largest of the California oaks. The hike follows the ridge separating Cheeseboro Canyon from Las Virgenes Canyon through native chaparral and coastal sage scrub communities. It then drops back down to the shaded valley oak savannahs, live oak woodlands, and picnic areas on the canyon floor. For a longer loop, the hike can be continued along the ridge to Shepherds' Flat—Hike 100.

Driving directions: AGOURA HILLS. From the Ventura Freeway/Highway 101 in Agoura Hills, exit on Chesebro Road. Continue one block straight ahead, past the stop sign, to Palo Comado Canyon Road and turn left. Drive 0.3 miles to Chesebro Road again and turn right. Continue 0.7 miles to Cheeseboro Canyon Road and turn right. The trailhead parking lot is 0.2 miles ahead.

Hiking directions: Take the well-marked Cheeseboro Canyon Trail, and hike through the rolling hills filled with groves of stately oaks. Pass the Modelo Trail on the left to a posted junction with the Canyon View Trail at a half mile. Bear right, leaving the canyon floor, and climb the grassy canyon hillside. At 0.9 miles,

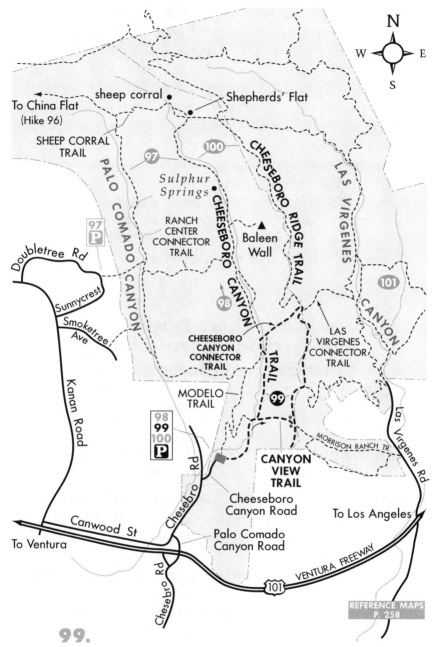

99.
Canyon View—Cheeseboro Canyon Loop
CHEESEBORO/PALO COMADO CANYONS

the Canyon View Trail ends at a T-junction and a trail gate on Cheeseboro Ridge. Pass through the gate. The right fork leads 0.3 miles to an overlook of the canyon. Bear left (north) on the Cheeseboro Ridge Trail. Follow the ridge uphill to a Y-fork, enjoying the great canyon views. Stay left on the undulating ridge, passing power poles. Slowly descend to the Las Virgenes Connector Trail on the right. Stay left 120 yards to the Cheeseboro Canyon Connector Trail on the left. The Cheeseboro Ridge Trail—Hike 100—continues straight ahead along the ridge to Shepherds' Flat. Bear left and descend 0.7 miles down the grassy, sage-covered hillside to the canyon floor and a picnic area. Bear left on the Cheeseboro Canyon Trail, an old ranch road, and stroll through the oak groves, completing the loop at the Canyon View Trail junction. Return down canyon to the trailhead. ◼

100. Cheeseboro Ridge— Cheeseboro Canyon Loop
CHEESEBORO/PALO COMADO CANYONS

Hiking distance: 10-mile loop
Hiking time: 5 hours
Elevation gain: 900 feet
Maps: U.S.G.S. Calabasas
      N.P.S. Cheeseboro/Palo Comado Canyons

Summary of hike: This canyon-to-ridge loop explores a large tract of the Cheeseboro/Palo Comado Canyons site. The Cheeseboro Ridge Trail follows the ridge separating Cheeseboro Canyon and Las Virgenes Canyon in the Simi Hills above Agoura. From the ridge are bird's-eye views into both canyons that extend to the Santa Monica Mountains and across the San Fernando Valley. The hike returns through the shaded oak savannah, following a stream through Cheeseboro Canyon.

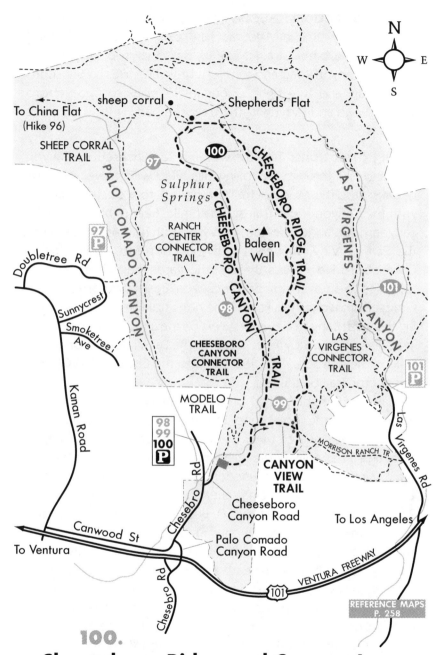

100.
Cheeseboro Ridge and Canyon Loop
CHEESEBORO/PALO COMADO CANYONS

Driving directions: AGOURA HILLS. From the Ventura Free-way/Highway 101 in Agoura Hills, exit on Chesebro Road. Continue one block straight ahead, past the stop sign, to Palo Comado Canyon Road and turn left. Drive 0.3 miles to Chesebro Road again and turn right. Continue 0.7 miles to Cheeseboro Canyon Road and turn right. The trailhead parking lot is 0.2 miles ahead.

Hiking directions: Take the well-marked Cheeseboro Canyon Trail, and hike through the rolling hills filled with groves of state-ly oaks. Pass the Modelo Trail on the left to a posted junction with the Canyon View Trail at a half mile. Bear right, leaving the canyon floor, and climb the grassy canyon hillside. At 0.9 miles, the Canyon View Trail ends at a T-junction and a trail gate on Cheeseboro Ridge. Pass through the gate. The right fork leads 0.3 miles to an overlook of the canyon. Bear left (north) on the Cheeseboro Ridge Trail. Follow the ridge uphill to a Y-fork, enjoy-ing the great canyon views. Stay left on the undulating ridge, pass-ing power poles. Slowly descend to the Las Virgenes Connector Trail on the right. Stay left 120 yards to the Cheeseboro Canyon Connector Trail on the left.

Stay to the right (north) on the old ranch road to begin the upper end of the loop. Wind up the ridge and skirt around the right side of a water tank. Gradually descend to the canyon floor and a trail split. Curve left and head west along the base of the mountain to a signed junction at Shepherds' Flat. The Sheep Corral Trail continues straight ahead to China Flat (Hike 96) and Palo Comado Canyon (Hike 97). Bear left on the Cheeseboro Canyon Trail (also called Sulphur Springs Trail), and follow the canyon floor steadily downhill. At Sulphur Springs, easily identi-fied by its smell, walk beneath the white sedimentary cliffs of the Baleen Wall on the east canyon wall. Continue down canyon through oak groves and past shaded picnic areas. Pass the Ranch Center Connector Trail and the Palo Comado Connector Trail on the right, completing the loop at the Canyon View Trail junction. Return down canyon to the trailhead. ▪

101. Upper Las Virgenes Canyon Open Space Preserve

from the Las Virgenes Trailhead

Hiking distance: 3.3-mile loop
Hiking time: 2 hours
Elevation gain: 400 feet
Maps: U.S.G.S. Calabasas
Trails of the Simi Hills map
Upper Las Virgenes Canyon Open Space Preserve map

map
page 273

Summary of hike: The Upper Las Virgenes Canyon Open Space Preserve (formerly the Ahmanson Ranch) is a sprawling, unspoiled landscape in the Simi Hills that straddles the Los Angeles—Ventura county line. Dirt ranch roads lace through the rolling grasslands and oak-studded hills of the 2,983-acre park. The bucolic open space contains nine miles of seasonal streams that form the headwaters of Malibu Creek. The streams flow through the ranch land en route to Malibu Lagoon in the Santa Monica Bay, one of the last remaining coastal wetlands in the county. The diverse land boasts shady streamside riparian habitat, walnut woodlands, valley oak savannah, coastal sage scrub, and native perennial grasslands. The elevations range from 870 feet to 1,840 feet.

This hike begins at the northern end of Las Virgenes Road in Calabasas. The loop hike begins by following a creekbed through a gorgeous oak woodland, then gently winds through rolling grasslands with great vistas. En route, the trail crosses a saddle and drops into a lush, forested canyon. The trail connects with the adjacent loop to the east—Hike 102.

Driving directions: CALABASAS. From the Ventura Freeway/ Highway 101 in Calabasas, exit on Las Virgenes Road. Drive 1.5 miles north to the posted trailhead at the end of the road. Park along the curb.

Hiking directions: Walk through the trailhead gate at the end of the road. Follow the west edge of seasonal Las Virgenes Creek 0.3 miles to a T-junction. Begin the loop to the right on the East Las Virgenes Canyon Trail. Gently wind up the open rolling hills through vast grasslands with distant views up the wide canyon. At a half mile, a short side path drops down to the stream in a pocket of stately oaks. The main trail continues north to a distinct junction by a wooden post. The East Las Virgenes Canyon Trail continues straight ahead to Laskey Mesa and the Victory Trailhead (Hike 102).

Veer left on the two-track trail. Head up the side canyon, and curve around a hill to an 1,100-foot saddle. Drop down into the next drainage to the west to a posted junction at the base of the steep hill. Bear left and cross the canyon bottom to a second saddle with more great vistas of the surrounding hills. Descend to a posted T-junction with the Upper Las Virgenes Canyon Trail. The right fork leads up canyon to Bell Canyon, Runkle Canyon, and to upper Cheeseboro/Palo Comado Canyons.

Bear left and walk gently down canyon among stately stands of oaks. Cross Las Virgenes Creek to a fork with the Las Virgenes Connector Trail, leading one mile to the Cheeseboro Canyon floor (Hikes 98—100). Continue following the canyon floor on the Las Virgenes Canyon Trail, completing the loop at 3 miles. (Along this section, an unsigned one-mile footpath curves up and over the hill, returning to the main trail 40 feet shy of the trailhead.) After completing the loop, return 0.3 miles to the right. ■

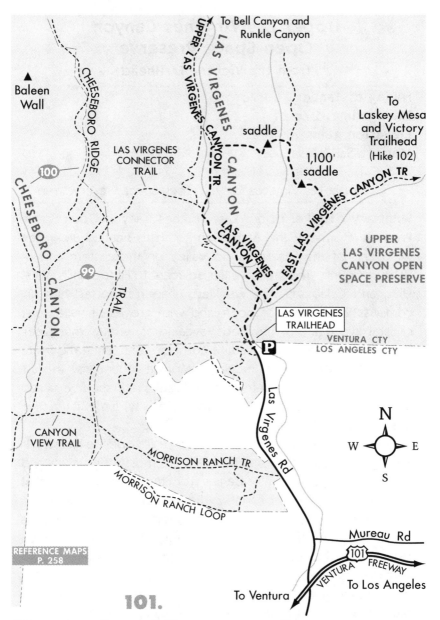

101.
Upper Las Virgenes Canyon
Open Space Preserve
Las Virgenes Trailhead

102. Upper Las Virgenes Canyon Open Space Preserve
from the Victory Trailhead

Hiking distance: 3.6-mile loop
Hiking time: 2 hours
Elevation gain: 400 feet
Maps: U.S.G.S. Calabasas
Trails of the Simi Hills map
Upper Las Virgenes Canyon Open Space Preserve map

Summary of hike: Upper Las Virgenes Canyon Open Space Preserve (formerly the Ahmanson Ranch) is nestled along the west end of the San Fernando Valley on the eastern end of Ventura County. The preserve lies adjacent to Hidden Hills, West Hills, and Calabasas. The wrinkled, chaparral-dotted hills encompass 2,983 acres of open land with groves of valley oak, coastal live oak, cottonwoods, sycamores, and walnut trees. The area is an important wildlife corridor connecting the Santa Susana Mountains with the Santa Monica Mountains. The unspoiled ranchland within the Malibu Creek watershed was used as a backdrop for such classic films as *Gone With the Wind*, *Duel In the Sun*, and *The Charge of the Light Brigade*.

There are more than 15 miles of hiking trails open to hikers, bikers, equestrians, and dogs. The trails are mostly fire roads and some single track. This hike begins from the Victory Trailhead at the western terminus of Victory Boulevard in West Hills in the San Fernando Valley. The hike forms a loop along three trails: Las Virgenes Canyon Trail, Laskey Mesa Trail, and Ahmanson Ranch House Trail. The scenic route crosses gently rolling hills dotted with majestic oaks and circles Laskey Mesa, a broad plateau on the southern portion of the park. From Laskey Mesa are far-reaching vistas of the San Fernando Valley and the Simi Hills.

Driving directions: WOODLAND HILLS. From the Ventura Freeway/Highway 101 in Woodland Hills, exit on Mullholland Drive/Valley Circle Boulevard. Drive 2.2 miles north on Valley Circle Boulevard to Victory Boulevard. Turn left and drive 0.6 miles to

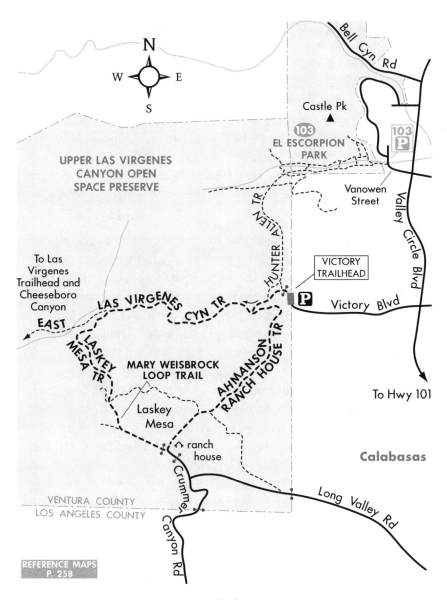

102.
Upper Las Virgenes Canyon Open Space Preserve
Victory Trailhead

the gated entrance. For free parking, park outside the gate on Victory Boulevard. For the pay parking lot, drive 150 yards past the gate to the lot.

From Highway 118/Ronald Reagan Freeway in Chatsworth, exit on Topanga Canyon Boulevard. Drive 2.5 miles south to Plummer Street. Turn right and continue 6.3 miles to Victory Boulevard. (En route, Plummer Street becomes Valley Circle Boulevard.) Turn right on Victory Boulevard and drive 0.6 miles to the gated entrance. For free parking, park outside the gate on Victory Boulevard. For the pay parking lot, drive 150 yards past the gate to the lot.

Hiking directions: Walk past the entrance gates into the pay parking lot to the trailhead. Pass through the trailhead gate to an immediate junction. To the right, the Hunter Allen Trail heads north one mile to El Escorpio Park (Hike 103). Go straight on the East Las Virgenes Canyon Trail. Gently descend into the open canyon to a U-bend and junction with the Ahmanson Ranch House Trail, our return route.

Begin the loop to the right, and continue on a long, gently winding downward slope. Curve right and make an S-shaped bend with minor dips and rises. Continue through the open, oak-dotted hillsides to a junction at 1.1 mile. The right fork, straight ahead, leads to the Las Virgenes Trailhead (Hike 101) and Cheeseboro Canyon (Hikes 97-100). For this hike, bear left on the Laskey Mesa Trail and steadily loose elevation. At 1.4 miles, ascend the slope and pass under a couple of old growth oaks. Make a sweeping U-shaped bend to a junction with the Mary Weisbrock Loop Trail. Both the Laskey Mesa Trail and the Mary Weisbrock Loop circle Laskey Mesa, a large flat grassland.

For this route, take the right fork (the longer route), and cross the south side of Laskey Mesa. Bear left on the old ranch road and skirt the east side of the mesa to water tanks and a vehicle gate at 2.3 miles. The right fork, straight ahead, passes the ranch buildings and leads out of the park, heading down Crummer Canyon on a paved road. Bear left on the signed Mary Weisbrock Loop Trail, and follow the east side of the mesa 0.3 miles to the east corner of the loop, where the two route options rejoin. Continue straight while overlooking the rolling hilly terrain, and stay left at a Y-fork 60 yards ahead. Curve left to a view of the trailhead and descend to a junction, completing the loop. Return to the trailhead on the right. ▪

103. El Escorpion Park

Hiking distance: 2 miles round trip
Hiking time: 1 hour
Elevation gain: 150 feet
Maps: U.S.G.S. Calabasas
       Trails of the Simi Hills map

map
page 279

Summary of hike: El Escorpio Park (also known as Castle Peak Park) is located in the West Hills of the San Fernando Valley. The small park sits in the Simi Hills adjacent to the expansive 2,900-acre Upper Las Virgenes Canyon Open Space Preserve. The three-acre park is open to hikers, bikers, equestrians, and dogs. It has two main trails that run the length of the park along El Escorpion Creek, with a network of connecting trails that leave the park. To the north, a path leads to caves on the hillside canyon wall. Also to the north, a rough, dangerously steep path ascends the south slope of Castle Peak, the prominent rocky mountain towering over the landscape. (The trail gains 1,000 feet in a short distance.) To the south, the El Escorpion Trail connects with the Upper Las Virgenes Canyon Open Space Preserve (Hike 102). A third trail heads west, connecting with the Las Virgenes Trailhead (Hike 101) and Cheeseboro Canyon (Hikes 97–100).

Driving directions: WOODLAND HILLS. From the Ventura Freeway/Highway 101 in Woodland Hills, exit on Mullholland Drive/Valley Circle Boulevard. Drive 3 miles north on Valley Circle Boulevard to Vanowen Street. Turn left and drive one block to the trailhead on the left, located as the road curves right onto Sunset Ridge Court. Park along the curb.

From Highway 118/Ronald Reagan Freeway in Chatsworth, exit on Topanga Canyon Boulevard. Drive 2.5 miles south to Plummer

Street. Turn right and continue 5.5 miles to Vanowen Street. (En route, Plummer Street becomes Valley Circle Boulevard.) Turn right on Vanowen Street, and drive one block to the trailhead on the left, located as the road curves right onto Sunset Ridge Court. Park along the curb.

Hiking directions: Walk through the trailhead gate and curve right. Follow the old dirt road west along the base of the oak-studded hillside to a Y-fork. Begin the loop to the right beneath jagged Castle Peak. Cross the seasonal El Escorpion Creek drainage and veer left, continuing up canyon. A couple of side paths on the right ascend Castle Peak. Connector paths on the left recross the drainage and join the parallel return path to the south. Meander through a mixed forest with palms, oaks, chaparral, and riparian vegetation. At the trail's west end is an open fence that separates the city portion of the park from the Santa Monica Conservancy land. Pass through the fence to a junction. The right fork leads up a side canyon a quarter mile to the base of weather-carved sandstone formations pocketed with caves. This route invites exploration.

Back at the drainage floor, the left (south) fork, leads 100 yards to another junction. The Hunter Allen Trail heads west and curves south, leading one mile to the Upper Las Virgenes Canyon Open Space Preserve at the Victory Trailhead (Hike 102). A short distance past this junction, a path veers right and heads west, winding through the oak-dotted rolling hills and sycamore-lined canyons to Cheeseboro Canyon (Hikes 97–100) and the Las Virgenes Trailhead (Hike 101). To return, head back down canyon on the south canyon wall, completing the loop near the trailhead. ▨

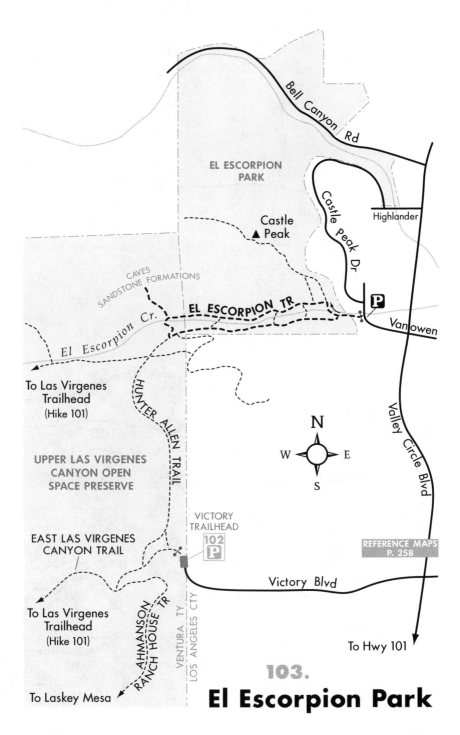

EL ESCORPION
PARK

Bell Canyon Rd

Castle Peak Dr

Highlander

Castle
▲ Peak

CAVES
SANDSTONE FORMATIONS

EL ESCORPION Cr.

EL ESCORPION TR

P

Van Owen

To Las Virgenes
Trailhead
(Hike 101)

HUNTER ALLEN TRAIL

UPPER LAS VIRGENES
CANYON OPEN
SPACE PRESERVE

N
W   E
S

Valley Circle Blvd

VICTORY
TRAILHEAD

102
P

EAST LAS VIRGENES
CANYON TRAIL

REFERENCE MAPS
P. 258

To Las Virgenes
Trailhead
(Hike 101)

AHMANSON RANCH HOUSE TR

VENTURA TY
LOS ANGELES CITY

Victory Blvd

To Hwy 101

To Laskey Mesa

103.
El Escorpion Park

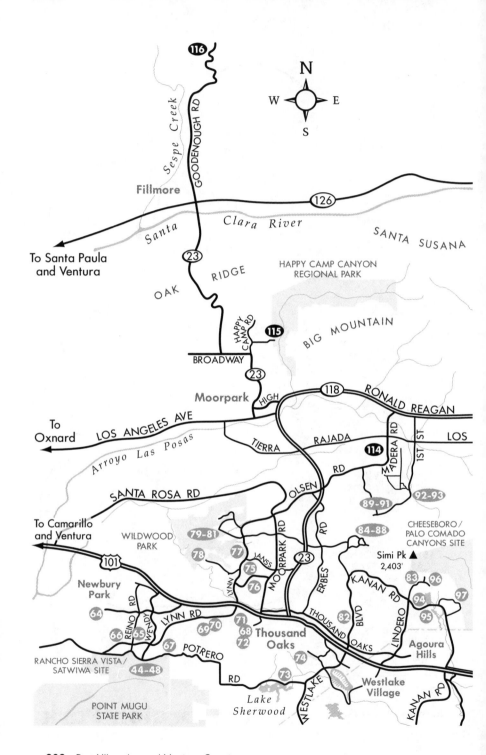

Simi Hills to
Santa Susana Mountains
SIMI VALLEY • MOORPARK • FILLMORE

MOUNTAINS

LOS ANGELES COUNTY
VENTURA COUNTY

5

5 MILES

8 KILOMETERS

GOLDEN STATE FREEWAY

REFERENCE MAPS
P. 12

ROCKY
PEAK
PARK

113
112
111

SANTA SUSANA
PASS ROAD

TO
LOS ANGELES

FREEWAY

YOSEMITE
KUEHNER

110

118

ANGELES AVE

109
108
107
106

Simi Valley

SAN FERNANDO
VALLEY

SAN DIEGO FREEWAY

PLUMMER

BOX CYN

105

Chatsworth
Reservoir

WOOLSEY
CANYON RD

ROSCOE

104

SIMI HILLS

VALLEY CIRCLE BLVD

TOPANGA CANYON BLVD

Los Angeles River

103
102

405

UPPER LAS VIRGENES
CANYON OPEN
SPACE PRESERVE

98-100
101

VENTURA FREEWAY

VENTURA BLVD

101

To
Los Angeles

SANTA

LAS VIRGENES
MONICA MTNS
MULHOLLAND HWY

MULHOLLAND DRIVE

104. Orcutt Ranch Horticulture Center

23600 Roscoe Boulevard · West Hills
Open daily 8 a.m. to 5 p.m.

Hiking distance: 1 mile round trip
Hiking time: 45 minutes
Elevation gain: Level
Maps: U.S.G.S. Calabasas and Canoga Park
Orcutt Ranch Horticulture Center map

Summary of hike: Orcutt Ranch Horticulture Center is tucked away at the west end of the San Fernando Valley in West Hills. The 200-acre estate was the vacation home of William and Mary Orcutt, dating back to 1917. The tree-studded estate, designated as a historical monument, was purchased by the Los Angeles Parks and Recreation Department in 1966 and opened to the public. The mission-style home with 16-inch thick adobe walls and a large patio area is nestled under the shade of ancient oaks, including a 700-year-old coastal live oak with a 33-foot circumference. Exotic plants and trees are planted on several acres around the former residence. Amid the fountains and statues are rattan palms, cork oaks, dogwoods, sycamores, birch, bunya bunya trees, purple lily magnolias, Chinese wisterias, bamboo, and a rose garden. An orchard of citrus and walnut groves covers the adjacent rolling hills.

Driving directions: CHATSWORTH. From Highway 118/Ronald Reagan Freeway in Chatsworth, take the Topanga Canyon Boulevard exit. Drive 3.2 miles south to Roscoe Boulevard and turn right. Continue 2 miles to the posted park entrance on the left.

WOODLAND HILLS. From the Ventura Freeway/Highway 101 in Woodland Hills, drive 3.4 miles north on Topanga Canyon Boulevard to Roscoe Boulevard and turn left. Continue 2 miles to the posted park entrance on the left.

Hiking directions: From the parking area, walk to the Parks and Recreation adobe buildings and the Orcutt estate house. After strolling through the patio areas, take the nature trail into the gardens. Dayton Creek flows through the south end of the gardens in a lush woodland. Along the creek are footbridges, statues and benches. Design your own route, meandering through the historic estate and gardens. ■

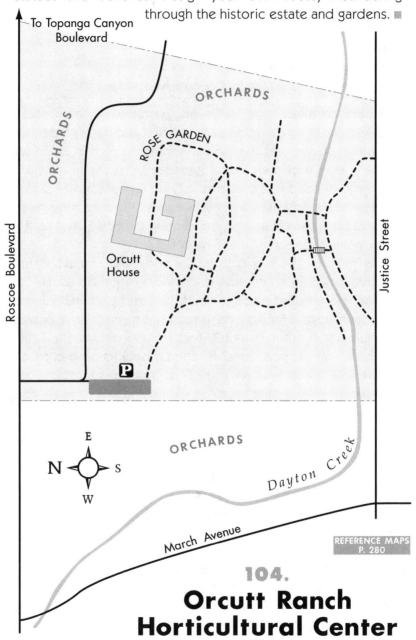

104.
Orcutt Ranch Horticultural Center

105. Sage Ranch Park

1 Black Canyon Road · Simi Valley

Hiking distance: 2.6-mile loop
Hiking time: 1.3 hours
Elevation gain: 300 feet
Maps: U.S.G.S. Calabasas
　　　Santa Monica Mountains Conservancy: Sage Ranch Park

Summary of hike: Sage Ranch Park, perched high in the rocky Simi Hills, sits at an elevation of 2,000 feet and has a garden-of-the-gods appearance. The old cattle ranch served as a film set for early Hollywood westerns. Previous to its use as a filming site, the park road was part of the Old Stagecoach Trail linking the San Fernando Valley with Simi Valley. The area remains an intermountain habitat linkage, connecting the Simi Hills with the Santa Monica and Santa Susana Mountains.

This 635-acre park is rich with world-class sandstone formations, including an endless display of unique boulders, tilted sandstone outcroppings, and metamorphic backdrops. Sandstone Ridge, a long, steep, weathered formation with caves and natural sculptures, rises 300 feet from the 2.6-mile trail that loops through the park. Beautiful carved boulders and eucalyptus trees fill the canyon. En route, the trail meanders past oak woodlands, prickly pear cactus, bracken and sword ferns, and orange and avocado groves.

Driving directions: SAN FERNANDO VALLEY. From Highway 118/Ronald Reagan Freeway in the San Fernando Valley, exit on Topanga Canyon Boulevard. Drive south and turn right on Plummer Street. Continue 2.4 miles to Woolsey Canyon Road and turn right. (Along the way, Plummer Street becomes Valley Circle Boulevard and Lake Manor Drive.) Continue west on Woolsey Canyon Road 2.4 miles to Black Canyon Road and turn right. The Sage Ranch parking lot is 0.2 miles ahead on the left.

From Ventura Freeway/Highway 101 in the San Fernando Valley, exit on Valley Circle Boulevard. Drive north to Woolsey Canyon Road and turn left. Continue on Woolsey Canyon Road

2.4 miles to Black Canyon Road and turn right. The Sage Ranch parking lot is 0.2 miles ahead on the left.

Hiking directions: From the parking lot, hike west up the park service road. Proceed through the gate, passing orange groves on both sides. At the top of the hill next to the sandstone formations, the trail leaves the paved road and takes the gravel road to the right (north). Continue past a meadow dotted with oak trees and through an enormous garden of sandstone rocks. Watch for a short path on the right to a vista point overlooking Simi Valley. Back on the main trail, the trail parallels Sandstone Ridge before descending into the canyon. Once in the canyon, the trail curves back to the east past another series of large rock formations. Near the east end of the canyon is a trail split. Take the left fork, heading uphill and out of the canyon, back to the parking lot. ■

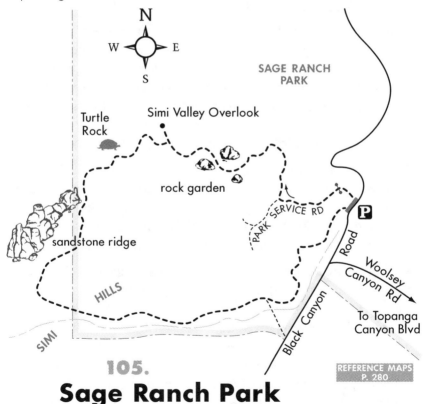

105.
Sage Ranch Park

106. Stoney Point

11000 Topanga Canyon Boulevard · Chatsworth

Hiking distance: 0.7-mile outer loop
Hiking time: 1 hour (allow extra for exploration)
Elevation gain: 100 feet
Maps: U.S.G.S. Oat Mountain

Summary of hike: Stoney Point (also known as the Stoney Point Outcroppings) is a dramatic sandstone formation that rises more than 300 feet from the valley floor in Chatsworth. The circular landmark is the centerpiece of 76-acre Stoney Point Park. The picturesque formation was designated as a historic-cultural landmark in 1974. Originally the site was an ancient Indian village. It was also used by outlaw Tiburcio Vasquez as a hideout in the 1870s. From the 1930s until today, it has been a popular climbing and bouldering site.

The natural rock outcropping is made up of a maze of weather-carved boulders that merge to form alcoves, caves, and dens. A wide hiking trail circles the perimeter of the mountain, weaving through large boulders dispersed along its base. A small stream trickles southeast of the formation. Several side paths lead up the cluster of boulders to an endless display of caves. Several paths also head up to the summit. The park is dog friendly.

Driving directions: CHATSWORTH. From Highway 118/Ronald Reagan Freeway in Chatsworth, exit on Topanga Canyon Boulevard. Drive 0.9 miles south to Chatsworth Street, passing the distinct Stoney Point on the left. Turn around and return 0.3 miles on Topanga Canyon Boulevard. Park along the curb.

Hiking directions: Walk past the vehicle gate and descend to the base of the extraordinary mountain. Many intertwining footpaths weave up and around Stoney Point. Take the wide (main) path, following the southern base of the magnificent formation. Parallel the small stream and the horse stables lined with eucalyptus trees. Meander among the embedded house-size boulders, passing natural caves and alcoves. Continue along the east side of Stoney Point, passing endless routes into the finely etched rocks and caves. At the northeast corner, by the railroad tracks, curve left and climb the slope among additional outcrops and access routes up the mountain. Cross up and over the rise, reaching Topanga Canyon Boulevard by Santa Susana Pass Road. Just before reaching the boulevard, veer left into the massive formation and descend to the sidewalk along the road. For a loop back to the trailhead, follow the paved and gravel path south, paralleling the road for 0.2 miles. ◼

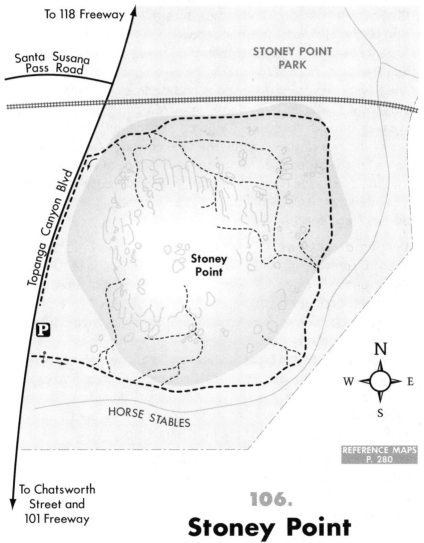

106.
Stoney Point

107. Old Stagecoach Trail
22360 Devonshire Street · Chatsworth

Hiking distance: 2.6 miles round trip

Hiking time: 1.5 hours

Elevation gain: 600 feet

Maps: U.S.G.S. Simi Valley East and Oat Mountain

*map
page 290*

Summary of hike: The Old Stagecoach Trail begins in Chatsworth Park South and climbs through an undeveloped portion of the Simi Hills. The trail follows a segment of the historic Santa Susana Stage Road that once linked Los Angeles with San Francisco from 1859–1890. The hike utilizes the old route, lined with interesting formations and bedrock worn down by stagecoach wheels. A web of unmarked and confusing trails weaves through rounded, fractured sedimentary rock to vistas of the city of Chatsworth, the San Fernando Valley, and the Santa Susana Mountains. Near the ridge is a plaque embedded into the sandstone rock. The marker was installed by the Native Daughters of the Golden West in 1937, designating the Old Santa Susana Stage Road.

Driving directions: CHATSWORTH. From Highway 118/Ronald Reagan Freeway in Chatsworth, take the Topanga Canyon Boulevard exit. Drive 1.5 miles south to Devonshire Street and turn right. Continue a half mile to the end of Devonshire Street and enter Chatsworth Park South. Curve right and drive 0.2 miles to the main parking lot.

WOODLAND HILLS. From the Ventura Freeway/Highway 101 in Woodland Hills, drive 5 miles north on Topanga Canyon Boulevard to Devonshire Street and turn left. Continue a half mile to the end of Devonshire Street and enter Chatsworth Park South. Curve right and drive 0.2 miles to the main parking lot.

Hiking directions: Follow the fire road/trail on the south (left) edge of Chatsworth Park South, skirting the wide park lawn. At the west end of the open grassland, take a gravel path towards the towering sandstone formations, just below the water tank on the right. Wind up the hillside past large boulders to an old paved road. Take the road 50 yards to the right, and bear left on the dirt path by two telephone poles. Climb to the ridge and a junction surrounded by the sculpted rocks. The left fork loops back to the park. Continue straight 50 yards and curve left towards Devil's Slide, a natural sandstone staircase. Follow the east edge of the chaparral-covered slope to an unsigned junction on the left. Bear left and climb the Devil's Slide, stair-stepping up the mountain on the stagecoach-worn bedrock. The sandstone slab leads to a huge rock with a historic plaque cemented into its face. From this overlook is a view into the Santa Susana railroad tunnel and across the San Fernando Valley. A quarter mile beyond the overlook is the 1,630-foot ridge atop the Devil's Slide, located near the Los Angeles—Ventura county line. Several trails wind through the hills and connect to Corriganville Park (Hike 32) and Rocky Peak Park (Hikes 110—113). Return on the same path or explore some of the side trails. ■

108. Stagecoach Trail Loop

Hiking distance: 2-mile loop
Hiking time: 1 hour
Elevation gain: 300 feet
Maps: U.S.G.S. Simi Valley East and Oat Mountain
        Rancho Simi Trail Blazers Stagecoach Trail map

map
page 293

Summary of hike: A network of trails runs through the northeast corner of the Simi Hills near Chatsworth. The area, adjacent to the Santa Susana Mountains, straddles the Ventura—Los Angeles county line. This loop begins on the Stagecoach Trail off of Lilac Lane and climbs over a chaparral-covered hill to Santa Susana Pass Road. Along the way, the trail weaves through massive, grey-colored sandstone outcroppings over 70 million years old. This hike continues as a loop with the upper (north) end of the Old Stagecoach Trail, the historic route that once linked Los Angeles with Santa Barbara during the last half of the

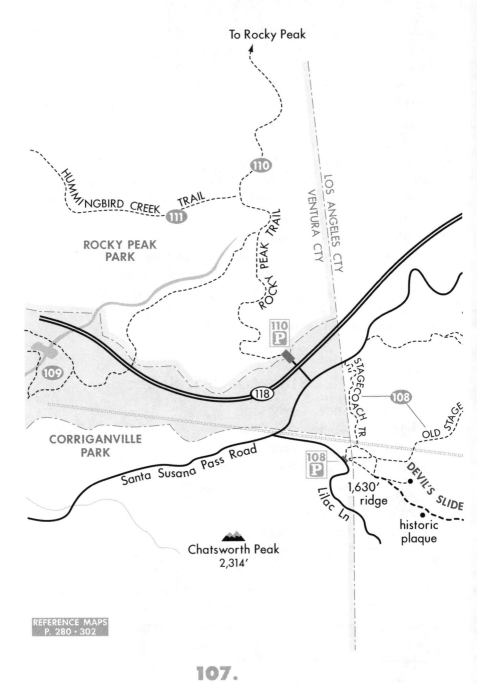

To Rocky Peak

HUMMINGBIRD CREEK TRAIL

110

111

ROCKY PEAK
PARK

ROCKY PEAK TRAIL

LOS ANGELES CTY
VENTURA CTY

110
P

109

118

STAGECOACH TR

108

OLD STAGE

DEVIL'S SLIDE

CORRIGANVILLE
PARK

108
P

Santa Susana Pass Road

Lilac Ln

1,630'
ridge

historic
plaque

Chatsworth Peak
2,314'

REFERENCE MAPS
P. 280 - 302

107.
Old Stagecoach Trail

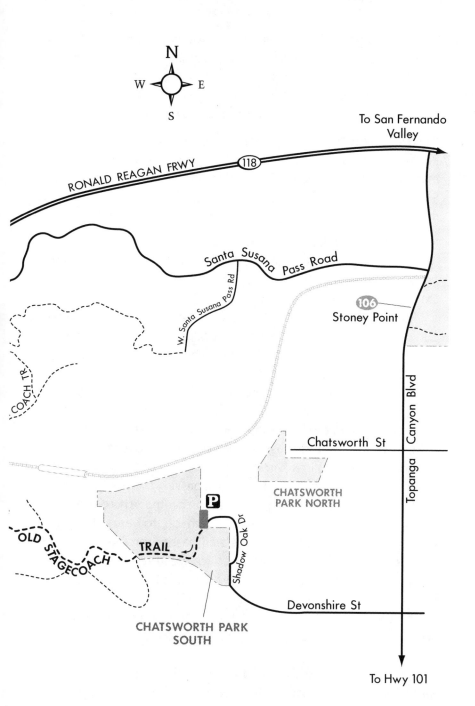

1800s. Throughout the hike are a series of magnificent overlooks of the San Fernando Valley, the Santa Susana Mountains, the San Gabriel Mountains, and the Santa Monica Mountains. The hike can be continued along the lower end of the Old Stagecoach Trail—Hike 107—leading down to Chatsworth Park South.

Driving directions: SIMI VALLEY. From Highway 118/Ronald Reagan Freeway in Simi Valley, exit on Kuehner Drive. Drive 2.8 miles south to Lilac Lane. (En route Kuehner Drive becomes Santa Susana Pass Road.) Turn right on Lilac Lane. Continue a quarter mile, and turn left into the dirt parking area.

Hiking directions: The signed trail, located at the back end of the parking area, is our return route. Begin the loop at the front of the parking area on the left (north). Traverse the hillside among gorgeous sandstone boulders. Curve right and drop into a wide gulch as the homes along Lilac Lane disappear from view. Surrounded by a jumble of weather-sculpted outcrops, the path leads to an overlook of Simi Valley, high above the 118 Freeway. The serpentine path curves right to an overlook of Rocky Peak Park (Hike 110). Head east through the low-growing chaparral while marveling at the spectacular landscape. Slowly descend, zigzagging down the hillside to Santa Susana Pass Road at a half mile, located 120 yards east of the 118 Freeway overpass.

Bear right and follow the road 0.1 mile to a fire road, closed off to vehicles by boulders. Bear right, passing the boulders, and gently descend, overlooking the canyon on the left to a Y-fork. The left fork continues down the canyon towards Topanga Canyon Boulevard. (En route, this trail passes through the 500-acre Spahn Ranch. The area was used for western films, including *Bonanza* and *The Lone Ranger*. However, it is best known as the site where serial killer Charles Manson and his infamous cult lived during their 1969 killing spree. All the ranch structures were destroyed in a wildfire one year later. The land is currently owned by the state.)

For this hike, veer right and head up the slope. Curve right and traverse the hillside while expansive views span across the San Fernando Valley. One hundred yards shy of the trailhead parking area is an unsigned fork. Detour left 0.2 miles to an overlook atop a knoll, offering 360-degree vistas across the valley to the San Gabriel Mountains and Santa Monica Mountains. To extend the hike, the trail descends on the Old Stagecoach Road to Chatsworth Park South (Hike 107). ■

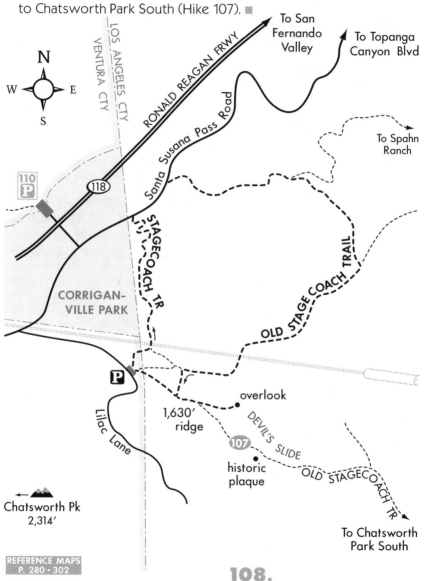

108.
Stagecoach Trail Loop

109. Corriganville Park

Hiking distance: 2 miles round trip
Hiking time: 1 hour
Elevation gain: 100 feet
Maps: U.S.G.S. Simi Valley East
Rancho Simi Open Space: Corriganville Park

Summary of hike: Corriganville Park, at the eastern end of Simi Valley, was an old movie ranch. It is named for Ray "Crash" Corrigan, who purchased the ranch in the 1930s. The area was the setting to about a thousand movie and television shows between 1937 and 1965, including *The Lone Ranger, Gunsmoke, The Fugitive, Lassie, Mutiny on the Bounty, African Queen, How the West Was Won*, and *Fort Apache*, to name just a few. Old stone and concrete foundations from the sets still remain. The oak-shaded paths lead through the 225-acre park past prominent sandstone outcroppings, cliffs, caves, a stream, Jungle Jim Lake, and the Hangin' Tree, a towering oak used to "execute" countless outlaws.

Driving directions: SIMI VALLEY. From Highway 118/Ronald Reagan Freeway in Simi Valley, exit on Kuehner Drive. Drive 1.1 miles south to Smith Road and turn left. Continue 0.4 miles into Corriganville Park and park on the left.

Hiking directions: From the far east end of the parking lot, take the wide trail past the kiosk. The forested trail heads northeast up the draw past coast live oaks and sculpted rock formations on the left. Cross a bridge to a junction. The left fork crosses a wooden bridge, passes a pool, and loops back for a shorter hike. Stay to the right to the next junction. The right fork is a connector trail to Rocky Peak Park (Hike 110) via a concrete tunnel under the freeway. Curve to the left and cross the stream to another junction. Both trails lead west back to the trailhead. The footpath to the right travels between the sandstone cliffs to a dynamic overlook and a junction. The left fork descends to the old movie sets and the site of Fort Apache. From the sets, cross the bridge back to the parking lot. ■

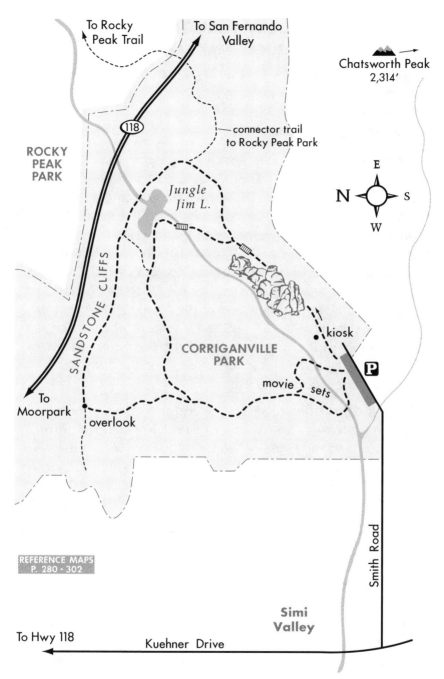

To Rocky Peak Trail

To San Fernando Valley

Chatsworth Peak
2,314'

118

ROCKY PEAK PARK

connector trail to Rocky Peak Park

N E S W

Jungle Jim L.

SANDSTONE CLIFFS

CORRIGANVILLE PARK

kiosk

P

movie sets

To Moorpark

overlook

REFERENCE MAPS
P. 280 - 302

Smith Road

Simi Valley

To Hwy 118

Kuehner Drive

109. Corriganville Park

110. Rocky Peak Trail
ROCKY PEAK PARK

Hiking distance: 5–6 miles round trip
Hiking time: 2.5 hours
Elevation gain: 1,100 feet
Maps: U.S.G.S. Simi Valley East

Summary of hike: Rocky Peak Park is aptly named for the dramatic sandstone formations, fractured boulders, overhangs, caves, and outcroppings. The 4,815-acre wilderness park is located in Simi Valley by Santa Susana Pass. The park is a critical wildlife habitat linkage between the Simi Hills and the Santa Susana Mountains. Rocky Peak Trail follows a winding fire road on the north side of the 118 Freeway to Rocky Peak, which lies on the Los Angeles-Ventura county line. There are a series of vista points along the route and at the jagged 2,714-foot peak, the highest point in the Santa Susan Mountains. The vista points include top-of-the-world views of the San Fernando Valley, Simi Valley, the Santa Monica Mountains, and the many peaks of the Los Padres National Forest.

Driving directions: SIMI VALLEY. From Highway 118/Ronald Reagan Freeway in Simi Valley, exit on Kuehner Drive. Drive 3 miles south to the Highway 118 East on-ramp. (Along the way, Kuehner Drive becomes Santa Susana Pass Road.) Turn left, crossing over the freeway, and park 0.1 mile ahead at the end of the road.

Hiking directions: Hike past the trailhead kiosk up the winding fire road to an unsigned trail split at 0.9 miles. Stay to the left on the main trail, hiking steadily uphill to a signed junction with the Hummingbird Creek Trail on the left (Hike 111). Proceed straight ahead on the Rocky Peak Trail, which levels out. The winding trail offers alternating views of the San Fernando Valley to the east and Simi Valley to the west. At the base of the final ascent is a singular, large oak tree. Begin the steep ascent, gaining 450 feet in a half mile, to the Rocky Peak Cutoff Trail. This is a good turn-around spot. However, if you wish to hike to the summit, the trail takes off to the right across the plateau for a half mile to Rocky Peak. The last section of the trail is a rock scramble to the peak. To return, reverse your route. ■

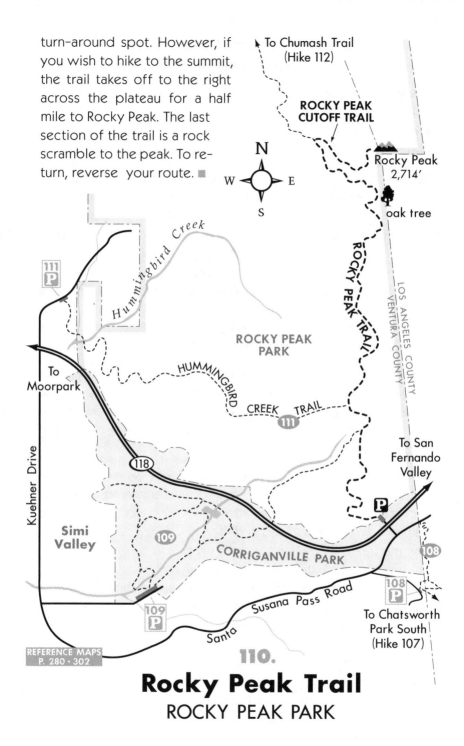

110.
Rocky Peak Trail
ROCKY PEAK PARK

111. Hummingbird Creek Trail
ROCKY PEAK PARK

Hiking distance: 4.6 miles round trip
Hiking time: 2 hours
Elevation gain: 1,000 feet
Maps: U.S.G.S. Simi Valley East

Summary of hike: Rocky Peak Park, in the Santa Susana Mountains, straddles the Los Angeles–Ventura county line at the eastern end of Simi Valley. A network of hiking trails weaves through the 4,815-acre park that is home to deep oak-lined canyons, trickling streams, and massive, sculpted sandstone formations with a moonscape appearance. The Hummingbird Creek Trail, at the base of Rocky Peak, crosses Hummingbird Creek and climbs up a narrow canyon through open chaparral to the Rocky Peak Trail (a fire road), passing stacks of giant sandstone boulders, sculpted caves, and dramatic rock outcroppings.

Driving directions: SIMI VALLEY. From Highway 118/Ronald Reagan Freeway in Simi Valley, exit on Kuehner Drive. Drive 0.3 miles north to the signed trailhead on the right. Park in one of the pullouts alongside the road. If full, additional parking is available just north of the freeway.

Hiking directions: From the trailhead kiosk, head downhill. The trail soon U-turns southeast into the canyon to a defunct rock dam from 1917 and Hummingbird Creek. Proceed past the dam into an oak woodland and meadow. Once past the meadow, the trail crosses Hummingbird Creek and begins the ascent up the mountain through chaparral. Switchbacks lead up to sandstone caves and rock formations. After the rocks and caves, the trail levels out before the second ascent. Switchbacks make the climb easier as it heads up the canyon. At the head of the canyon, the trail levels out and passes more rock formations. The trail ends at a junction with the Rocky Peak Trail. Return to the trailhead by retracing your steps.

To hike farther, the Rocky Peak Trail continues 1.7 miles north to the summit of Rocky Peak—Hike 110. ■

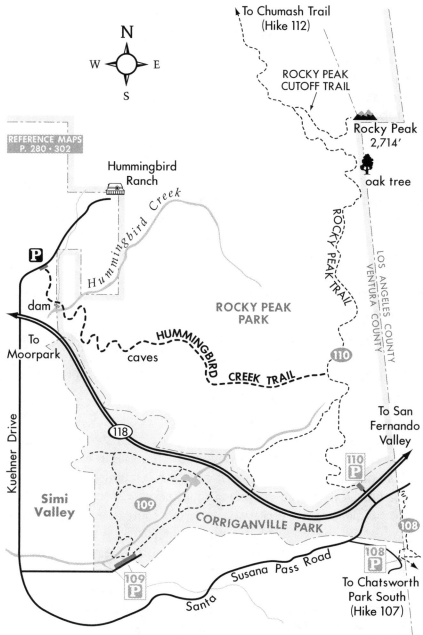

To Chumash Trail
(Hike 112)

ROCKY PEAK
CUTOFF TRAIL

Rocky Peak
2,714'

oak tree

ROCKY PEAK TRAIL

LOS ANGELES COUNTY
VENTURA COUNTY

REFERENCE MAPS
P. 280 · 302

Hummingbird
Ranch

Hummingbird Creek

P

dam

ROCKY PEAK
PARK

HUMMINGBIRD

caves

CREEK TRAIL

110

To
Moorpark

To San
Fernando
Valley

118

110
P

Kuehner Drive

Simi
Valley

109

CORRIGANVILLE PARK

108

108
P

109
P

Santa Susana Pass Road

To Chatsworth
Park South
(Hike 107)

111. **Hummingbird Creek Trail**
ROCKY PEAK PARK

112. Chumash Trail
ROCKY PEAK PARK

Hiking distance: 5 miles round trip
Hiking time: 2.5 hours
Elevation gain: 1,100 feet
Maps: U.S.G.S. Simi Valley East

Summary of hike: The Chumash Trail is located in Rocky Peak Park in the Santa Susana Mountains east of Simi Valley. This trail ascends the west flank of Rocky Peak, winding up the chaparral-cloaked mountainside to the ridge north of the peak. En route, the trail passes sculpted sandstone outcroppings, caves, and a series of scenic overlooks and highland meadows. From Hamilton Saddle and the Rocky Peak Trail junction are panoramic views of the Simi Hills, Simi Valley, San Fernando Valley, the Santa Susana Mountains, the Santa Monica Mountains, Blind Canyon, and Las Llajas Canyon.

Driving directions: SIMI VALLEY. From Highway 118/Ronald Reagan Freeway in Simi Valley, exit on Yosemite Avenue. Drive 0.4 miles north to Flanagan Drive and turn right. Continue 0.8 miles to the trailhead at the end of the road.

Hiking directions: Head north past the kiosk along the rolling hills and grassy meadows. The trail climbs steadily as you round the hillside to the first overlook of Simi Hills to the south. Continue uphill through coastal sage scrub, curving left around the next rolling hill and passing sculpted sandstone formations. Arrow signposts are placed along the route. Continue to the east along the edge of the canyon to Hamilton Saddle. From the saddle, the trail sharply curves left (north), gaining elevation before leveling out again at Flat Rock. From Flat Rock, begin the final ascent through chaparral, curving around the last ridge to the top. The trail ends at a junction with the Rocky Peak Trail at an elevation of 2,450 feet. Sixty yards to the left of the junction are views of Blind Canyon and Las Llajas Canyon. Reverse your route to return.

For a longer hike, the Rocky Peak Trail continues 1.3 miles southeast to the summit of Rocky Peak (Hike 110). ■

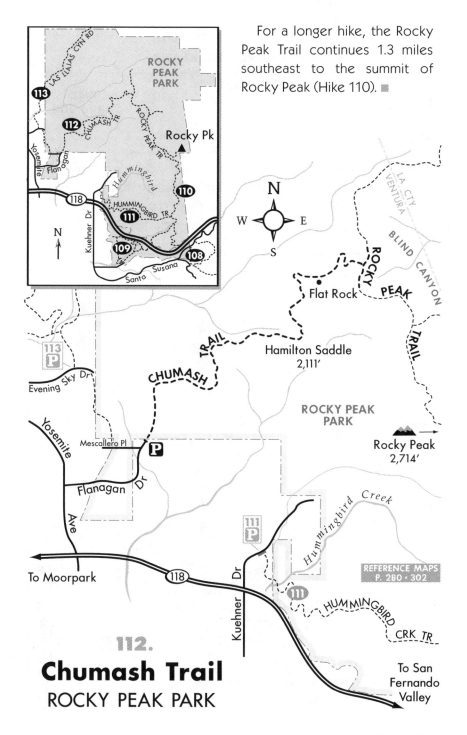

112.
Chumash Trail
ROCKY PEAK PARK

113. Las Llajas Canyon
MARR RANCH PARKLAND

Hiking distance: 8.8 miles round trip
Hiking time: 4.5 hours
Elevation gain: 1,200 feet
Maps: U.S.G.S. Simi Valley East

map
page 304

Summary of hike: The Marr Ranch Parkland in Simi Valley is tucked into the foothills of the Santa Susana Mountains adjacent to Rocky Peak Park. The publicly owned parkland and open space encompasses 1,842 acres, which includes Chivo Canyon

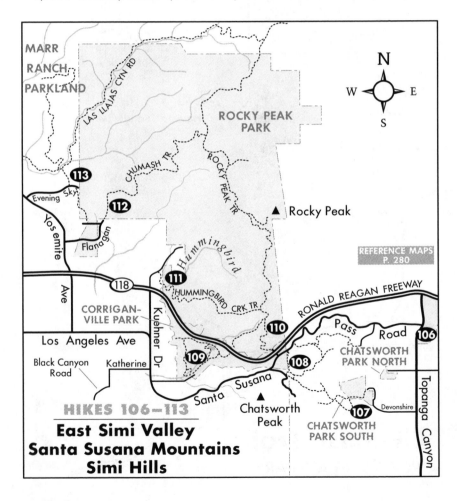

and Las Llajas Canyon, both stream-fed canyons. The Las Llajas Canyon Road, a vehicle-restricted road, heads up the canyon through scenic, unspoiled landscapes. The hike meanders along the valley floor along the road, parallel to the creek and under groves of old oak trees. The trail climbs out of the canyon on Oil Well Road (part of an active ranch) to Rocky Peak Trail atop the ridge. From the ridge are sweeping vistas, including views of Oat Mountain and its distinctive radio towers.

Driving directions: SIMI VALLEY. From Highway 118/Ronald Reagan Freeway in Simi Valley, exit on Yosemite Avenue. Drive 2.8 miles north to Evening Sky Drive. Turn right and continue a half mile to the signed trailhead on the left. Park along the curb.

Hiking directions: Pass the trailhead kiosk and descend 300 yards on the paved road, dropping into Las Llajas Canyon. At transient Las Llajas Creek, veer to the right and cross over the east fork of the creek. Follow the east side of the main fork, weaving along the canyon bottom as the canyon walls narrow. Pass pockets of oak trees on the easy uphill grade. Cross over the creek at 1.2 miles, then cross over the creek for the third time. Meander past shaded streamside oak groves, continuing up the serpentine canyon. Traverse the north canyon slope above the waterway, then return to the canyon floor. Cross the invisible line from Ventura County into Los Angeles County without noticing an increase in the population. Continue to a Y-fork at 3.4 miles. To the left is a gated access into La Quinta Ranch. Curve right on the Oil Well Road, a partially-paved but mostly dirt road, and ascend the north-facing wall overlooking Las Llajas Canyon. Weave up the hillside, passing oil wells, holding tanks, and grazing cattle. Gain 700 feet over the next mile to Rocky Peak Trail, a fire road. After savoring the well-earned vistas, return along the same route.

To extend the hike and form a 9.5-mile loop, take Rocky Peak Trail 1.6 miles to the right. Head south to the Chumash Trail. Bear left and descend 2.5 miles (Hike 112) to the Chumash trailhead on Flanagan Drive. Go right on Mescallero Place, and weave to Evening Sky Drive, completing the loop. ▪

113.
Las Llajas Canyon
MARR RANCH PARKLAND

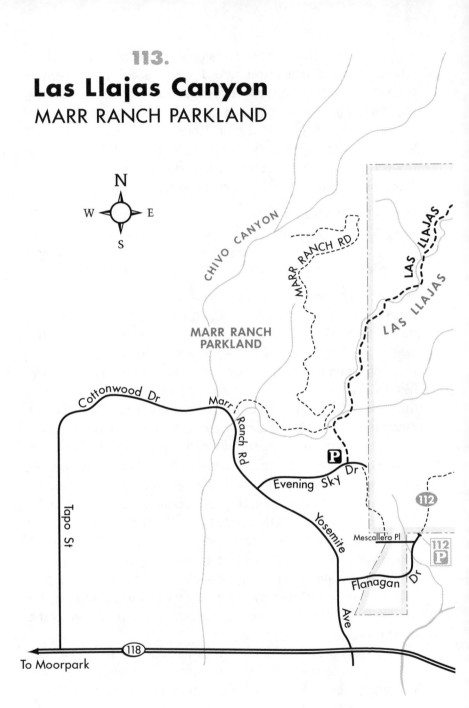

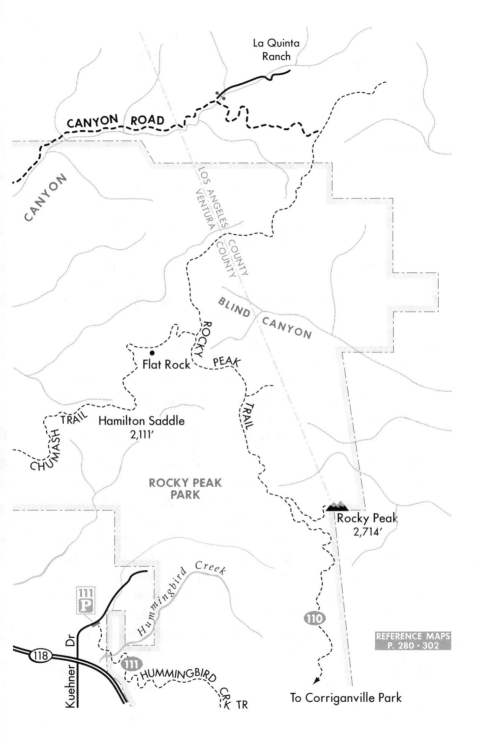

La Quinta Ranch

CANYON ROAD

CANYON

LOS ANGELES COUNTY
VENTURA COUNTY

BLIND CANYON

ROCKY

Flat Rock

PEAK

TRAIL

CHUMASH TRAIL

Hamilton Saddle
2,111'

ROCKY PEAK
PARK

Rocky Peak
2,714'

Hummingbird Creek

111
P

Kuehner Dr

118

111

110

HUMMINGBIRD CRK TR

To Corriganville Park

REFERENCE MAPS
P. 280 · 302

114. Mount McCoy

Hiking distance: 2.6 miles round trip
Hiking time: 1.5 hours
Elevation gain: 600 feet
Maps: U.S.G.S. Simi Valley West

Summary of hike: Mount McCoy is an isolated 600-foot knoll in a 200-acre open space at the west end of Simi Valley. A white, concrete cross, erected in 1941, sits atop the 1,325-foot summit and is a visible landmark throughout the valley. The wide trail to the summit is composed of a series of switchbacks for an easy, gradual climb. From the summit are 360-degree panoramas of Simi Valley, the Ronald Reagan Presidential Library, the Santa Susana Mountains, the Conejo Ridge, the San Gabriel Mountains, and the Santa Monica Mountains. The trail was engineered and is maintained by the Rancho Simi Trail Blazers.

Driving directions: SIMI VALLEY. From Highway 118/Ronald Reagan Freeway in Simi Valley, take the Madera Road South exit. Drive 1.6 miles south to Royal Avenue and turn right. Immediately turn right on Acapulco Avenue, then quickly turn left on Washburn Street. Drive one block to the end of the street at the junction with Los Amigos Avenue. Park near the trailhead on the left.

Hiking directions: From the trailhead, an old steep path heads nearly straight up the east flank of the mountain. For a longer but more enjoyable hike, take the lower path to the left, skirting the base of Mount McCoy across the grasslands. Cross to the south side of the drainage filled with coastal live oaks. Ascend the slope on a series of long, sweeping switchbacks through coastal sage scrub and chaparral. The northern switchbacks skirt the edge of the oak-studded canyon, but the trail never enters the shaded canopy. Cross over volcanic rock to an old dirt road on the ridgeline. To the left, the dirt road leads to the Ronald Reagan Presidential Library. Take the route to the right, soon merging with the steep, direct route. At 100 yards, the path reaches the concrete cross at the summit. After taking in the views, return on the same path. ■

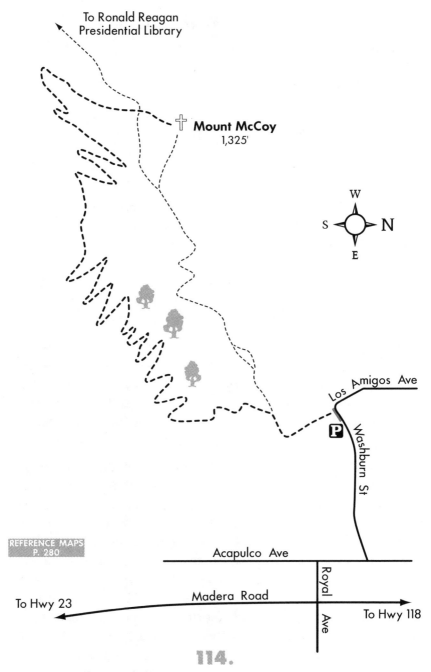

To Ronald Reagan
Presidential Library

✝ **Mount McCoy**
1,325'

W
S ✦ N
E

Los Amigos Ave

P

Washburn St

REFERENCE MAPS
P. 280

Acapulco Ave

Royal Ave

To Hwy 23

Madera Road

To Hwy 118

114.
Mount McCoy

115. Happy Camp Canyon

Hiking distance: 10 miles round trip
Hiking time: 5 hours
Elevation gain: 1,300 feet
Maps: U.S.G.S. Simi Valley West

Summary of hike: Happy Camp Canyon Park, north of Moorpark in the Santa Susana Mountains, was once part of a large cattle ranch. The 3,000-acre park has retained its natural setting and is an important wildlife corridor linking the Simi Hills with the Santa Susana Mountains. Happy Camp Canyon is a lush riparian oak woodland with an intermittent stream. The canyon is sheltered by Oak Ridge to the north and Big Mountain to the south. The remote park has miles of hiking, biking, and equestrian trails. This hike follows the Happy Camp Trail through the interior of the park on an abandoned ranch road. The trail winds through open grasslands and the gorgeous stream-fed canyon.

Driving directions: MOORPARK. From the town of Moorpark, take Moorpark Avenue (Highway 23) 2.5 miles north to a sharp left bend in the road. (En route, Moorpark Avenue becomes Walnut Canyon Road.) Continue straight ahead 30 yards on Happy Camp Road to Broadway and turn right. Drive 0.3 miles to the Happy Camp Canyon parking lot at the road's end.

Hiking directions: Overlooking the valley, the trail heads downhill past the trailhead sign. Cross the hillside to the grassy valley floor, joining the old ranch road at one mile. Turn left up canyon a quarter mile to the Happy Camp Canyon Nature Trail kiosk. One hundred yards beyond the kiosk is a trail split. The right fork heads up Big Mountain, the return route. Take the left fork and begin the loop, curving east into the shady canyon. Parallel the stream, then walk across it. At 3.5 miles is the first of several road forks. The left (north) forks are powerline maintenance roads. Take the right fork each time, staying in the canyon. At 4.5 miles, the trail passes a gate, entering an oak grove with picnic tables and horse corrals. Continue east to a junction.

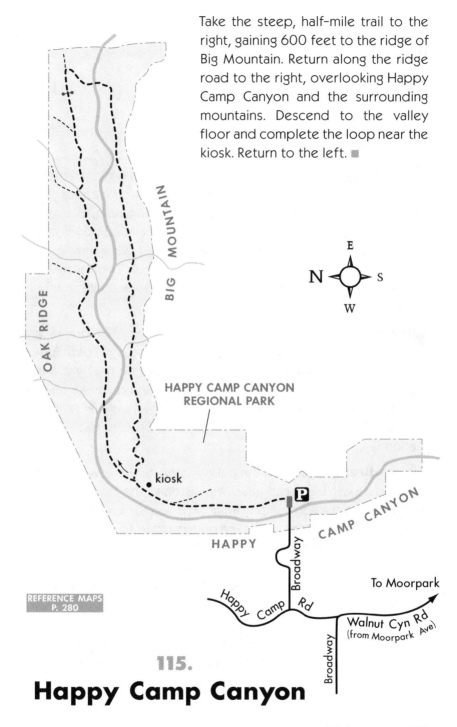

Take the steep, half-mile trail to the right, gaining 600 feet to the ridge of Big Mountain. Return along the ridge road to the right, overlooking Happy Camp Canyon and the surrounding mountains. Descend to the valley floor and complete the loop near the kiosk. Return to the left. ▰

HAPPY CAMP CANYON
REGIONAL PARK

kiosk

BIG MOUNTAIN

OAK RIDGE

HAPPY   CAMP CANYON

REFERENCE MAPS
P. 280

To Moorpark

Broadway

Happy Camp Rd

Walnut Cyn Rd
(from Moorpark Ave)

Broadway

115.
Happy Camp Canyon

116. Tar Creek

Hiking distance: 4 miles round trip
Hiking time: 2 hours
Elevation gain: 700 feet
Maps: U.S.G.S. Fillmore
Sespe Wilderness Trail Map
Los Padres National Forest Trail Map

Summary of hike: Tar Creek is in the Los Padres National Forest and the Sespe Condor Sanctuary, a reintroduction area for the California Condor. The creek flows through a grotto of sculptured, sandstone boulders with smooth, water-filled bowls and mossy rocks. This hike follows a well-defined but lightly used trail, descending into a deep canyon to Tar Creek. The trail meanders along the stream to pools, cascades, and waterfalls. A mile downstream, Tar Creek joins with Sespe Creek.

Driving directions: FILLMORE. From the town of Fillmore, take A Street (Highway 23) one mile north to Goodenough Road. Turn right and continue 2.7 miles to Squaw Flat Road on the right. It is marked as the Dough Flat turnoff. Turn right and drive 4.8 miles up the winding mountain road to the unsigned parking pullout on the left. It is located 1.5 miles beyond the Oak Flat Guard Station.

Hiking directions: From the parking area, take the wide path northwest past the metal gate. Wind around the mountainside, with views of the surrounding mountains and the canyon below. As the trail begins its descent, the path narrows to a single track. At the final descent, the trail overlooks Tar Creek. Once at the creek, explore up and down the stream. There are more waterfalls and pools downstream, but the hike becomes demanding and technical. After enjoying the creek, return along the same path.

To hike farther, head upstream and curve away from Tar Creek. The trail weaves along the contours of Sulphur Peak, reaching Sespe Creek in 3 miles. ∎

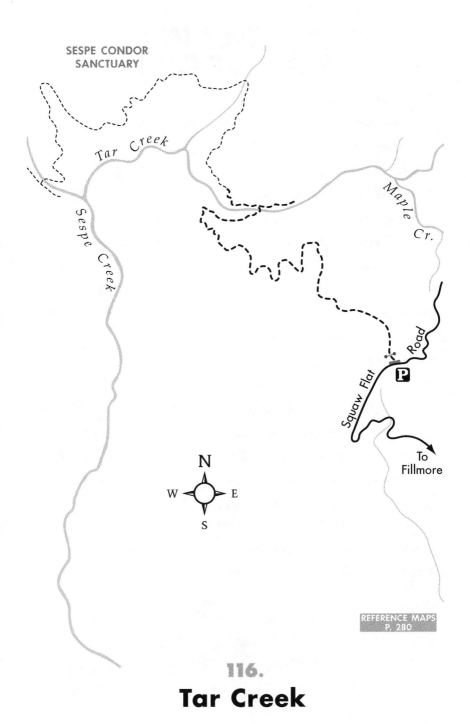

SESPE CONDOR
SANCTUARY

Tar Creek

Sespe Creek

Maple Cr.

Squaw Flat Road

P

To
Fillmore

N
W · E
S

REFERENCE MAPS
P. 280

116.
Tar Creek

DAY HIKE BOOKS

Day Hikes On the California Central Coast.....978-1-57342-058-7 ....17.95

Day Hikes On the California Southern Coast ..978-1-57342-045-7 ... 14.95

Day Hikes In the Santa Monica Mountains .....978-1-57342-065-5 ... 21.95

Day Hikes Around Sonoma County ....978-1-57342-053-2.....16.95

Day Hikes Around Napa Valley...................978-1-57342-057-0 ....16.95

Day Hikes Around Monterey and Carmel.......978-1-57342-067-9.....19.95

Day Hikes Around Big Sur............................978-1-57342-068-6 ....18.95

Day Hikes Around San Luis Obispo ....978-1-57342-070-9 ... 21.95

Day Hikes Around Santa Barbara................978-1-57342-060-0....17.95

Day Hikes Around Ventura County................978-1-57342-062-4.....17.95

Day Hikes Around Los Angeles.....................978-1-57342-071-6.... 21.95

Day Hikes Around Orange County ....978-1-57342-047-1.....15.95

Day Hikes In Yosemite National Park ....978-1-57342-059-4 ....13.95

Day Hikes In Sequoia and Kings Canyon N.P...978-1-57342-030-3 ....12.95

Day Hikes Around Sedona, Arizona..............978-1-57342-049-5 ... 14.95

Day Hikes In Yellowstone National Park........978-1-57342-048-8 ....12.95

Day Hikes In Grand Teton National Park........978-1-57342-069-3.... 14.95

Day Hikes In the Beartooth Mountains
Billings to Red Lodge to Yellowstone N.P.....978-1-57342-064-8 ....15.95

Day Hikes Around Bozeman, Montana ....978-1-57342-063-1.....15.95

Day Hikes Around Missoula, Montana ....978-1-57342-066-2.....15.95

These books may be purchased at your local bookstore or
outdoor shop. Or, order them directly from the distributor:

National Book Network

800-243-0495 DIRECT   **800-820-2329** FAX

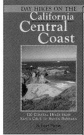
DAY HIKES ON THE
California
Central
Coast
120 COASTAL HIKES FROM
SANTA CRUZ TO SANTA BARBARA
Robert Stone

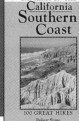
DAY HIKES ON THE
California
Southern
Coast
100 GREAT HIKES
Robert Stone

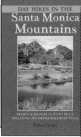
DAY HIKES IN THE
Santa Monica
Mountains
FROM LOS ANGELES TO POINT MUGU
INCLUDING THE ENTIRE BACKBONE TRAIL
Robert Stone

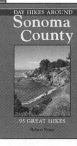
DAY HIKES AROUND
Sonoma
County
95 GREAT HIKES
Robert Stone

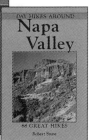
DAY HIKES AROUND
Napa
Valley
88 GREAT HIKES
Robert Stone

DAY HIKES AROUND
Monterey
& Carmel
125 GREAT HIKES
Robert Stone
3rd EDITION

DAY HIKES AROUND
Big Sur
99 GREAT HIKES
Robert Stone
2nd EDITION

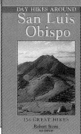
DAY HIKES AROUND
San Luis
Obispo
156 GREAT HIKES
Robert Stone
3rd EDITION

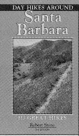
DAY HIKES AROUND
Santa
Barbara
113 GREAT HIKES
Robert Stone
3rd EDITION

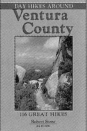
DAY HIKES AROUND
Ventura
County
116 GREAT HIKES
Robert Stone
2nd EDITION

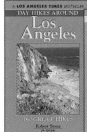
A LOS ANGELES TIMES BESTSELLER
DAY HIKES AROUND
Los
Angeles
160 GREAT HIKES
Robert Stone
4th EDITION

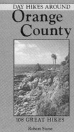
DAY HIKES AROUND
Orange
County
108 GREAT HIKES
Robert Stone

DAY HIKES IN
Yosemite
NATIONAL PARK
80 GREAT HIKES
Robert Stone
2nd EDITION

DAY HIKES IN
Sequoia
&
Kings Canyon
NATIONAL PARKS
Robert Stone

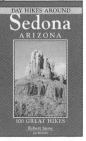
DAY HIKES AROUND
Sedona
ARIZONA
100 GREAT HIKES
Robert Stone
2nd EDITION

DAY HIKES IN
Yellowstone
NATIONAL PARK
82 GREAT HIKES
Robert Stone
4th EDITION

DAY HIKES IN
Grand
Teton
NATIONAL PARK
84 GREAT HIKES
Robert Stone
2nd EDITION

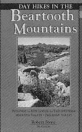
DAY HIKES IN THE
Beartooth
Mountains
RED LODGE to YELLOWSTONE
BOULDER VALLEY - PARADISE VALLEY
Robert Stone

DAY HIKES AROUND
Bozeman
MONTANA
INCLUDING THE GALLATIN
CANYON AND PARADISE VALLEY
Robert Stone

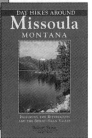
DAY HIKES AROUND
Missoula
MONTANA
INCLUDING THE BITTERROOTS
AND THE SELECT-SWAN VALLEY
Robert Stone

Day Hikes Around Santa Barbara

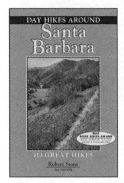

Santa Barbara is a captivating community located in a beautiful setting along California's Pacific coast. The temperate climate and gentle ocean breezes have distinguished this area as "the jewel of the American Riviera." The surroundings include mountainous terrain, forests and wilderness areas, and stretches of undeveloped coast, allowing the area to have miles of quiet, secluded hiking trails.

320 pages • 113 hikes • 3rd Edition 2010

Day Hikes Around Los Angeles

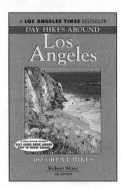

Now in its 6th edition, this book has made the LA Times Bestseller List for many years. Residents and travelers alike will find the book essential to discovering an amazing number of hiking opportunities. Despite the imminent presence of the city, there are thousands of acres of natural, undeveloped land with hundreds of miles of trails. Includes 160 hikes and walks within a 50-mile radius of the city.

544 pages • 160 hikes • 6th Edition 2015

Day Hikes On the Calif. Southern Coast

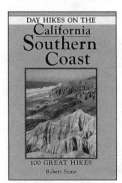

This guide is a collection of 100 great day hikes along 240 miles of southern California coastline, from Ventura County to the U.S.—Mexico border. The area has some of the most varied geography in the state...a blend of verdant canyons, arid bluffs, and sandy coastline. Discover hundreds of miles of trails in scenic and undeveloped land, despite the expansive urban areas.

224 pages • 100 hikes • 1st Edition 2004

INDEX

ADRIENNE METTER

About the Author

Since 1991, Robert Stone has been writer, photographer, and publisher of Day Hike Books. He is a Los Angeles Times Best Selling Author and an award-winning journalist of Rocky Mountain Outdoor Writers and Photographers, the Outdoor Writers Association of California, the Northwest Outdoor Writers Association, the Outdoor Writers Association of America, and the Bay Area Travel Writers.

Robert has hiked every trail in the Day Hike Book series. With 20 hiking guides in the series, many in their fourth and fifth editions, he has hiked thousands of miles of trails throughout the western United States. When Robert is not hiking, he researches, writes, and maps the hikes before returning to the trails. He spends summers in the Rocky Mountains of Montana and winters on the California Central Coast.